# HANDBOOK FOR PATROL LEADERS

## By William Hillcourt

·ANDY JANSON·

BOY SCOUTS OF AMERICA
2 Park Ave., New York, N. Y.

HILLCOURT
RIDING HIS HOBBYHORSE

*Copyright* 1929 *by*
*BOY SCOUTS OF AMERICA*

FROM the very start of the Boy Scouts of America, we have strongly advocated the Patrol System as essential to real Scouting. For the last ten years we have more aggressively urged the Patrol System as an absolute fundamental of Scouting.

In 1923 in a foreword to a pamphlet on the Patrol Method, I stated that this method does not relieve the Scoutmaster of responsibility for maintaining standards of Scouting, but that it does very definitely open up a way whereby the Scoutmaster may share his leadership responsibility with his Patrol Leaders.

I am happy to state that never before in the History of the Boy Scouts of America has the Patrol Method been used more universally or with better success than at the present time. It is not an experiment, but a practical method—the only practical method—of conducting a Troop, that has been tried and found successful. Hitherto most of the literature published has been for the benefit of Scoutmasters. This is a Handbook for Patrol Leaders, though the Scoutmaster will find much of value in it. Its practical value will be realized in the degree in which the Patrol Leaders actually make use of it in the conduct of their Patrols.

*James E. West*

*Chief Scout Executive.*

THE Editorial Board takes great satisfaction in presenting to the Scout Field this Manual for Leaders of Patrols—whether Troop Patrols, Sea Scout Patrols, or Farm or Home Patrols—as it was prepared in response to an insistent demand for a Handbook of this type. The author, William Hillcourt, has himself served as a Scout, a Patrol Leader and a Scoutmaster. The book offers in simple boy language a working plan of Patrol organization, procedure and leadership, based on the "learning by doing" method. Every project recommended has been tried and tested and found workable and worth while. It is a real boys' book, as well as a genuine contribution to the whole field of Scouting.

To you Patrol Leaders, to whom this Handbook is dedicated, we offer it in the hope that it will prove of service and inspiration in your task of leadership. We sincerely believe it will help you to feel more strongly the responsibility of the work you have undertaken and the joy that goes with it.

Scouting is "Forward," as the author reminds us. May this book be a pleasant comrade for your journey and may happiness and good luck attend you as you go!

WM. D. MURRAY
*Chairman, Editorial Board*

FRANK PRESBREY                    HENRY VAN DYKE

E. S. MARTIN
*Secretary*

ONCE upon a time there was a boy who wasn't much of a boy.

He wasn't physically strong. He didn't care very much for games such as other boys played. Indeed he didn't care very much for other boys. He lived mostly in a dream world of his own.

Then one clear January day a good many years ago, he became a Scout because his father gave him the "Handbook for Boys" for a Christmas present.

Little by little he became absorbed in the life of the Scouts, in the things that Scouts do, in the ideals of the Scout Movement.

He was lucky enough to have a very wise Scoutmaster who understood the minds and moods and abilities of his boys and tried to give each one an opportunity to grow. And so, one day the Scout found himself appointed a Patrol Leader.

And right then and there, a new life started for him.

His responsibilities developed his character. His life with his Patrol in the open strengthened his body. The realness of the boys in his group made him into a real boy himself.

For a long time he carried on his job.

Slowly he learned its many phases. Slowly he made himself a leader somewhere near worthy of those wide-awake, very much alive boys of his, that Patrol group with its splendid spirit of loyalty, unity and "togetherness."

And as he worked he came to wish that he might some day give to other Patrol Leaders the benefits of some of his experiences, to help them along on their path to successful leadership.

This book which you boys now have in your hands is that other boy's dream come true.

*William Hillcourt*

# CONTENTS

# CHAPTER I.

## THE PATROL LEADER AND HIS JOB

**Y**OU have been elected a Patrol Leader. Congratulations!

There are some splendid times ahead for you and your boys, plenty of fun and adventure, plenty of work, plenty of play, plenty of one of the best things in the world—comradeship. A good Patrol is a group of good comrades, "All for one, one for all"— a real unit, standing shoulder to shoulder whatever comes.

Get all the fun and satisfaction you can out of being a Patrol Leader—and there's a lot of both to be had. But don't forget—for a good Patrol Leader cannot forget an instant, any more than the captain of a ship at sea can forget—that there is much more to it than that.

Every one of your boys is going to be a decisive factor in making the Patrol into whatever it turns out to be, but the biggest responsibility, the biggest trust is yours. *Your* leadership, *your* ideals for yourself and the Patrol, *your* example and attitude as a Scout, *your* sympathy with and understanding of the group, individually and as a whole, are going to make all the difference in the world to the rest of them.

1

Under the right kind of a leader almost any Patrol can make itself into the right kind of a Patrol. So Mr. Patrol Leader, it's up to you to get straight to the heart of this job of yours, from the beginning.

## What Makes the Right Kind of a Patrol Leader?

Well, for one thing, the right kind of a leader *believes tremendously in his Patrol.* He has the enthusiasm and the faith to see it in his mind's eye beforehand, *as the best Patrol in the Troop,* made up of the best all-round Scouts, living up to the Scout Oath and Law, better and better all the time. He gets this ideal, this possibility, so firmly planted in his mind and heart, that it is behind everything he says and does and is, and the first thing he knows, the other boys will feel precisely the same way that he does about it.  Enthusiasm is contagious and if you expect the best of your Scouts you go a long way toward getting it.

A Scoutmaster once asked a Scout why it was that he and the other boys in his Patrol followed their Patrol Leader so eagerly and loyally whatever he asked, or wanted them to do.

The boy thought it over for a minute.

"I don't exactly know," he said, at last. "But maybe it's mostly because we feel he's the kind of fellow we'd like to be ourselves."

That gives the key to the situation.  It also leads up to the next point. *The right kind of leader is also the right kind of Scout.*

A Patrol Leader who doesn't care very much whether he goes on from Second Class to First Class rank is likely to have a Patrol that is satisfied to stand still or slip back.

A Patrol is very much like a train. If the engine keeps moving, the whole train moves. If it stops, the whole train stops. If it gets off the track, the whole train may be wrecked.

You are the locomotive in your Patrol train. If you forge ahead so will your boys. If you stop moving so will they. If you let yourself slip off the track from laziness or carelessness or indifference or any other reason, you may have a Patrol "bust up."

## Be a Leader in Scoutcraft

Generally speaking, you will want to try to keep a little ahead of the other boys in your Patrol in Scout tests. It is easier and more effective for a leader to say, "Come on," than "Go on." If you are a bit in advance they will want to catch up. If you lag they will probably lag too. You will want to be a Patrol Leader like tne one whose boys wanted to be the kind of fellow he was. And you can do that best if you show that you, yourself, have "pep," initiative, persistence and ambition in every phase of Scout advancement and service.

The Patrol Leader who has his mind set from the beginning on getting on to Eagle rank himself, will find he has a Patrol who wants to go along with him

SLIGHT EFFORT WILL SHAKE DOWN A FEW, PERHAPS —

—WHILE ENTHUSIASM WILL WORK WONDERS.

to the summits. Here, too, enthusiasm is contagious, and nobody will want to be left behind on the upward trail.

## Be a Leader in Scout Spirit

Even more important, you will find, is to be a leader not a lagger in other phases of Scout training and spirit. A "grouchy" leader may and probably will have a "grouchy" Patrol but a cheery one who does what he has to do willingly and with enthusiasm even if the job is a hard one is likely to have a Patrol that the Scoutmaster can count on every time, a Patrol that it is a pride and satisfaction to lead.

If your boys see that you are making an honest effort yourself to live up to the Scout Law to the best of your ability, if you take the Good Turn seriously as a real obligation, do your utmost to make and keep yourself "physically strong, mentally awake and morally straight," it will seem more worthwhile to the others to do the same. This is one of the biggest parts of the trust that has been re-

posed in you. You can't lead in Scouting if you, yourself, haven't learned to follow the Scout ideals, through and through. If you are a real leader, your boys will look to you for guidance and example not only in the activities but also in the inner spirit of a Scout.

## The Patrol Leader Understands

Sometimes we hear a boy say about some older person, "Oh, he doesn't understand." Well, a very real part of your job as a Patrol Leader is to understand.

to get so close to the minds and hearts of your boys that they will feel your sympathy, give you their confidence.

Naturally, this doesn't come all at once. It is a matter of time and patience and earnest thought—a matter often of silence and waiting. You know from your own experience that if somebody tries to force your confidence before you are ready to give it, you shut up like a clamshell, and it is a long time before anybody has a chance to really get at you again. When the time comes, if you are the right kind of a leader and have made each boy in the Patrol understand by your manner and attitude even  more than by your words, that you are "standing by," ready to help if need be; made them feel sure of your loyalty and sympathy, you will, in time, have won the voluntary confidence of each and when you have, you may well feel happy, for you will have proved yourself a true leader and friend.

One of the tests of a Patrol Leader's real power of understanding his boys is his power to get inside their moods, so to speak, to know not only *how* a certain boy feels at a particular time but *why* he feels that way, to notice not only *how* he acts but also *why* he believes he has to act that way.

In this matter of understanding you will find it a great help if you take the trouble to go to the boys' homes, learn all you can of their background, their parents, their school, their jobs, their habits and hobbies and ambitions. All this takes time and tact and effort, but it is part of your work as a Patrol Leader. Only a leader who understands can truly lead his boys.

So far, so good. In looking this job straight in the eye, we have discovered these important points:

¶ A good Patrol Leader is enthusiastic, has unlimited faith in his boys and in the Patrol.

¶ He keeps moving, himself, along the Scout Trail of advancement and inspires the rest of the Patrol to come along with him, as fast and far as they can go.

¶ He leads in Scout Spirit as well as in Scoutcraft; sincerely tries to set a good example for the rest to follow.

¶ He does his best to understand his boys, to give them all the help and sympathy he can because he really cares for each and all of them from the depths of his heart.

There are a few other points which we shall need to consider briefly.

## An Active Patrol

We have compared a Patrol to a train. It is clear enough that a train that didn't go anywhere, had no destination or schedule would be a useless thing. And a Patrol that could be described the same way, would be equally useless. Only an *active Patrol,* a Patrol with plenty of *things to do,* and a planned schedule for getting them done, definite goals and purposes, is a live Patrol. And it is the Patrol Leader's job— and a big

one it is, too, as well as a stimulating and interesting one—to see that his Patrol is alive in just these things. He plans meetings and programs, looks up Good Turns and projects, works out all kinds of ways and means for keeping his boys interested and progressing in Scouting, getting somewhere, doing something, being something. This Handbook for Patrol Leaders, we hope, will be a help along this line. It is enough at this point to indicate the Patrol Leader's responsibility as the organizer and executive officer of the group which has been entrusted to his leadership, because somebody —several somebodies—believed he could do the job and do it well.

## Share Your Leadership

In all this, of course, it doesn't mean that the Patrol Leader is simply to be the "Big Boss" of the Patrol, planning everything that is to be done, ordering everything accomplished as he wants it, whether it suits the rest or not. Far from it. One of your responsibilities as a Patrol Leader is to help train your boys in leader-

ship, also, letting them learn by doing things themselves, letting them help to plan things and put them through, seeing that they are "in" on everything that is attempted, eager for its success because it is something they want to see done and enjoy doing, not merely something you and possibly your Assistant have arbitrarily decided on. Remember: "Come On," not "Go On."

## A Part of the Whole

Some Patrol Leaders get so interested in their Patrols and Patrol work that they forget sometimes that their Patrol has a definite responsibility and duty to the Troop as a whole. Leadership isn't a one-sided thing. It has to face many directions, work along many lines.

If you are thoroughly filled with that faith in your Patrol and ambition for its success, which we spoke of earlier, you will take immense pride in seeing to it that your Patrol takes an active and spirited part in all the Troop's life and work and play. You will want to make your boys want to be out in full attendance at every Troop meeting, not only present, but. willing, loyal, interested participants in whatever is being done in the Troop, whole-heartedly co-operating with your Scoutmaster and the other Patrols, ready to give service, comradeship and team play all along the way.

## Representing Your Patrol

At the Troop Leader's Council you represent your

Patrol, and are responsible for your Patrol to that Council. It is here, meeting with your Scoutmaster and the other leaders, that plans for the Troop life as a whole are made, Troop problems considered. Here you will get guidance and help in conducting your Patrol affairs and from here bring over to your boys who are not present, the spirit of these leaders' meetings, your Scoutmaster's ideal and wishes for the Troop, of which your Patrol is an active and loyal unit.

## The Real Issues

But coming back to your special, personal job as leader of your Patrol. Don't let yourself be frightened by the bigness of the task which lies ahead of you. It *is* a big task, but you are going to be equal to it if you go at it the right way, learning as you go along, and always keeping the ideal in your heart, even if you do not always find it possible to live up to it or keep your Patrol up to it at every point.

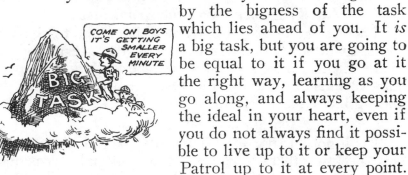

"Not failure but low aim," is most to be avoided. "You can if you think you can."

The main thing to remember is that your chief job is to help your boys *to be happy,* happy in their Patrol life. That very happiness will bring with it a good deal of the rest. It has been said, "A happy citizen is a good citizen." A happy Scout is also undoubtedly a good Scout. So let happiness be your first aim for yourself and the others, not happiness in selfishness, which isn't happiness at all, but happiness in service and friendliness which is the real kind.

You are, for a time, to be the leader of a group of sturdy, alert, impressionable boys. It is "up to you" to keep them happy, interested, eager Scouts, to help them to follow to the best of their ability the great ideals of Scouting.

It is a trust and a responsibility well worth working for, giving the best one has to give to the service.

Let us close this chapter with a Patrol Leader's Creed written by a real Patrol Leader,—a boy like yourself—John Bruce Innes, of Philadelphia, Pa.

## A Patrol Leader's Creed

### *I will develop spirit in my Patrol*

"I will be cheerful constantly. I will be the fast friend of all the Patrol Members and be ready at all times to serve them. They can count on me to have a new song, a fresh idea or a stunt at my finger's end and we will all be as thick as the Forty Thieves.

### *I will advance along the Scout ladder*

"I will steadily step up from Tenderfoot to Second Class, to First Class and through all the Merit Badges to the Eagle Rank, so that I may be a guide and perhaps the inspiration for the rest of my fellows to go and do likewise.

### *I will do a Good Turn Daily*

"I will not let the Good Turn Idea be a thing like my best necktie, that I use only on special occasions.

Neither will I automatically stop looking for and doing Good Turns after the first one of the day. Just because I have already done my Good Turn for the day is no reason at all why I should refuse to grab the opportunity to help grandmother find her specs or put ice in the refrigerator for mother.

### *I will live the Scout Oath and Law*

"I will remember always that I must be loyal and I will not misjudge Bill when he plays me what seems to be a dirty trick. And I will be exceedingly cheerful, even when it hurts, when it would do my old heart good to backbite and be sarcastic or even just plain grouchy. I will take time, once in a while, to sit down and think what it means to do my duty to my country (perhaps it even means picking up carelessly spilled trash—who knows?) and to other people and to God (is it possible that I really ought to go to Church on my own account?). In addition, next to Godliness comes our old friend Cleanliness, and I will remember that it is a part of the Scout Law and make good old soap my constant companion. I will remember that it works just as well on my uniform as on my hands and neck and behave accordingly. I will be thrifty, even though it hurts and my heart yearns for an extra tennis racquet and I have just about twelve dollars in the bank. The best

thing I can do, then, is to sock another dollar in there to make a lucky thirteen and go whistling on my way. I will be trustworthy and absolutely reliable always and my Scoutmaster may count on me to be on time for every meeting and hike.

### I will lead my Patrol

"I will remember that I am the Patrol Leader and that I am responsible for what my fellows do and how they act and I will take steps to make sure that they respect my leadership. I will plan carefully all my Patrol Meetings and the parts of the Troop Meetings for which I am responsible. I will take an active interest in all my Patrol projects and stunts and contribute my fair share of all Patrol work. I will be fair to my Assistant and train him in Patrol management to the best of my ability. I will be alert to the possibilities of all my fellows in my Patrol and will call upon them frequently to add their share to the Troop and Patrol work.

### I will plan my work

"I know that there is only one way to be a successful director and leader and that is to know what I am trying to accomplish and how I want it done. I will not hold a Patrol meeting without first being very sure that I know just what I want Tom and John to do in connection with the song-fest and the games the Troop is to pull at the next meeting, and how I am going to get Frank to see that he ought to pass First Aid to clear up his work on the First Class tests.

*I will be generous and give credit where it is due*

"I know that there is nothing that helps a fellow so much as a word of encouragement and to cheer when he has done a job well. I want to be on the lookout for fellows who do more than their share of the work and let them know that I appreciate their spirit. I will not take credit for their work and when Ed has a particularly fine First Class map I will be very sure that all the fellows in the Troop get a chance to look it over and congratulate him on his good work."

If this creed is yours too, splendid! Sign the dotted line:

. . . . . . . . . . . . . . . . . . . . . . . . . . . . . . . . . . . . . . . . . . . .

And let's go!

## CHAPTER II

## PATROL SPIRIT

IN THE previous chapter we have looked a little into the Patrol Leader's job. In later chapters we shall go more specifically into the various details of that job. Right here let us pause and look at the fellows in your Patrol themselves. Here they are—husky, wide-awake boys, looking to you to lead them into the fun and adventure and comradeship of Scouting. You want to make them into a real Patrol. How are you going to start? What are the first essentials of a real Patrol?

Just consider your boys a moment, try to see what they are really like, inside and out. Some are tall, some are short; some fat, some lean. Some are so quick to act and think that they are always a jump ahead of the others. Some are so slow they have to be pushed and pulled along whatever they do. Some are eager, willing workers. Some are just naturally lazy. Some are sunny tempered, some positively "ornery." They will come from all sorts of homes, have all sorts of queer quirks of disposition and ways, all their own.

That's all right. You wouldn't want them to be just alike. It is much more of a challenge to your ability as a leader, much more interesting to the Patrol as a whole to have them all so different though it cannot be denied the differentness does make complications and difficulties at times.

But luckily they all have one thing in common with each other and with you.   They are all Scouts and Scouts because they want to be, not because anybody said they had to be.   There is that to start with and it is a great help, too.   So long as you can keep them wanting to be Scouts you are a good leader.

Consider them again, these Scout pals of yours. Think how much all this is going to mean to them and to you.   For a year, perhaps several years, their lives and yours will be running along the same trail.   You will have the same interests, the same ambitions, the same hopes.  Together you will undertake great things, enjoy many adventures, share disappointments and triumphs and satisfactions as Scouts, as a Patrol of Scouts, in which everything that affects one affects all.

Notice that word *together*.

It means everything to the life of a real Patrol.

You can't grow into a real Patrol unless you have that together feeling.

"Together" is the key word, the secret pass to that all desirable thing—Patrol Spirit.

## What Is Patrol Spirit?

Patrol Spirit isn't a thing you will find defined and analyzed in dictionaries and encyclopedias. It isn't a thing that can be confined to the pages of a book. Patrol Spirit is a little like personality, something to be felt rather than defined. You recognize it when you meet it. You know when it is present. You miss it when it isn't there. But you cannot easily tell in words what it is.

Suppose then we go at it another way.

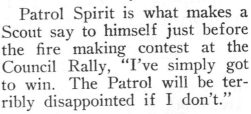

Patrol Spirit is what makes a Scout say to himself just before the fire making contest at the Council Rally, "I've simply got to win. The Patrol will be terribly disappointed if I don't."

It is what makes a Scout say to another boy, "Sorry, but I can't go to the movies with you tonight. It's Patrol meeting night."

When two Scouts get their heads together to think out some way by which Bill who hasn't much spare pocket money can earn his camp fee so that the Patrol can go to camp full force, it is Patrol Spirit that is operating.

A Patrol Leader turns to his Scoutmaster who has asked for volunteers for a Good Turn and says, "I can promise for my fellows. I know they'll be glad to help." There is Patrol Spirit sure of itself, to be depended upon to meet the demand.

It is Patrol Spirit that puts enthusiasm and "pep" into whatever the Patrol undertakes, whether it is building a totem pole, passing tests or guarding a street crossing. It is what puts fun and interest into Patrol meetings, real meaning into a Patrol camp fire, loyalty and good comradeship into all Patrol relationships.

It is Patrol Spirit that makes it seem more than worth while for its members to sacrifice their own comfort or wishes if need be for the good of the whole, that keeps out personal bickerings and jealousy, that makes every fellow feel the fineness and realness of standing together through thick and thin, rain and shine.

Patrol Spirit is a living thing. It goes on. When you have, in years to come, forgotten the particular hikes and camps and tests and competitions and Good Turns—the ups and downs of Patrol life which seem so important now to all of you, you will remember the spirit of it all, how wonderful a thing it was to be together as a Patrol for all that time, how much it meant to you all. And it should mean most of all to you who as the leader had most to do with creating that unforgettable thing—Patrol Spirit.

## How Patrol Spirit Grows

Without Patrol Spirit a Patrol is just a bunch of boys, who happen to be together at the moment, a group that may fall apart the instant the passing interest subsides. With Patrol Spirit, the thing coheres, grows, counts—in the life of the Troop and the community as well as to its members.

From the beginning then you will want to do all you can to make your fellows feel the importance of developing this sense of "togetherness" without which Patrol Spirit cannot be. You will want from the beginning to make each one realize that he is an indispensable part of the whole group and that the spirit of the whole Patrol depends absolutely upon the spirit of the individual Scouts in it.

Nevertheless, do not be discouraged if Patrol Spirit doesn't spring up like a mushroom, over night, in the group. It isn't a thing to be manufactured to order. Still it can be helped to grow and develop just as a plant put in the earth can be assisted, by faithful watering, by fertilizing of the soil, by letting plenty of sun and air get to it, by patiently and persistently pulling up the weeds which rise up to choke out its very existence.

Many small details go into the building up of a genuine Patrol Spirit. The Patrol Leader will try to see that none of them is overlooked.

## Believe In Your Patrol

We have spoken already of the importance of a Patrol Leader's own attitude from the beginning. If he believes with all his might that the Patrol can and will grow into the best Patrol in the Troop or even the community, the chances are it will. If you have the courage to stand up in front of your Patrol the very first meeting and put it up to your fellows, fair and square, what you expect of them and yourself, make a thundering speech that will serve to put them on their mettle, all set to live up to your hopes and determination for success, so much the better.

If you are a bit shy about doing that, let the fellows at least *feel the spirit* of your faith anyhow. They'll catch it from you if you believe in your ideal firmly and sincerely enough, even if you never get it put into words. It isn't a bad idea to make your "thundering" speech anyway, if you only make it in the privacy of your own room, to the mirror.

"Golly! We'll show 'em what a live Patrol is!" you declare, banging your fist down on the table till everything rattles.

And Golly! You probably will—going into it in that spirit. So there's that—an important first step.

## Leader Not Boss

Another thing which helps to foster a lively Patrol Spirit from the start is getting your boys to feel you count on each and every one to help put through this ideal of yours, of the best, most up-on-its-toes Patrol in town. As we say elsewhere, Patrol Leadership isn't a one man job. It certainly isn't. You will need the help of every fellow in your Patrol and you will get

it, too, once they get the idea that you want to be their leader but not their boss. There will be times, of course, when you will have to give orders and expect them to be obeyed. But it won't be blind obedience. They have a right to know the "why" of the whole thing. Little by little, if the thing grows as it should, the whole Patrol will come to see that if you put Bob or Bill or Jack at a certain task and expect him to perform it, it isn't just because you want to show your authority but because this particular arrangement and division of work is best for the Patrol as a whole. And naturally you will not ask the boys to do anything you wouldn't or couldn't do yourself. It is the "Come on" attitude, not the "Go on" attitude that makes for successful Patrol organization and real Patrol Spirit. The boys will follow where you lead when they see that your leadership is for the happiness of all.

## DISCIPLÍNE

Few boys like the sound of the word "Discipline." Probably you don't like it very much yourself. Yet a Patrol which isn't well controlled, *self controlled,* isn't a happy Patrol, or a successful Patrol, or a Patrol with the spirit that sticks together.    Instead it is a Patrol which is headed for the rocks which naturally isn't the direction you want it to set out for.

But this discipline—necessary everywhere throughout the world, wherever a group of people, small or large, come together—isn't a matter of force or bossing.    The word we have used above, "self controlled" gives the secret.    If you can get your boys to do the right thing in the Patrol, not because you have made them do it, but because they want to do it and see the sense of doing it, you have made a real step toward successful leadership and the creation of true Scout and Patrol Spirit.

### "Why Can't Joe Do It?"

Explaining the "why" of a situation or an order as suggested above goes a long way toward smoothing out any difficulties or friction.    If the boys don't understand what is behind it all you will soon be pestered and the whole order of the Patrol upset by "I don't see why I should have to do it?   Why can't Joe do it?" "Why don't we do this, that, or the other thing instead of what we are doing?" "Why this?" "Why not that?" A little sympathetic attention to "Whys" in advance will save a disastrous attack of "Whys" later.    A wise Patrol Leader takes the boys of his Patrol into his confidence and, in turn, earns theirs.

"Discipline?"    said    a    Patrol Leader not long ago.  "Don't know the word.  Doesn't exist in our Patrol.  We rely on the Patrol Spirit instead."

Naturally, he did not mean quite

literally that there was no discipline in his Patrol. Problems of discipline will come up in the best regulated Patrols, since boys are neither saints nor blocks of wood, all carved exactly alike. What he did mean was that in a Patrol in which there was the real stick-together spirit a natural discipline was created which did not need enforcement.

## Varieties of Species

In order to minimize the risk of friction and bring about a really unified Patrol, the Patrol Leader must thoroughly understand his fellows, at least he must make a sympathetic and patient attempt to do so. If he isn't willing to go that far he won't make much of a success as a leader.

We have said earlier in this chapter that the very diversity of types of boys which is sure to occur even in a small group like a single Patrol makes a part of

the problem of the Leader's task as well as its interest. It may be helpful to run briefly through some of the more familiar types which every Patrol Leader may have to deal with and understand.

Naturally it is always true that these types may overlap to a considerable extent and it is also true that the same boy may react quite differently and show quite different sides of himself at one time than he does at another. These things also have to be taken into consideration.

This matter of studying personality isn't at all a simple thing. Indeed it is often very complex and baffling. Yet a Patrol Leader can and must make a study, first hand, of the particular boys in his Patrol and the more he studies, the more he understands and sympathizes and is able to help and be a real friend to each and every one of the group. He doesn't have to generalize. He just has to look and learn and love

## Familiar Types

In almost any Patrol one is likely to find the "Wise Guy," the "Bully" and other recognizable varieties of the species which call for special tact and patience in trying to convert them into valuable adjuncts of the Patrol instead of a possible total loss. On the other hand you will also happily enough usually find several boys who naturally "play the game," fit well into Patrol life and who not only present no particular problem but are often a tremendous help to the Patrol Leader.

## These Are All Right

Among the easy-to-handle types of boys you will first of all discover the one whom we may describe as *smooth running*. He probably comes from a pleasant, sympathetic home where he has acquired a certain amount of social ease and tact and consideration for others. He takes things about as they come in an agreeable happy-go-lucky fashion. He is, as a rule, easily led and quick to conform to suggestion. He may or may not have initiative and ambition. If he hasn't, it will be up to you to stir him up, to see that he gets interested enough to forge ahead and assume leadership on his own in some phase of Patrol work for which he is fitted. This last naturally applies to all the types or combinations of type.

Another easy-to-handle type is the naturally *passive* boy, who has no initiative at all but who will follow with docility and even eagerness where somebody else leads. He has to be told to do everything. He never thinks of doing it by himself. Naturally he never starts trouble. You sometimes almost wish he would. In one way he isn't a problem. In another he is. You will need to study him closely, keep after him, put

THE PASSIVE BOY NEEDS BOOSTING

him on his own wherever possible. If by chance, he has an idea of his own listen to it sympathetically and encourage him to execute it, help him to express himself.

In between the types that are easily handled and those that are not comes the *clever boy*. The clever boy is the analyzer for the whole Patrol. He can not only size up a situation, he can also size you up. He is often your keenest critic. He knows exactly where you failed at a given point and precisely what you should have done or said, instead of what you did do and say. Rather an alarming individual as you will see. If you don't look out you will find him quietly taking over the Patrol reins in his own capable hands, running everything, including yourself. What are you going to do with him? Easy enough. Utilize his cleverness, turn it to good account. Put responsibility on his shoulders and a whole lot of it. Give him enough to do to exercise his brains and energy and personality on. Get him on your side by taking him fully into your confidence, recognizing his ability, asking his advice. Often when this is done you will find him your ablest, most loyal helper. Very often he by all odds is the best fellow to serve as your Assistant. Be thankful you have him and let him know it. In turn he will play the game with you.

## These Are Not So Easy

Among the least difficult of the not-so-easy group comes the *lazy* boy. The lazy boy is almost sure to turn up in any group. Indeed, you are lucky if you have not more than one of him. The lazy boy usually means very well.

He doesn't intend to make trouble. It is just his natural

inertia that makes him postpone the job he has to do
or never do it at all or, at most, half do it. You will
have to do your best to fire his enthusiasm. Get him
really interested in Patrol work or some phase of it
at least. When this happens you will be surprised
to see him actually wake up, show amazing energy and
thoroughness. Somebody has said that all the time and
labor saving devices of civilization were invented by
lazy folks. Of course that isn't strictly true but it has
an idea behind it. Another way to get at the lazy boy is
through appealing to his loyalty. If he once sees that
his slipshod ways bring down the credit and standing
of the Patrol and is made to feel that the rest really
count on him to rise to the standard of the whole Patrol
and are disappointed in him if he doesn't, it will make
a considerable difference. Anyway whatever you do,
you can't afford for his own sake or the Patrol's to let
the lazy boy stay lazy. When you have him pepped up,
keep him that way, never give him a chance to slip back.
Keep him permanently busy and interested and on
the job.

Then there is the *mischievous* boy. He isn't the least
bit in the world malicious. He is just fearfully and
wonderfully lively, simply can't help playing tricks on
everybody, getting himself and the Patrol into trouble.

He is as quick in his thoughts
and actions as the lazy boy is
slow. He can be turned into
a real asset to the Patrol if
he is treated the right way.
Let him use his wits inventing Patrol stunts, thinking
up things for the Patrol to
do, keep him busy. Give him
hard things to do. Keep him
interested all the time. Place enough responsibility on
him to steady him, keep him out of mischief. Never
let him have a dull minute. If you do—hoop la!
He's off and Heaven help the Patrol! The mischiev-

ous boy is usually also the lovable, popular boy. It is just his gaiety and high spirits that spill over and make difficulty. Gaiety and high spirits are fine things in the life of a Patrol. Don't try to squelch them. Direct them where they will do the most good. Before you know it your mischievous boy isn't a problem but your right hand man.

## And These Are Really Difficult

The lazy boy and the mischievous boy and even, at times, the clever boy present some difficulties in the life of the Patrol. But these types aren't really disagreeable. They simply need adjustment. But unluckily there are two or three types that are definitely disagreeable, types that offer a real trial to the Patrol Leader, a challenge to all the patience and self control he can muster.

First there is the *grouchy* boy. He is a regular killjoy, a born pessimist or if he isn't a born one he has let himself get that way.

He always looks on the dark side of everything. He doesn't think there is any use of going on a hike because it may rain and since the Patrol is bound to lose anyway there is no good in their even planning to enter the contest. He doesn't like the eats that have been provided. The smoke gets in his eyes and the flies into his soup. If somebody says, "Let's do so and so," he can find ten reasons for not doing it or doing something else instead and is quite willing to argue it out along that line if it takes all summer. He is moody and glum when everybody else feels gay and cheerful. In short, he is more or less of a pest to himself and everybody else. If he doesn't make the rest of you feel any too good, you may be sure he isn't any too

happy himself.  Try to get behind this grouchiness.
For this boy you and the others will need patience,
patience, and yet more patience.  Sometimes the best
possible thing to do is to ignore him entirely and
go on as if everything were quite all right.  If he finds
not too much attention is being paid to him, ten to one
he will follow the others, even have a good time doing it
in spite of himself.

Another inconvenient and trouble-making type is the
so-called *"wise guy."*  He has sarcastic remarks ready
to shoot at precisely the wrong moment.  He "gets your
goat" if he possibly can.  He's simply built that way.
He thinks he knows everything in the world generally,
and particularly how the Patrol ought to be run.  The
*clever* boy knows too.  That's why he's clever.  But
he really knows while the "wise guy" merely thinks he
does, which makes all the difference.  The "wise guy"
is just another kind of "bone-head," only he doesn't
suspect it.  He really believes himself a fine fellow and
loves to show off.  Maybe you can't straighten this chap
out all by yourself.  Very often you will need the help
of the rest of your Patrol to put him where he'll do the
most good to himself, as well as to the Patrol.  In releas-
ing a drowning person, whom you are trying to save
and who has got hold of
you in his struggle for
dear life, it is some-
times advised to sub-
merge his head, be-
cause that will
make him use
his arms to

try to climb to the surface again. The same method may be used figuratively to great advantage in the treating of the "wise guy." And when you duck, duck well. Wait until the opportunity comes—when he shows a weak point—and use the time to prove to him his own failings. It won't do him any harm if he can see himself for once as a punctured balloon, flat as a pancake, instead of all puffed up. He has got good stuff in him. Every boy has. But he needs to catch a glimpse of his own littleness and be put in a place where his show-

offness won't help him a bit. It is only when we see ourselves as little, that we start to become big.

And last but not least —there is the *bully*.

The bully tries to dominate the whole Patrol. He is the master braggart, the tyrant of all he can handle. Don't let him bluff you. His noise means nothing, and the strength he brags about very often exists only in his own imagination. You will need all your skill to handle this special type. You must be strong in your opposition to his bullying and never give in, and you will have to get your boys' assistance in the treatment of him. If you can make the rest see behind his bluff, you can weaken the effect of it. But as in the case of the "wise guy," it is only by making him feel his unimportance that you can deal with him; and even then his bragging may continue even if it has lost its effect, until he discovers that it's no fun bragging if nobody listens.

The types mentioned are naturally only a few of the many boy types that exist and even these are overlapping. If we set out to treat them all it would make a book by itself. We can only discuss a few of the common types which you may find in your Patrol.

## This Applies to Them All

In the above we have explained some of the methods of handling the individual types, but there are rules that can be applied to every boy in the Patrol, and we can put them down in brief:

1. *Keep the boys busy with things that interest them.*
2. *Give them responsibilities.*
3. *Be patient and sympathetic. Try to understand.*

To keep them busy you must plan your Patrol meetings and hikes very carefully so that there will be no pauses in which the difficult boys can run wild.

Responsibilities are very often able to "make" a boy. Even the "wise guy" and the "bully" type often can be changed by placing responsibilities on their shoulders. A Patrol organization that divides the duties and gives some of them to each boy to perform usually will mean quite a bit in creating the right kind of spirit in the Patrol. We shall describe such an organization in detail in another chapter.

And then patience, and sympathy! You will never make your Patrol into a well-controlled and self-controlled group if you get impatient. You don't get anywhere by scolding. It will only put the boys on the defensive and create the opposite effect from what was desired and intended.

## Try to Understand

As has been previously suggested you will need to study the boys and try by every means in your power to understand them. If you are able to have some short sincere talks with them in private it will help immensely. Very often boys are entirely different when you are alone with them from what they are in public. Boys like to act, to seem something they really aren't. And their behavior  isn't always exactly improved when they act. To get to the bottom of a boy's heart you have to be alone with him. Walking home from a meeting with one, sitting with another at the camp fire, going with a third on a short walk before Taps may mean learning to know the real boy—not only the sometimes ugly looking mask he may use to disguise himself with,

but the boy himself. Understanding a boy's family life and background, as has been said elsewhere, is also a great help in understanding the boy himself.

But even if you do your best, there may be times when your diplomatic efforts will be in vain.

There may come misunderstandings, "scraps," even the beginning of a fight inside the Patrol.

Don't be discouraged if this should happen. Do your best to get everything smoothed out again. Usually a scrap is only a passing incident. It will soon be forgotten and, queerly enough, it sometimes even benefits the Patrol. You may some day find a wild fight going on between two of the boys. Possibly they have been on unfriendly terms for some time, or their fighting spirit has suddenly been aroused in them by some special provocation. Anyway there is fight. Your interference might easily make things worse. On the other hand, interference at the right moment might clear the thunder clouds away. Here your tact and common sense will have to tell you what to do.

But every time there has been a break in the discipline, try to make the boy or boys understand that they did something that wasn't worthy of the Patrol—and then forget about it. Don't try to take it up time and again and rub it in. That will only stir up the bad spirit again.

## A Rare Occurrence

The occasion might come when it may seem necessary to drop a boy from the Patrol. If he repeatedly conducts himself in a way far from the spirit you want to have rule in your Patrol, you may be forced to ask him to withdraw. Speak to the other members of your Patrol and first of all to your Scoutmaster about it and remember that no Scout should ever be removed from a Patrol until you have tried out every sound advice the other boys or your Scoutmaster might give you. To be dropped from his Patrol puts a bad stamp on a Scout, even if it can be arranged that he join another Patrol. But, after all, it is better to cut a sick branch off the tree than to have the whole tree destroyed.

## The Honor of the Patrol

There must be discipline in the Patrol, but the thing is to create the discipline from the inside out, i.e., from the boys themselves, instead of having it impressed upon them from the outside in, i.e., from you.

By letting the boys feel that discipline is only a means to make the Patrol better and stronger, it will some time turn out that the discipline has grown into Patrol Spirit. Then the boys will do the things not as a matter of discipline, but "for the honor of the Patrol." There will be no falling down on the jobs, because each boy will realize that the execution of your orders as a Patrol Leader will only make himself—as a part of the Patrol—have a better time all round.

That was what the Patrol Leader meant when he said: "Discipline doesn't exist in our Patrol."

While the right understanding of Patrol discipline helps largely in creating Patrol Spirit, there are several other things that help likewise. Some of them are big things; some of them are just small details. But it is the rule in creating Patrol Spirit that not even the smallest details must be overlooked. Therefore, let us be careful in our procedure. Let us try to follow a Patrol as it works along and let us try to find out the details that enter into a Patrol's life, which may help in the development of Patrol Spirit.

# THE NAME OF THE PATROL

Very often the name of the Patrol is the first thing which is decided upon at the very first meeting of the boys. You get hold of a Handbook for Boys, find a list of Patrol animals, and choose one. And that's that.

But what does a name *chosen like that* mean to a Patrol?

Less than nothing!!

A name is an important thing. You will rarely hear of a baby being baptized without its name having been the subject of discussion by the entire family for weeks. The members will weigh the different names, think out reasons for using one and not another, until it is finally decided upon and given to the defenceless child. And even so you will very often find that when the baby grows up the name doesn't fit its character at all.

Why not use some time and thought for the selection of a real Patrol name—a name that will mean something to the Patrol in the future, maybe have a hidden meaning that nobody outside the Patrol will know about?

Let the boys be on the lookout for a good name and it is certain to come some day—one way or another.

## How One Patrol Got Its Name

One Patrol we know of had been trying in vain to find a name and it came to them on their first big hike.

They had been hiking through the forest when suddenly one of them came across a spot where the old leaves had been turned over, where many tracks told them that a fight had taken place, and fresh blood marks hinted at a tragic tale. In a minute the Patrol was collected around the place trying to find out what had really happened, and by the help of loose hairs which the Scouts found on the ground and on the branches of a couple of bushes, they found out the encounter had been between a fox and a muskrat. By careful investigation they discovered that it was possible to follow the trail of the fox dragging its bleeding prey along through the underbrush. Fortunately the wind helped them and they started on their tracking expedition. After having walked for a little while they stopped short. From a distance they heard the sharp bark of a fox, almost as a strange sound from an unreal world. They went on and by extreme carefulness they succeeded in getting near enough to the fox's den to see t h e cubs having their meal while the old fox was on g u a r d , watching them and listening for intruders.

This incident gave the Patrol its name: "Barking Fox." And you may well believe that every mention of that name makes the boys remember the day when they tracked their first fox through the underbrush.

## And Another

Another Patrol got its name in a funny way. It had been building a bridge over a broad ditch as a pioneering stunt. It was a good day's work and the bridge looked fine. But anyway its Patrol Leader decided that its strength had to be tested. He ordered the whole Patrol on the bridge and everything seemed to be all right until suddenly a crack sounded, and down came the bridge with its human weight of seven Scouts. Fortunately the ditch wasn't deep and the only thing that happened to the boys was that they got into water up to their knees.

But at the same time the Patrol was baptized: "Wet Moccasin," a name that doesn't convey much to a person outside the Patrol, but one that means everything to the boys inside.

If nothing worthy of perpetuating happens inside a reasonable time it may be necessary for you to invent a name, but consider it carefully.

## Color Names

The first idea that comes to you may be to choose the favorite color of the boys in the Patrol; use it for the color of the shoulder knot or medallion and use its name as the Patrol name. How do you like "Green Patrol," "Blue and Grey Patrol." Not bad sounding, eh?

## Animal Names

Or maybe you would prefer the name of an animal for a Patrol name. What you ought to think of then is, "Which animal will best represent the place where we live or best represent the virtues we want to develop in our Patrol?" If you live in the Rocky Mountains, a bear might be your choice, or even living where bears do not appear except in a zoo you might choose the bear because of its strength (or maybe its sweet tooth?). If you live in Florida the alligator or the pelican may be the favorites, while living in Maine, you would prefer the moose or the deer.

When you think it over you may find it inappropriate to name your Patrol for the hippo or the rhinoceros, for instance. You won't find them in your locality and as to their significance . . . .

Probably the kangaroo, the hyena, the elephant and others you could think of would be equally unsuitable.

In trying to find an animal for whom to name your Patrol don't forget that the animals mentioned in the Handbook for Boys are only suggestions. The Patrol may choose any name it finds fitting.

And why stick to the rather over-used "Beaver Patrol," "Owl Patrol," "Wolf Patrol"? Why not put a little personal touch into it and call the Patrol "Busy Beaver," "White Owl," "Wary Wolf." Or use any other appropriate adjectives that come to your mind. Make the name distinctive, something that belongs peculiarly to your Patrol. Here are a few suggestions:

"Leaping Antelope"      "Arrow Hawk"
"Seeing Bat"            "Flying Horse"
"Roaming Buffalo"       "Speedy Otter"
"Spreading Eagle"       "Silent Panther"
            "Swift Swallow"

And let people expect to find the "Seeing Bat" Patrol capable of pathfinding in the dark; the "Roaming Buffalo" Patrol filled with strength and wanderlust, the "Speedy Otter," a Patrol of swimmers and life savers, and the "Silent Panther" consisting of expert stalkers.

Choosing an animal or bird as a Patrol name has the advantage in some cases of suggesting an appropriate and distinctive call.

**Tree Names**

Local trees may also suggest a name for your Patrol. The "Pine Tree Patrol" is well known, and names like "Yucca Patrol," "Sequoia Patrol," "Hemlock Patrol," "Dogwood Patrol" all sound well, and it isn't difficult to increase the list.

"Birch Patrol"          "Hickory Patrol"
"Cedar Patrol"          "Maple Patrol"
"Chestnut Patrol"       "Oak Patrol"
"Hazel Patrol"          "Sumach Patrol"
            "Willow Patrol"

## Star Names

Maybe again the name of a constellation or a single star or planet would appeal to you:

"Algol Patrol"      "Orion Patrol"
"Capella Patrol"      "Scorpio Patrol"
"Corona Patrol"      "Taurus Patrol"
"Dragon Patrol"      "Ursa Patrol"
            "Vega Patrol"

## Racial and Historical Names

The above names are all taken from nature, but you might be able to find a Patrol name somewhere else. Human races and history may suggest some names to you. What about "The Buccaneers", "The Vikings", "The Pioneers", for example? Or how would you like using the name of an Indian tribe?

"The Apaches"      "The Kiowas"
"The Blackfeet"      "The Mohicans"
"The Cheyennes"      "The Navajos"
"The Comanches"      "The Senecas"
            "The Sioux"

## Using the Names of Persons

Another splendid way of getting a Patrol name would be to choose the name of the person for whom you have the greatest esteem. It might be a hero from the olden days, or a man of our own times. You may use it in connection with the word Patrol, as for example "The James E. West Patrol" or you may use a combination like "Lindbergh's Own," letting the own mean "Own Boys," "Own Patrol." Here are just a few suggestions:

"B. P.'s Own"
"Dan Beard's Patrol"
"The Daniel Boone Patrol"
"The Columbus Patrol"
"Edison's Patrol"
"Kit Carson's Own"
"Lincoln's Own"
"Roosevelt's Patrol"
"The Washington Patrol"

You yourself can increase that list with hundreds of names.

## Secret Names

And as a last idea we might consider a secret name for your Patrol. Secrecy is a thing which appeals to all boys and if you can surround the Patrol with some mystery so much the better. Your Patrol may be able to make its own hidden name, that has a meaning only to the Patrol itself but if you can't find one, here is a suggestion:

Choose a slogan like "Stick To It" or "Do It Now," or "Hit The Line" or any other of a similar inspiring kind, reduce the slogan into initials and let that be the name of the Patrol. Who else but the Patrol's own boys will be able to penetrate into names like the "The S. T. I. Patrol" or "The D. I. N. Patrol" or "The "H. T. L. Patrol"? You don't necessarily have to stick to slogans to make up an initial name. You may

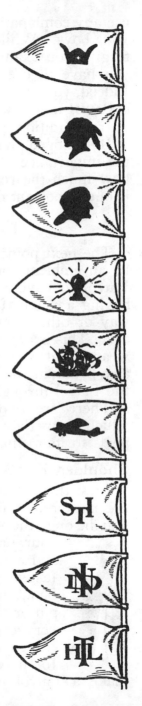

use any combination of words if they mean something to your boys. While in the other cases we have been able to give you examples of groups of Patrol names, here you have to use your own imagination and initiative. Indeed, you will need to use these in any case. *Choosing a Patrol name is a very personal matter.* With it your Patrol tradition gets under way.

It is hoped that all this has opened your eyes as to the importance of a Patrol name and made you realize how much the real name can mean to a Patrol. This is one important detail. There are many others.

## PATROL EMBLEMS

The next point which it is necessary to consider may be an emblem for the Patrol. It is all right for your Patrol to have a fine name. But what is the use of having a name if nobody ever calls you by it? Some way or other you will have to tell the world who you are. This is done by having all the boys of your Patrol wear a Patrol emblem of some kind. It may be done also by having a Patrol flag or totem pole which follows the Patrol through all of its exploits.

There are two kinds of individual emblems from which your Patrol may choose the one that most appeals to its members.

### Shoulder Knots

First there is the shoulder knot. Just as the color of the neckerchief designates to which Troop or Council you belong, the color of the shoulder knot designates

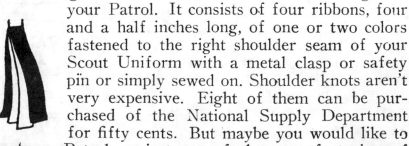

your Patrol. It consists of four ribbons, four and a half inches long, of one or two colors fastened to the right shoulder seam of your Scout Uniform with a metal clasp or safety pin or simply sewed on. Shoulder knots aren't very expensive. Eight of them can be purchased of the National Supply Department for fifty cents. But maybe you would like to make a Patrol project out of the manufacturing of

them and that is entirely all right as long as you stick
to the official measurements.

## Medallions

Another way of indicating to which Patrol your boys
belong is by the wearing of a Patrol medallion, a small
disc of red felt, two inches in diameter with the Patrol
animal (or whatever the emblem is) embroidered on it
in black. It is worn two inches below
the right shoulder seam. The Supply
Department offers some of these medallions for sale but if your Patrol
has selected a special and peculiar
animal, tree, constellation or initials
as we discussed earlier, you may have
to make the medallions for your-
self. And here is immediately another Patrol project
which it might be worth while working on.

To cut the discs out of red felt is easy enough. The
trouble starts when you want to put the emblem on
them. You probably can't embroider it so you will have
to use oil paint. Get hold of a picture of the Patrol
animal's head, the tree or whatever you have chosen.
The most important thing is to have the picture simple
enough so that you can make a satisfactory looking sil-
houette outline of it. It must also, of course, be the
right size. Transfer the outline to a piece of thin cardboard. The next step is to cut out the outline with a

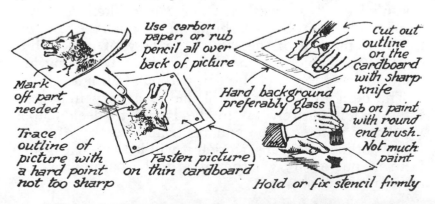

Use carbon paper or rub pencil all over back of picture

Cut out outline on the cardboard with sharp knife

Mark off part needed

Trace outline of picture with a hard point not too sharp

Fasten picture on thin cardboard

Hard background preferably glass

Dab on paint with round end brush. Not much paint

Hold or fix stencil firmly

sharp penknife. The remaining mask is placed on the felt disc. All the red felt shown through the opening is filled in with a short-haired stiff brush dipped in black oil paint. Apply the paint, not with the ordinary stroke used in painting, but with an up-and-down movement of the brush. This done, the disc is put aside to dry while the next is being made. When the medallions are dry they are sewed on the uniforms.

## Patrol Flags

You will easily understand that the wearing of the Patrol's colors or insignia will help to make the boys feel that they really "belong," which fosters Patrol Spirit, but in the long run you will soon find that a Patrol flag or a Patrol totem pole will mean even more to the boys.

Not a Patrol flag on a *de luxe* polished, mahogany flag pole that has to be handled with care so that no scratches will show, and with a brass emblem on top that has to be "shined up" every once in a while, but a real flag on an honest-to-goodness Scout staff that will stand rain and snow, wind and sun, that can follow the Patrol through thick and thin.

You might start with a flag such as you can purchase of the Supply Department for 25 cents, but you will very likely find that the Patrol will like to make its own flag.

Choose a comparatively dark color, so that the flag doesn't have to be washed after every hike. Green is a splendid color. So is light khaki. Or maybe you will prefer to make it of the same color as your neckerchief or the Patrol colors. The material must be strong and the color able to stand the sun without fading.

The designing of a Patrol flag is a very important thing. It is entirely up to the Patrol to decide upon its shape; if it is to be square, triangular, or of some fancy outline; what inscription it will bear; what design is to be put on it; whether it is to be painted or embroidered, and so forth.

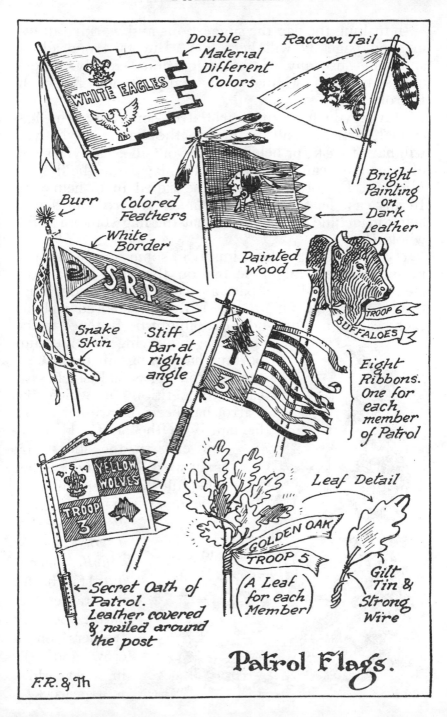

Double Material Different Colors

Raccoon Tail

WHITE EAGLES

Colored Feathers

Burr

White Border

S.R.P.

Snake Skin

Stiff Bar at right angle

Bright Painting on Dark Leather

Painted Wood

TROOP 6

BUFFALOES

Eight Ribbons. One for each member of Patrol

B.S.A.

YELLOW WOLVES

TROOP 3

GOLDEN OAK

TROOP 5

(A Leaf for each Member)

Leaf Detail

Gilt Tin & Strong Wire

←Secret Oath of Patrol. Leather covered & nailed around the post

Patrol Flags.

F.R. & Th

In making the flag the suggestions and working drawings on page 39 will help you. But take our advice and don't use any of the suggestions exactly. Work out something original that really stands for your Patrol.

Maybe you have in your Patrol some boy who has enough artistic skill to design the flag. Maybe you will have to ask for help from the outside. Maybe some of your boys can manufacture the flag from the design. Maybe a Patrol mother may be called in to help you. In any case let the boys *feel that it is their flag* that is being made and let them feel that the flag stands for the whole Patrol.

If a boy distinguishes himself in some way his initials in small letters might be put on the flag. If all the members of the Patrol pass a certain Merit Badge, that badge might be put on it. Different colored ribbons each bearing a name and a date might be fastened to the

flag pole signifying the most important happenings in the life of the Patrol. A small shield for each competition in which the Patrol has been the winner might be nailed to the staff. There is no end to the ideas you may work out. There is but one rule to be remembered. *Whatever you put on your flag or flag pole it must have a definite meaning.* If it hasn't it is rather like putting peacock feathers on a crow and telling the world it is a peacock.

## Totem Poles

In regard to the Patrol totem pole the very same can be said. Every single bit of decoration on it must mean something to the Patrol. The totem pole, like the flag staff, must be strong enough to follow the Patrol everywhere. Fine and delicate designs, therefore, ought to be avoided, but even so, a Scout staff can be made into a beautiful totem pole as the illustrations in the chapter on Patrol Handicraft will prove to you.

Choose the boy in the Patrol who has proved himself to be the best whittler to make the totem pole. Have him go ahead and use his art on small pieces of wood until he has found a design that represents the Patrol worthily. It may contain the Patrol animal, a symbol of your city, or your state, or represent some phase of Scouting. It may be a reproduction of an old Indian totem pole. When the design has been approved by the Patrol, the whittler is supplied with an ash pole from which to make the final project, ash being light and strong and, easy to carve. After the carving has been completed the pole is painted in bright colors.

If you want the Patrol flag or totem pole to mean something, it should follow your Patrol wherever it goes. The dates on the pole or on the ribbons are not only put there to signify where the Patrol has been, but also to make the flag able to say, "I was there too," and before you know it your boys will instinctively feel that something is wrong when their emblem isn't with them, a feeling that contributes definitely to developing Patrol Spirit.

## PATROL SONG, YELL AND CALL

You may have attended a football game between a couple of colleges. Did you hear the boys cheer up their team by thundering yells and fiery applause? Did you see what effect it had on the players? Likewise, every Patrol ought to have its yell and practice it. It helps its bit to the fostering of Patrol Spirit. So does a real Patrol song. Lucky the Patrol that has both. Songs and yells will be treated in more detail in the chapter on "Patrol Stunts."

The distinctive Patrol call, as has been already said, has its special interest and picturesque value—something by which a member of a Patrol will always recognize a fellow member. It is understood that Scout honor forbids any Scout to use the call of another Patrol for any purpose.

## THE SCOUT UNIFORM

There is no doubt that the right name and emblem mean a great deal in creating team spirit. Still more important is the uniform.

If you have once seen a crowd open up willingly to let a boy in a Scout uniform pass through it to the help of an injured person in its midst, if you have seen that the Scout uniform was the pass that permitted a boy to go back and forth in flood- or tornado-stricken areas, where other boys, and men, too, were kept away almost for miles; if you have ever been present at big national gatherings where Boy Scouts were the honor marshals, you will have realized what the khaki uniform means to the public.

### An International Uniform

If you have considered that two million boys scattered over the world all wear similar uniforms and even if their languages and customs are different, consider each other as brothers; if you have felt the thrill of being a part of a Troop of Scouts performing an important civic duty, then you know what the khaki uniform means to team spirit.

And what the uniform means to all these other boys you can make it mean in concentrated form to the boys of your Patrol.

## When and How to Get It

As soon as your boys have passed their Tenderfoot tests you will find them eager to get their Scout Uniform. Some day one will bob up with a Scout hat, another one with a Scout shirt, still another with a pair of khaki breeches and you will find yourself surrounded by a number of queer looking "critters."

Stop that!

Tell your boys as they get near the stage when they want to get the uniform, how much it will mean to each one of them and to the Patrol to which they belong if they stick to each other in this matter as in all other matters. Make them see that it isn't fair to the other fellows if one turns up at a meeting one day in a complete uniform, while the others have only been able to save enough to buy the broad-brimmed hat. By getting the fellow with the uniform to sacrifice a little of his desire for showing off until his friends can show off too, he will  catch something of the spirit of the Patrol, and, by having the other boys feel that somebody is willing to sacrifice something for their sake, they will work even harder to earn money enough to buy their own uniforms. And then when the great day has arrived when *all* the boys have their Scout Uniforms complete, what a joy! What tremendous satisfaction and comradeship!

# BADGES AND INSIGNIA

Metal Badge of highest rank worn on hat (Tenderfoot, Second Class, First Class, Star, Life, Eagle, or Achievement)

"Boy Scouts of America" embroidered in red silk over right pocket

Patrol Medallion worn on right sleeve—top 2 inches below shoulder seam

Special Temporary Insignia (Camp emblems, etc.) worn centered on right pocket below flap

*ON LONG SLEEVED SHIRT ~*

Merit Badges in rows of two each, if worn on sleeve instead of on Merit Badge Sash

Veteran Insignia centered on right cuff 1½ inches above lower edge

Service Stars ⅜ inches above left pocket flap, point up, ¾ inches from the center to center of stars

Community Name Strip worn on left sleeve above Troop Numeral

Troop Numeral on left sleeve, top two inches below shoulder seam

Embroidered Badge of Office worn on left sleeve top 4 inches below shoulder seam

Embroidered Badge of highest rank centered on left pocket. If metal badge of rank is worn on shirt it is centered on left pocket

# OFFICIAL UNIFORM

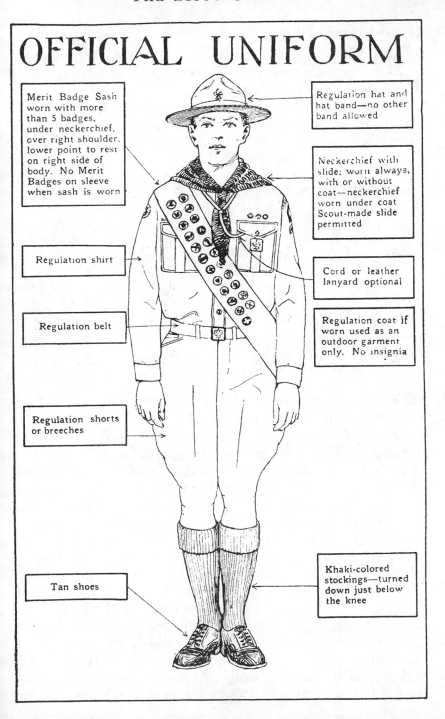

Merit Badge Sash worn with more than 5 badges, under neckerchief, over right shoulder, lower point to rest on right side of body. No Merit Badges on sleeve when sash is worn

Regulation hat and hat band—no other band allowed

Neckerchief with slide; worn always, with or without coat—neckerchief worn under coat Scout-made slide permitted

Regulation shirt

Cord or leather lanyard optional

Regulation belt

Regulation coat if worn used as an outdoor garment only. No insignia

Regulation shorts or breeches

Tan shoes

Khaki-colored stockings—turned down just below the knee

## U-n-i-f-o-r-m ! ! !

And when we say "uniform," we mean *"uniform."*
*There is only one Boy Scout Uniform and there is only one way of wearing that Uniform.*

If you saw a football player with a baseball cap on his head, if you saw a postman in a street cleaner's "white wings" or a West Point cadet wearing a sailor's

flaring trousers you would think that he was crazy. Why not then consider a Scout "batty" if he wears a green cap, red sweater, a pair of grey knickers while the rest of his uniform is seemingly correct?

It says in the Handbook for Boys that it is not necessary for a boy to have a uniform in order to carry out the Boy Scout Program. That is true, of course. You have to act like a Scout, *be* a Scout, whether you are in uniform or not. You can't take off and put on the spirit of Scouting as you can a Scout shirt. Off on a hike, you can have just as good a time, build just as good a camp fire, signal just as effectively if you and your boys are just wearing everyday old clothes instead of the Scout uniform, but somehow you'll find after you've tried both ways that the very wearing of the Scout Uniform knits you all more closely together, makes you more of a unit. Moreover you'll also find that old clothes aren't always the best for hiking. The

Scout uniform is tried and tested, durable, comfortable, just right, every way.

## Either—or

But the main point is, either wear the uniform or don't wear it. Don't make any half-way-betweens. It is a case of "to wear or not to wear that is the question," to misquote Shakespeare. Go in your old clothes or in your Scout Uniform. Don't mix the two.

And when the members of your Patrol wear their uniforms, insist on having them *wear them the only correct way.* Make them understand that there is only one (1) way of tying the neckerchief, one (1) way of wearing the Patrol medallion, one (1) color of stockings to wear, and so forth.

If you make them conform strictly to this, your pride in looking at your boys when they line up at Troop meeting will prove to be contagious. Your Scouts will become proud, too, of belonging to the neatest Patrol in the Troop and they will do their best to wear the uniform right and keep it in order.

## MEETINGS AND HIKES

The right name, the right emblems, the right uniform are all things that will help the Patrol Leader in building the Patrol Spirit in his unit. But after all they are only things. Their value depends upon the life you put into them.

The Patrol flag means nothing if it is kept tucked away in a dark corner of the meeting room. It is when it is carried at the front on a hike, when it is raised outside the tent when the day's trip is over, when it waves from the top of the cliff which the Patrol has conquered, that its worth is appreciated.

And it is the same with all the other Patrol possessions. Without life they are without meaning.

### It's Life That Counts

It is the living things that count. And a *living*

*Patrol* is the one, which has its own meetings, hikes, camps, that works and plays in the *right Scout Spirit*.

It is by being together time and again that your boys begin to feel that they stand really together, that they begin to realize that there are ties which bind them to each other and to the Patrol. When they have helped each other through a hard task, when they have fought their way together, through a storm to their camp site, when they have sat around a camp fire, without talking, just looking into the leaping flames and listening to the sounds of the night around them, then they will have felt the spirit of unity which is growing among them.

But that feeling depends very much upon the Patrol Leader and his abilities. Just as much as a successful hike or meeting will mean to the development of Patrol Spirit, just so much may the hike or meeting that was a failure because of poor leadership mean the lowering of that spirit.

## You Are the Leader

You are the one that has the chief responsibility. You must be sure that when the Patrol starts a thing it brings it through to the finish. You must have all meetings and hikes so well prepared that they simply have to be successes. You must inspire your boys in their work. And you must always keep your Patrol on the go by bringing new ideas and plans to execution.

The boys must know that when they go to a Patrol meeting some pleasant hours are in store for them. They are willing to help in making them so but they expect you to be the one to pull the wires.

If the boys feel that to be together in the Patrol means that they are having a corking good time, they

will stand with the Patrol. They will consider their Patrol the best in the world, and if difficulties should arise they will not be afraid of helping the Patrol along, working and fighting for its honor.

It is the life at the meetings, on hikes and in camp that develops Patrol Spirit more than anything else. And with the spirit you will see Patrol traditions grow, which in their turn again with a curious reciprocal action deepen the spirit.

## PATROL TRADITIONS

A tradition might start as pure accident as was the case with one Patrol we know of who, coming home from a rainy camp trip started to unfold their tent in order to hang it up for drying and discovered that one of the forked sticks, which had been used for the fire place, had, by chance, been wrapped into it. They were going to throw it away when suddenly one of the boys exclaimed: "Don't, that's a souvenir from *that* trip!" And it was kept for a souvenir with the result that the Patrol decided to bring a remembrance home to the meeting room from every one of their hikes. And now in their den you can see a wall decorated with crude camp implements, with rare minerals, a couple of old bird's nests, and as the most valued souvenir the antlered head of a deer which had been found lying dead in the forest by the Patrol. And all this history-filled collection started from a pure accident.

A good Easter holiday hike or a successful Columbus Day camp on a certain spot may mean the start of a tradition to spend those particular days of each year on the same spot. A certain way of celebrating the Patrol's birthday once may become the tradition for all coming birthdays.

Traditions usually grow up by themselves. Some people believe that traditions are never created by will. Nevertheless, it is possible to help get them started and to keep them alive.

You may begin all your Patrol meetings with a short

silence and close them with Taps. Or you may find some other form of beginning and ending which suits you all well enough to use over and over. In the beginning it may be considered routine but before you realize it, it will have grown into being a tradition. The boys will feel that something is wrong if these simple ceremonies are ever left out. And the same may be the case with other ceremonies which the Patrol develops for itself.

You may create traditions if your mind is sympathetically adjusted to things your boys like, and traditions will help you in building the spirit of your Patrol.

Sometimes a custom or routine may start with some of your boys, and be caught up and liked by the whole group. In which case it is up to you to help to develop it into tradition. Don't let any of these small everyday happenings escape you. Maybe they contain the seed of something that will help your Patrol to grow into a stick-together-through-everything group of boys with will to conquer in everything they undertake. And it will be a joy for you to be their leader even if that goal has cost you many hours of worry and hard work.

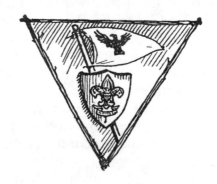

# CHAPTER III

## THE PATROL AND THE TROOP

WHEN we speak of the life of a Patrol, we are speaking about a very definite and significant, very real, and vital thing. But we must remember that no Patrol exists for and by itself alone. It has another part to play aside from its important individual life.

The Troop is the sum of its Patrols and every Patrol has its obligation toward, and its share in *the larger life of the Troop*. Your Patrol could never have the truest kind of Patrol Spirit unless it also had in a very active way genuine Troop spirit, pride in the Troop as a whole, eagerness to help the Troop make a good showing in whatever it undertakes, devotion to Troop traditions, Troop ideals and especially to Troop Leaders.

### The Patrol Leader's Responsibility

The Patrol Leader has a special responsibility in this matter. He is the link between the Patrol and the Troop. He represents the Patrol at the Troop Leaders' Council. Through him Troop plans and ideas are communicated to his own special group; and through him also what his Patrol stands for, what it is doing, what it hopes to do, its whole spirit is communicated to the Troop. He is responsible for the conduct of his Scouts at Troop meetings and rallies, in camp, on the hike—wherever they go as a group. His leadership determines to a large extent, the part the Patrol plays in the Troop life, its attitude toward Troop life.

## Getting the Idea Across

In telling his fellows, or telling himself that he means the "Bisons" to *be the very best Patrol* in the Troop, the Patrol Leader must not feel, nor let grow up in the

KEEP YOUR PATROL AHEAD

Patrol any jealousy or opposition or superiority toward the others, any "Beat 'em at any cost" attitude. This would be as fatal as not to care whether his Patrol showed up well or not, to say "Aw, what's the difference? What if the 'Foxes' can do first aid better than we can? We're too busy making a Patrol totem pole to bother with a first aid contest."

The ideal is something quite different from either of the above points of view. You do want the "Bisons" to be the best Patrol in the Troop, not because you have any unfriendly spirit toward the other Patrols or want to feel superior and vainglorious, but because you want it to be best, for its own sake and out of loyalty too, to the Troop and the Scoutmaster, because you owe it to them to get the most out of Scouting, which is only another way of saying that you mean to put the most of yourselves into Scouting.

And you certainly don't want to say, "What's the difference?" It makes all the difference in the world, not only to the Troop but even more to the Patrol, if you never let the fellows get so absorbed in their Patrol projects and life of the Troop. That attitude isn't fair to the Scoutmaster. It isn't fair to the Troop. It isn't fair to the Movement. But most of all, it isn't fair to your fellows themselves.   They are getting out of it all only half of what they might get out of it, perhaps much less than half.

Enter fully into all the Troop's life.   See that your fellows do the same.   If the Troop is putting through an entertainment or a rally, or a community Good Turn, take active part in it.   Plunge into the fun. Plunge into the work.   Don't be afraid even if you have to neglect or postpone Patrol undertakings to do it.   Patrol Spirit will gain rather than lose by it in the long run.   The fellows will feel themselves more, not less of a unit, if they work and play and compete and serve with other units, for a common end.   Their Patrol life, as well as the rest of their Scout life, will mean more to them afterward.

## Competitions

Speaking of competitions, you will find them undoubtedly a great help in inspiring your fellows to take an interest in all phases of Scouting, learning to do their "Scout stuff" just right, in the best, most efficient way.   They are a great help also in developing Patrol Spirit, the feeling of "togetherness," the determination never to "let down" the rest, no matter what happens.

Be winners, always, if you can.  But win fairly and generously. And if you win don't "crow" over the other fellows who didn't win.  If you lose—and even losing together may help to deepen Patrol Spirit—lose gallantly, without whining or complaint.  "Hit  the line hard" and take the breaks as they come.  It's all part of the game.  See that you congratulate the victors, too, and do it sincerely in the spirit of "Let the best man win." It takes courage to be a good loser. As a matter of fact, it isn't so important whether you win or lose, as it is how you have played the game.

These are ideas to be somehow "got across" to your Patrol. If you don't succeed in getting them across, you will never have the best kind of a Patrol, and never be the kind of leader your Patrol ought to have. If you have the ideas firmly planted in your own head and heart, however, be sure the rest will get them, too.

Whatever you do in your Patrol, make team-play, loyalty, co-operation, a vital part of Patrol life.

## The Patrol and the Scoutmaster

The third part of the Scout Law says, "A Scout is loyal to all to whom loyalty is due," and first in the list of these is mentioned the Scout Leader—the Scout-master.

It is your job and the Patrol's to stand by your Scoutmaster all along the line, to follow his leadership, give him one hundred per cent loyalty, devotion, obedience, service. In this, as in other respects, your fellows will get their cue from you. It is upon your attitude toward him that theirs will largely depend. You can and must, if you are to be true to your trust of leadership, get them to see the thing precisely as you do. The Scoutmaster is a mighty fine fellow. He is giving up a whole lot of his time, spending a lot of thought, putting a lot of effort into trying to make your particular Troop a success. The least you can all do is to meet him more than half way. Make it a point of pride, individually and as a group, to let him know he can count on you all the time, any time, for the best you have to give.

This is the idea you want your fellows to get. This is the way you want them to act. How is it to be done? Well, primarily, as we have said, by your having the idea yourself and having it good and strong. Second, by telling them how you feel about it, right out loud when the right moment comes. And third—by the way you conduct yourself.

"What you do speaks so loud, I cannot hear what you say."

It wouldn't do much good for you to make impressive speeches about what the Patrol owed to your Scoutmaster unless you showed you meant it by the way you acted yourself at Troop meeting and elsewhere.

## Ways to Help at Troop Meeting

There are many ways by which a Patrol and a Patrol Leader can help a Scoutmaster at his job and contribute to the success of Troop life.

One way and a very important way is to have the Patrol out full strength and on time at every Troop meeting. Have your boys so well trained that they come to attention instantly upon order. See that they take personal pride in being properly uniformed, neat in appearance, courteous in manner. These things are your responsibility. If your fellows come up to this standard you are living up to what your Scoutmaster has a right to expect of you.

You can help, also, by being ready yourself and seeing that your Patrol is ready to take part in everything that goes on at all of the Troop's meetings whole-heartedly and to the best of your ability, whether it is getting the most out of an instruction period, putting on a stunt or entering a competition. It is not only good team-play in a Troop to have a good stunt or song or yell or "what have you?"—ready to spring at a

moment's notice. It rebounds splendidly back in the life of a Patrol, builds up Patrol Spirit, adds to the Patrol's faith in itself and in you as the leader.

Develop the reputation and live up to it of being a live Patrol "all there" every minute, a Patrol that can be counted on to meet any demand loyally, efficiently, cheerfully and modestly, a popular Patrol if you can achieve it, anyway a Patrol *to be trusted*.

## On Hikes

Hikes are strenuous affairs, as a rule, for a Scout-master. It's up to you to answer, at least for your Patrol, to see that they not only present no problem, but are actively alert to be of service. Naturally you will see to it that your gang is at the appointed meeting place, precisely on time, properly costumed and

equipped with everything you have been told to bring along for the outing, whether it be food, signal flags, notebooks, compass, or what not. Let's have no "Oh, gee! I forgot this," or "I forgot that." Check up beforehand to be sure nothing has been forgotten. You owe that to the situation and the hike leader. Habitual "forgetters" are badly trained members of a Patrol.

On the trip, see that your group gets the very most out of it, that it observes discipline, obeys all orders promptly and cheerfully, doesn't make itself in any way obnoxious or conspicuous by shoving, rushing about heedless of whether one is in the way or not, by too noisy talk or singing, by any slightest lack of courtesy and consideration. No Patrol or individual gains in popularity by being a "show off." Indeed, one boy can damage the reputation of the whole Troop, if he lets himself run wild or his Patrol Leader lets him.

This doesn't mean, of course, that you are to keep your boys' bubbling spirits completely corked up, frown on any and all fun and gaiety. Far from it. If your Patrol has the reputation of being the jolliest in the lot, the quickest to start a song, when the trail is getting a little long and monotonous, the most cheerful when a sudden rainstorm arrives over the hill, when you haven't expected it—so much the better. Only keep the bubbling spirits a little in check. Make your conduct and your Patrol's fit the conditions.

On the hike, it will be natural to keep together as a Patrol. But avoid being too "clannish."

Mix with other Patrols, if it comes easy and natural to do so. You are all part of the Troop gang. While you are on the trail is often the best possible time to exchange ideas and get better acquainted with the other Patrol Leaders and their boys. This leadership business is a real give and take.

Keep your eye on the Scoutmaster to see if there is any little thing you can do for him. Make yourself responsible not only for your own Patrol but also for whatever you can contribute to the smooth running and enjoyment of the whole excursion. It is part of your job as a Troop Leader as well as a Patrol Leader. The Scoutmaster should at all times be able to count on his "Green Bar Men" as his right hand men.

## In Camp

Much of what has been said as to the Patrol's participation in the Troop meeting and hike applies equally to the Troop camp. It is your task to see that your Patrol takes its full share in all the work and play of the camp, is ready with stunts and songs around the fire, eager and interested during an instruction period, willing and prompt and thorough in getting its assigned jobs done. If you have helped your boys to see Scout Spirit for what it really is, you will have no difficulty in making them willing to help out anywhere, any time, not shirking the doing of even hard or disagreeable tasks, not afraid of doing more than somebody else, realizing that "anything that needs doing is everybody's job."

Naturally you will insist on good discipline among your boys. You will see that they are prompt to obey orders, first up at reveille, first to "pipe down" after "Taps." If you've given your Patrol a square deal in advance, given them the proper training, helped

them to self-discipline, all this will be nothing new. They will have got the idea that the happiness of everybody depends upon everybody's showing the right spirit. One musician playing out of tune can spoil the whole effect. They have learned all that already at Patrol meetings and hikes and camps, in all their Patrol contacts. If they haven't, then your bad hour is in store for you in the big camp. The responsibility has been yours. The reward of success is yours if you've earned it. Otherwise—expect trouble. But no. Don't expect it. Put your Patrol on its honor. See what happens. Remember that with real Patrol Spirit comes the absence of necessity for discipline in the disagreeable sense. Remember always that "The Scout Law is the Law of the Camp." Help your fellows to remember the same thing.

If real Patrol Spirit has come along with you to camp together with your Patrol flag and the makings of Patrol tradition, you will have little cause to be other than proud of the way your Patrol fits into the life of the Troop in camp. You will find the boys as eager as you to show their tent the neatest at inspection, their first aid and signaling the most efficient, their camp fire stunt the most effective,—their spirit the strongest, the most loyal.

## Patrol "Get Togethers"

We have already said that Patrol competitions are excellent things for both the Patrol and the Troop. Indeed, all kinds of Patrol Get Togethers are helpful, whether on a large or small scale. Invite other Patrols to your own meetings or hikes, now and then, not only Patrols from your Troop but from other Troops, even out-of-town ones if you can arrange it. You will all be better for the exchange of ideas, for the fun and good fellowship involved. Scouts should never live like snails, shutting themselves up in narrow, tight little houses.

Patrol Leaders, also, should take and make every opportunity to come into close, friendly contact with other Patrol Leaders, not only of their own Troops, but with all the Patrol Leaders of the community, Patrol Leaders anywhere. They should give all the help they can to other leaders and, in turn, be eager to learn from others. Attend Patrol

Leaders' courses and conferences whenever possible, get all you can out of them.

## The Troop Leaders' Council

We have spoken of the Troop Leaders' Council, or

"Cornertooth Meeting" as it is frequently called. For the Patrol Leader this meeting is of great importance. Through him it is of equally great importance for the Patrol.

Who is there? The Scoutmaster, of course, and his Assistants, the Junior Assistant Scoutmaster, the Senior Patrol Leader and the Patrol Leaders, you and the other three, the "Green Bar Men" of the Troop. You may be sure it is an interesting group and an interested group, too. Suppose the newest member of the group, the newest appointed Patrol Leader is there too, suppose he is feeling rather proud and happy to be there tonight for the first time.

What are the things that he will hear and see at such a meeting?

## Opening the Meeting

Perhaps a brief moment of silent prayer. These Green Bar Men and their older leaders approach this thing reverently, and seriously. Then follows a summary of what went on at the last Council Meeting, short and businesslike and to the point.

## Getting to Business

"Unfinished business?" asks the Scoutmaster looking around.

Oh, yes, several things under unfinished business. An Assistant Scoutmaster reports on what he and his committee have accomplished in getting ready for a first aid demonstration in connection with the Red Cross. Somebody else reports on the collecting of magazines for the Seaman's Institute as previously arranged for. Somebody else announces he has been lucky enough to secure the services of a nature expert and photographer to accompany the Troop on their next Saturday's hike. One after another reports on the various projects which had previously been assigned.

"New Business?"

A question of policy comes up. The Troop has been asked to sell tickets for a charity bazaar, a request that has to be courteously refused. Another request for Scouts to serve as ushers at a church concert. Of course.

"Bring that up at the next meeting. Ask for volunteers," rules the Scoutmaster.

"Excuse me, sir," says a Patrol Leader, "most of my boys go to that church. If you like, we could take on the job."

"Good," approves the Scoutmaster. "Find out the details and report to me definitely before the meeting Friday night how many of your fellows will turn out."

"You asked my Patrol to get up a five minute stunt for the next meeting," says another Patrol Leader to the Scoutmaster, "It's all ready, may I tell you about it after meeting, to be sure it's all right?"

"Sure," agrees the Scoutmaster. "How about Sam Ferris, Bob? Have you found out why he hasn't been coming to Troop meetings?" The Scoutmaster turns to the Junior Leader to ask this.

"His mother is sick. He has to do most of the house-work."

"I see. Anybody been helping him out?"

"Yes, he told me the 'Bob Whites' had been on the job right along, at least one of them goes over every day to see if any errands need doing. They've been washing dishes and scrubbing floors too, I hear. How about it, Johnny, you 'Bob White,' over there?"

Johnny, the Bob White Patrol Leader, blushes and looks a little "fussed."

"We haven't done much," he murmurs, "just sort of stood by. Please don't mention it at Troop meeting. 'Twasn't anything anyway."

The new Patrol Leader is interested, learning a whole lot. Other things come up for discussion, are ruled on, assigned to somebody to look up further or arrange for.

## The Patrol Leaders' Report

Then follows what is the most important and inter-esting part of the whole meeting to the new Patrol

Leader. Each leader of a Patrol stands up before the group and tells them what his Patrol has been doing since the last meeting, what meetings it has held, what Good Turns and projects have been accomplished, how many have passed tests and which tests they are. Everything, in short, that represents the life of the Patrol.

The new Patrol Leader feels a thrill hearing the others give these reports, thinks how proud they must be to lead Patrols that are doing such fine things, what real leaders they must be to have achieved such Patrol Spirit in their groups.

He can see that each leader takes the responsibility of his job seriously, that it means a lot to them to stand here representing their Patrols. He hopes some time he will be able to make as good a showing.

When his own time to speak comes he hasn't much to say. He has only just started. Shyly, however, he tells the group that he has had his first meeting. His boys know the Law and can tie three knots.

"Fine beginning," says the Scoutmaster, "If you need any help, let me know.

"Thanks, ·I'm getting on pretty well. Jim's been helping me, of course. I knew the knots myself, but I didn't know the best way to teach them to anybody else."

Jim was an Assistant Scoutmaster, assigned by the Scoutmaster to do this very thing. That was the way things went in that Troop. Either the Scoutmaster or some of his Assistants, taught the Patrol Leaders, the Patrol Leaders handed it on to the Patrol.

"May I see you a minute after this meeting?" asks another Patrol Leader of the Scoutmaster. "I've been having a little trouble with—well, with one of my crowd. I'm not sure I'm managing it right. I've about decided I'm 'all wet' myself. Was too easy on him first, then too hard. He doesn't know where he's at, and I'm sure, I don't," the Patrol Leader admits, with a perplexed shake of his head.

"All right," agrees the Scoutmaster, "I won't promise to prescribe—that's your job. But I'll help diagnose the case, if I can."

"He's great," thinks the new Patrol Leader. "He doesn't boss a bit, or make them all think he thinks he's the whole show. He just helps everybody to help themselves. Why that's all a Patrol Leader has to learn to do. He's just got to be their friend, the way the Scoutmaster is to this bunch here and to everybody in the Troop."

The Patrol Leader has stumbled on the answer to the whole problem. "You've just got to be their friend."

# CHAPTER IV.

## PATROL ORGANIZATION

ANY successful business man will tell you that his success is due to the fact that he has his business carefully organized and the right number of right people to take care of the different duties.

The same is the case with the successful Patrol.

Unless it is thoroughly and efficiently organized it will never get far.

### What Is the Right Size of a Patrol?

Eight boys is usually considered *the* number for a Patrol. A Patrol Leader, his Assistant, and six other Scouts who take care of the rest of the Patrol's duties is very often believed to be the ideal.

But this doesn't necessarily have to be so. It doesn't exactly mean that a Patrol is incomplete, if it has less than eight members. What is necessary is, that the Patrol shall have the right gang-formation.

Six might be just the figure for your Patrol. In fact, if you look around you will see that there are possibly more successful Patrols with a membership of six than there are with eight. It sometimes seems true that it is easier for the average Patrol Leader to handle five rather than seven boys.

Some Patrols are as small as four, and do wonderful work because the right team spirit is present, while at other places you will find successful Patrols with as many as ten Scouts in them.

No hard and fast rule can be laid down as to size, but as a general rule it can be said that the best number is from six to eight. Fewer than six will often mean inconvenience because there aren't enough boys to fill the places in Patrol competitions, on camp trips and so forth, while a number bigger than eight often will prove impossible for the Patrol Leader to handle.

Probably, the best thing would be to start with six in the Patrol. If it proves that you are able to lead any more and your boys would like to see the Patrol bigger, you will soon find it growing into eight. On the other hand, if six seems to be the number you and your boys like, then stick to it. If it is too big somebody is sure to lose interest in the Patrol some day and will drop out to join another Patrol. Then you automatically will have the right number in your own.

## Not a One Scout Job

You may have met the Patrol Leader who wants to be the center of the universe known as the Patrol, the sun around which the Scouts as planets have to revolve. He plans all the meetings and hikes himself, collects dues, has charge of diary, equipment and everything

else and believes that he is entirely living up to his duties as a Patrol Leader.

You must have met him somewhere and maybe you have observed the difference in the way his Patrol members acted when he was present and when he wasn't there. He might be able to run his Patrol and seemingly make a success out of it, but the day he doesn't attend a Patrol meeting, there is simply no Patrol meeting because nobody else knows how to run one, never having had the opportunity to try, and the day he is prevented from going along on the Patrol overnight hike, everything will fall flat, because only he knows what arrangements are necessary.

You will never get anywhere with a one-man system. The farthest it can bring your Patrol is into the ditch and one might assume that that is exactly the place of all places where you don't want to see it.

If you want it to succeed you will have to build up a system of organization in which every one of the boys is a part with special duties and special work to perform for the good of the Patrol.

As you work along you will soon find that the leading of a Patrol is much more than a one-man job, and you will soon find that you need the help of every one of your boys to take care of special details.

You might not need them all at the very start, and in fact it will be better for you to wait with the assigning of jobs to the different boys, until you have worked together with them for some time, during which you will have acquired some knowledge as to their abilities.

If you then believe that Bill might make a good Scribe and Ed a splendid Quartermaster and Joe an excellent Treasurer, then try them out—until you get your expectations verified or until they show their

inability to handle those special jobs which you assigned
them. In the first case, you let them continue, in the
second, you simply try them out at something else,
until you have them each placed in his right niche.
Many of your "difficult boy" problems, mentioned in
an earlier chapter will automatically disappear, when
this last result has been accomplished.

## A Word to the Wise

In the pages which follow we are going to work out
a practicable plan of organization for a Patrol, with
various officers and jobs. Before you begin to study
this, and try to fit it in your mind to your own Patrol
and its members, let us warn you, that the thing isn't
half so hard and complicated as it may sound at first.

It isn't meant to scare
you away from being a
Patrol Leader before you
have even started or to
simply pile up a list of
tasks and responsibilities
that threaten to topple
over and crush you. It
is merely intended to
suggest what can be done
by a Patrol Leader who
isn't looking for a one-
man job, but wants to
work up a real Patrol, with everybody in it interested and active and happy, with real Patrol Spirit
that will take the group as far as you like along the
Scout trail.

## Details of Organization

To have a basis for our organization plan, let us
assume that your Patrol consists of eight members. If
it happens to be smaller, you will simply combine some
of the offices and assign them to one boy. If it is
bigger you will find no difficulty in dividing some of the
posts into two.

There is the post of *Patrol Leader*. Quite easy. That's your job.

The first need that will arise is for you to have a helper who can work with you on planning the meetings and hikes, instructing the Patrol and doing all the hundreds of other odd jobs that are necessary to make the Patrol run. In other words you will need an *Assistant Patrol Leader*.

And as you go along, other needs will arise.

You will need a *Treasurer* to collect dues and keep the accounts, a *Scribe* for preparing the Patrol Reports, somebody to take care of the equipment—suppose we call him the *"Quartermaster"*—to arrange for camps and hikes a *"Hikemaster,"* a *"Grubmaster"* to buy the provisions for the Patrol, and a *"Cheermaster"* to bring the cheer into it.

Here is your list. It is for you to fill it out with the names of the boys best fitted for the different jobs and make up different names for the jobs if you prefer. These above aren't hard and fast prescriptions, merely suggestions for convenience.

Patrol Leader ...............................

Assistant Patrol Leader ......................

Treasurer ..................................

Scribe ....................................

Quartermaster ..............................

Hikemaster ................................

Grubmaster ................................

Cheermaster ...............................

## Fitting the Scout to the Job

It will require some study on your part to fit the boys of your Patrol into the jobs best suited to them.

but it will be worth while to give time and thougnt to it instead of making mistakes every time you assign a boy to a special job.

One of the best ways of being sure of your facts is by making notes about your boys in a notebook. Just a few words jotted down when they have shown you some of their characteristic features is enough to go on. Besides being a help to you in your appointments, such an analysis will be of great value for your understanding of the Scouts.

PATROL JOBS

NOT SO DIFFICULT

As an example, you may have observed the following traits in Roy:

"Good in arithmetic. Invented a Morse code, using different small figures. Has the funny idea of adding the digits in the number of automobiles to find their sum. Father gives him a certain amount of pocket money, he has to account for every Saturday. Is terribly orderly . . ."

There will be little doubt, Roy will be your first choice for Treasurer.

Or take the notes about Jack:

"Reads everything he can get hold of. Sent me a wonderful eight-page letter from camp. Wrote Patrol song for first overnight hike. Makes wisecracks out of everything. Showed me a book about Lindbergh, made up of articles and pictures from the newspapers . . ."

No wonder you think that he will be the ideal Scribe.

But let us look at all the different offices to study the necessity for them and the duties which their occupants will have to perform.

## ASSISTANT PATROL LEADER

The most important post in the Patrol next to the Leader's is that of his Assistant. Consider your "Clever Boy," if you have one, for this post.

As a token of his position he wears one green bar on his shirt sleeve. And unhappily enough, that green bar is, in many Patrols, the only thing that distinguishes him from the rest of the members.

You will want to be sure that that isn't the case in your Patrol. Your Assistant must show the world that he is not only wearing the Assistant's insignia, but also actually functioning as an Assistant, helping you to plan and execute the work of the Patrol.

The name itself suggests his duties.

### Actually Leading

He is your Assistant in everything you do in the Patrol. He must be completely in your confidence. He must know why you do certain things a certain way, why you let other things remain undone. Because without understanding you and your leadership he will never be able to take your place when you are prevented from being present, nor will there be the necessary sympathetic co-operation between you.

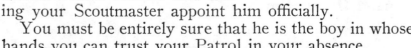

A careful consideration is necessary before you take the important step of choosing an Assistant Patrol Leader and having your Scoutmaster appoint him officially.

You must be entirely sure that he is the boy in whose hands you can trust your Patrol in your absence.

### His Qualifications

He must have the qualifications of a Patrol Leader. He must work well with you and he must, like yourself, have the confidence of the rest of the Scouts.

Often the mistake has been repeated that a Patrol

Leader has chosen the one who was his best friend in the Patrol as the Assistant.

No personal feelings should govern you in your choice. What you have to think of is, "Who will make the best Assistant for the Patrol?"

The all-round good of the Patrol must count more than your personal wishes.

If your best friend is the best qualified, nobody will think of criticizing your choice, but if he isn't you will create ill-feeling in your Patrol, which you will have difficulty in overcoming.

Use your judgment and think of your Patrol.

As said already your Assistant must help you in the planning of the Patrol's work, help with instruction and hikes. He must be ready to represent you in your absence, be the leader of the Patrol at Troop meetings and hikes, take the Patrol along without your assistance, if necessary, represent you at the Patrol Leaders' Council. The Assistant must be the Patrol Leader's shadow.

And he can only do these things if he knows exactly what you would have done in the different cases and has the same general ideas of Patrol management that you have.

## Depend Upon Him

Let him lead the Patrol once in a while when you are present, let him take charge of different activities. That is the only way in which he can be taught leadership and be really a help to you in the Patrol. With his consent, now and then, the other members of the Patrol may be asked to take charge in the same way so that other assistants may be in training.

A good thing would be to give him a definite job

as a leader. For example let him be the game leader. Let him collect games suitable for Patrol use. Let him be in charge every time a game period is called for, and let him feel his job as a real responsibility. This also applies to the other Scouts in a Patrol. Let every one have a chance to lead at something.

Let him check up on attendance with the Scribe and get in touch with absent boys to find out the reason for their absence. Let him help you keep in touch with the homes. Let him have the material ready which is necessary for use at the meetings. Let him work out the necessary orders for hikes and camps. In other words: let him relieve you of a lot of detail work and give him a chance to show his abilities.

In short let him really assist and help to lead the Patrol.

## TREASURER

Money is a necessary evil in this world even inside Scout circles.

The yearly registration has to be paid. There are Troop dues to be collected. Equipment can't be purchased without money, a long hike also requires some cash. These are cold, hard, familiar, pressing facts.

One of the first posts then that has to be filled by one of your Scouts is that of Patrol Treasurer.

Be very careful in this particular choice.

You must know that the boy is orderly, dependable, pretty good at figures, precise and accurate.

But there is another thing you must think of.

Boys sometimes have weak streaks. And sometimes it is a terrible temptation for a boy to be trusted with money. A boy who would not dream of being actually dishonest may through carelessness get his own and the Patrol's funds mixed up. "An ounce of prevention is worth a pound of cure." Have that in mind when you assign the Treasurer, and be sure you choose a boy for this office who will feel a real sense of responsibility in this important matter. In many Troops the actual Patrol funds are kept separately and accounted for by the Troop Treasurer or member of Troop Committee.

A Patrol Treasurer will usually have plenty to do keeping his accounts. Especially if your Patrol is industrious and earns its money by making handicraft articles or by taking odd jobs.

## The Patrol Budget

The first thing for him to do, when he takes over his job is to have a business conference with you and your Assistant. The Patrol budget has to be planned.

### BUDGET FOR THE BEAVER PATROL

| Income | | Expenditures | |
|---|---|---|---|
| Registration Fee - 8x $.50 | $ 4.00 | Registration Fee - 8x $.50 | $ 4.00 |
| Patrol Dues (Scouts pay 15¢ a mo.) - 8x12x15¢ | 14.40 | Boy's Life - 8x $1.00 | 8.00 |
| 5 Per Cent of Tickets to Be sold for Troop Entertainment Night, ap. | 16.00 | Troop Dues (10¢ a mo.) - 8x12x10¢ | 9.60 |
| | | Repair of Camp Equipment | 10.00 |
| | | New Patrol Flag | 2.00 |
| To Be Earned (at least) | 18.85 | 2 First Aid Belt Pouches | 1.50 |
| | | Extra Set of Signaling Flags | .65 |
| | | Christmas Gift for Scoutmaster | 1.50 |
| | | Sending Bill Jones from the Fox Patrol to Summer Camp | 12.00 |
| | | Thanksgiving Baskets | 4.00 |
| | $ 53.25 | | $ 53.25 |

Together you must estimate what expenses the Patrol will have inside a certain period, for example, inside a year, half a year, or three months, and then make out how much it is necessary for the Scouts to pay as dues and how much the Patrol has to earn extra.

The budget being decided upon, the next thing for the Treasurer to do is to collect the Patrol dues from the boys at the end of each month, say at the last Patrol meeting. That will make him ready to pay the Troop dues for the entire Patrol to the Troop Treasurer with punctuality at the first Troop meeting of the following month.

## Money Earning Ideas

Next he will try to find some ideas for the Patrol's earning of the necessary overdraught. The ideas are put up to the Patrol for open discussion and decision. The Treasurer keeps an accurate account of every cent that comes in or goes out of his box from this source.

He collaborates with the Grubmaster and Hike-master when the Patrol goes on hikes where expenses are incurred and he receives, pays and keeps bills coming in from such trips.

### CASH ACCOUNT

| Date | Item | Income | Exp. | Balance |
|---|---|---|---|---|
| 7-11 | Gauze Bandage | | 25 | 5 51 |
| 7-12 | Bill, Dues for August | 15 | | |
| 7-12 | Jack, Dues for August | 15 | | 5 81 |
| | Fare to Queens, 8 x $.47 | 3 76 | | 9 57 |
| 7-13 | Fare to Queens, 8 x $.47 | | 3 76 | 5 81 |
| 7-25 | Camp Trip Fees, 8 x $.60 | 4 80 | | 10 61 |
| 7-27 | Trolley Car to Jackson, 8 x $.05 | | 40 | 10 21 |
| 7-27 | Groceries (see Bill) | | 2 88 | 7 33 |
| 7-27 | Potatoes | | 32 | 7 01 |

## Account of Income and Expenses

He has a simple bookkeeping system, as shown above.

In connection with his bookkeeping he has a file of bills received and paid by the Patrol.

Every once in a while, maybe every three months, the Treasurer makes up an account for expenses and income.  He arranges them in general groups so that the boys of his Patrol may see at a glance how expenditures separate under different headings, how the income has been derived from different handicraft projects.

It may look something like:

### ACCOUNT FOR THE MONTHS OF APRIL, MAY, JUNE

| Income | | Expenditures | |
|---|---|---|---|
| Transferred from March | # 12.46 | Troop Dues - 3 x 8 x 10¢ | # 2.40 |
| Dues - 3 x 8 x #.15 | 3.60 | Handicraft Material | 1.26 |
| Handicraft | 6.42 | Tools | .78 |
| Patrol Job | 3.28 | Camps | 18.28 |
| Gifts | 1.14 | Balance (in Bank) | 19.17 |
| Camp Fees | 22.00 | | |
| | # 54.79 | | # 54.79 |

As you see, there will be enough to keep a Treasurer busy, and he must be a rather bright lad to make up the different accounts and keep them straight.  But it is a splendid experience for a boy and the training he gets in the Patrol might well mean something for him in the future.

## SCRIBE

The next post to fill will probably be the Scribe's.

Choose for this position the Scout who has most literary inclinations, the boy who has proved himself most interested in expressing himself in writing.

Sometimes it will be well to let the post be filled with the winner of a Patrol competition.  Announce that the Scribe's position is open and tell the boys that the one who makes the best report, if possible with photographs and sketches, of the Patrol's life during one month will be awarded the position.

It would be a queer Patrol in which at least half of the members did not go in for the competition.

Have a special committee of judges appointed consisting of, for example, your Scoutmaster, the Assistant Scoutmasters, Leaders of other Patrols, maybe a couple of members of the Troop Committee, and let the competitors feel that something real is happening.

The object is to find the boy who can tell the history of the Patrol in the most vivid form, who has sense for making his manuscript look neat and orderly, who isn't afraid of letting funny sketches follow his report, even if they are more well-intentioned than exactly resembling their subjects.

## The Patrol Log

The foremost duty of the Scribe is to keep the log of the Patrol, and bring it up to date immediately after an incident has happened worth relating. Not just by writing "started 9.30, arrived at Alderton 10.45, hiked to our camp site, pitched the tents, etc.," but by trying to put life into the story, by relating characteristic remarks and doings of the boys, by describing the scenery along the way, the discouragements, achievements and adventures of the Patrol.

He collects all the photographs he can get hold of depicting the life of his Patrol, photographs taken by Scout friends, by visitors, by acquaintances. If possible he gets hold of a cheap camera with which to record important moments in the Patrol's history.

He makes sketches of camp sites the Patrol has used—diagrams of hikes and journeys taken. If he has artistic skill, he will make sketches of the boys occupied with different activities, of nature objects found en route and of details of the Patrol Camp. All of which, put into the Patrol diary, will make it an interesting and graphic record.

## The Records of the Patrol

His next work of importance is the keeping of the Patrol's record book. He checks up with the Assistant Patrol Leader at the beginning of each meeting and each hike, be it Patrol or Troop, and writes down in his book the names of boys present and of those ab-

### ATTENDANCE RECORD

| NAMES OF SCOUTS | DATE 4-2 | 4-9 | 4-12 | 4-14 | 4-19 | 4-21 | | | | | | TIMES PRESENT | TIMES ABSENT WITH REASON | TIMES ABSENT WITHOUT REASON |
| KIND OF MEETING | P M | P M | T M | P H | T M | T H | | | | | | | | |
|---|---|---|---|---|---|---|---|---|---|---|---|---|---|---|
| Mike Brady | X | X | X | X | W | X | | | | | | 5 | 1 | |
| Dick Schotte | X | X | X | X | X | X | | | | | | 6 | 0 | |
| Vincent Reppe | X | X | X | X | X | X | | | | | | 6 | 0 | |
| Irving Fuller | X | S | S | X | X | X | | | | | | 4 | 2 | |
| Jack Holloran | X | X | X | X | X | X | | | | | | 4 | 2 | |
| Fred Egnes | W | X | X | X | X | X | | | | | | 5 | 1 | |
| Bill Miller | X | X | T | T | X | X | | | | | | 4 | 2 | |
| Oran Waggoner | X | X | X | | | X | | | | | | 4 | | 2 |
| | | | | | | | | | | | | | | |
| NUMBER PRESENT | 7 | 7 | 6 | 7 | 6 | 8 | | | | | | | | |
| NUMBER ABSENT | 1 | 1 | 2 | 1 | 2 | 0 | | | | | | | | |

INDICATE KIND OF MEETING WITH: P.M.(PATROL MEETING) P.H.(P, HIKE) P.C.( PATROL CAMP)T.M.(TROOP MEETING) ETC.
INDICATE PRESENCE WITH X, ABSENCE WITHOUT REASON BLANK, ABSENCE WITH REASON WITH S FOR SICKNESS, W FOR
WORK, T FOR TRAVEL ETC.

sent. If the reason for absences is known, that, too, has to be recorded.

In the record book he keeps a list of tests passed and Merit Badges acquired by the different members of the Patrol. Every Scout of the Patrol has his special page in the record book containing all information about his Boy Scout life, and as soon as requirements have been met for advanced rank, the Scribe will have them put down in his book.

## PAGE OF PATROL LOG

**Tuesday, May 14th**

Had our weekly meeting, this time at John's home. Six present. Phil absent because of work. Brissie's father met us and made a talk on First Aid and Signalling. Especially the first one was good. Second Class tests were discussed and after that we went into the yard for half an hour of star study.

**Saturday, May 18th**

Patrol Hike to Morrow Dale. We met at the Den, oh, so early in the morning i.e. 8 o'clock. Pete and Phil had to stay at home doing some work. The rest of us took the trolley to Jackson Place and walked from there to M.D. We had a fire-by-friction contest. John won. Brissie couldn't even make a spark and was very much embarrassed because he had been boasting of his wonderful set. We made a fire and started our luncheon.

camping M.D - friction fire

How Brissie looked after the Contest!

REPORTS
(.....N, PA.)

...at the homes of the Patrol. ...ercraft. The ...Merit Badges. ...McMullen and ...y and Conser... ...ing to have all ...McMullen has ...his award and ...his five Merit ...ss Scout may...

...trol ...following the ...our ex-Patrol ...cers. The re- ...Nagle, P.L.; ...L., and Louis ...weeks ago we ...Lehigh Moun- ...been reorgan- ...endance at the ...n of mobiliza- ...The results ...ber of Silver ...r of the meet- ...A. S. Watson.

...ol ...f our members ...o a new capacity of Assistant Scribe, our ...Patrol is left with a roll of five active ...members and we are looking for some new ...members who are active in Patrol work. ...We have chosen the subject for our pro- ...ject, which is Airplane Model building, and ...will soon be having planes to fly in the ...contest.—Paul Riemer, P. L.

At Eastern State Exposition, members of the Worcester Press Association published a daily newspaper The Press Club of the North Shore Area Council, Illinois, gets out two weekly news pages for local papers regarding Council activities. The Long Island Scout Press Club is acting as an agency for the distributing of Scout news to the newspapers of Long Island and the metropolitan district. The Bridgeport Press Club is instructing many Scouts in journalism and the Los Angeles Scout Press Association publishes a fine Local Council paper.

This Scout Handicraft Exhibit of the Eastern States Exposition roused tremendous interest among the public. Why not try something of this sort in your home town as a part of Anniversary Week celebration.

## PAGE OF PATROL SCRAP BOOK

## Monthly Reports to the Troop

Once at the end of each month the Scribe works out from his diary and his record book a report to his Scoutmaster about the Patrol's work in the past month, telling of meetings and hikes undertaken, tests passed, attendance of the boys, and so forth.

One copy is signed by the Patrol Leader and sent or given to the Scoutmaster, another is kept in the Patrol's files.

## Keeping the Patrol File

The Patrol file is just a piece of cardboard folded in the shape of a book binding in which documents and printed matter are kept. Troop bulletins have their place here, copies of letters sent by the Patrol and letters received by it, programs from Council rallies, from Father-and-Son banquets and so forth. The keeping of this file also is the responsibility of the Scribe.

But he has still other duties.

## Miscellaneous

He has a special scrapbook in which he collects clippings from the newspapers about the Boy Scouts of his city, reports of his Troop's or his Council's activities.

If the Troop publishes a monthly or weekly paper, it is the Scribe's duty to keep the editor of it provided with reports of his Patrol's activities by sending in articles, notes, programs, etc. He may even develop and publish a paper special for his own Patrol.

And as a last task:

If the Patrol is happy enough to own its own library, it is for the Scribe to take care of it, to keep track of the books and keep the whole library in good order.

The job of the Scribe is certainly not a lazy man's job. But on the other hand, it is one of the most interesting positions in the Patrol for the right boy.

## QUARTERMASTER

Next on our list comes the position of Quartermaster (or whatever you like to call him).

It is a splendid thing for a Patrol to have its own equipment, but what is the use of having it if it is spread to all winds and nobody knows anything about where the winds have blown the different articles?

Somebody must be responsible for the equipment and it falls to the Quartermaster's lot to take care of it.

Every Patrol has usually two groups of equipment:

(1) One which is purely the Patrol's own property.

(2) Another which is the private property of some of the boys but which is used for the common good and half way considered Patrol property.

The first group usually contains tents, cooking utensils, Patrol flag, totem poles, maybe a trek cart, etc., while the other consists of articles such as axes, bugles, first aid kits, signaling flags, etc.

However, it doesn't make any difference whose property it is, the Quartermaster has to know at any time in whose possession it is.

There are no special rules for choosing the Quartermaster, but it would be a good thing to let it be the boy who lives nearest to the Patrol or Troop headquarters where the equipment is stored. It is easier for him to get to it, to see if everything is there, if anything has to be repaired or replaced.

### List of Equipment

The first thing he will do as soon as he is appointed is to make a list of the Patrol's property. The reproduction from the Patrol Record Book on the following page will show how this may be done.

## Looking After the Equipment

As soon as the Quartermaster has made his list with the help of all the Patrol Members, he gets the articles collected in one place in order to look it over and see if anything needs to be repaired or perhaps even replaced with something new. He will report these points to his Patrol Leader who will provide him with

### PATROL EQUIPMENT
#### "TENTING" GROUP

| ITEM | WEIGHT | VALUE | Owned by | Where Kept |
|------|--------|-------|----------|-----------|
| Patrol Flag | 3 | 5.00 | Patrol | Patrol Den |
| Tents (2 4-pers. or 4 2-pers.) | | | | |
| 1 4 pers. Tent | 10 | 15.00 | Patrol | Patrol Den |
| 1 Pup Tent | 6 | 7.00 | Jack Jones | Jack's |
| 1 Baker Tent | 8 | 12.00 | Patrol | Patrol Den |
| Ground Sheets | | | | |
| 1 (big Tent) | 4 | 3.00 | Patrol | Patrol Den |
| 1 (pup) | 3 | 1.50 | Jack | Jack's |
| 1 (Baker) | 4 | 2.00 | Patrol | Patrol Den |
| Axes (2) 1 | 2 | 1.80 | Roy Shirley | Roy's |
| Spades (1) | 2 | .75 | Bill Moore | Bill's |
| Lanterns (1) | ½ | .50 | Bill Moore | Patrol Den |
| Guard ropes (2) | | | | |
| First Aid Kit (1) | | | | |
| Signaling Flags (2) 1 set | 1½ | .75 | Patrol | Patrol Den |
| Repair Bag | ½ | .50 | Patrol | Patrol Den |
| Shoe Cleaning Bag | 1 | .30 | Patrol | Patrol Den |
| Other Items | | | | |
| TOTAL | 45½ | 50.10 | | |

the necessary working force. The Quartermaster should not attempt to do everything himself but should get all the boys in the Patrol interested in the outfit and willing to help him keep it in the best order. If the right spirit rules in the Patrol any Scout will be glad to help, on request, on any job, even if it isn't his special assignment.

## Keeping the Check-up Book

When the Patrol goes out on an overnight hike or any other trip where parts of the Patrol equipment are required, the Quartermaster will put the necessary articles together and he will make a list in his notebook of everything taken along. When the Patrol returns he will check up on the equipment to see if just as much has been brought home as was taken away.

When the things are returned he will put them where they belong. With the help of his comrades, he will put the tent up for drying if it is wet, will grease the cooking utensils to keep them from rusting. If anything is missing he will investigate the matter immediately, and if something has been lost he will take steps to have it replaced.

## Making Inventory

At the end of each year the Quartermaster should be expected to make an inventory, i.e., a list of the Patrol's property with the estimated value of the different articles.

This list will not only contain the Scout equipment of the Patrol, but will also include all things of value which are kept in the Patrol Den.

### INVENTORY TAKEN OCT 31

| Number | Item | Estimated Value | Remarks |
|---|---|---|---|
| 1 | Tent | $ 5.00 | A-1 |
| 1 | Tent | 3.00 | Leaking, needs repair and water-proofing |
| 4 | Tentpoles | 0.80 | One broken and lashed |
| 24 | Tent pegs | 0.80 | 6 more necessary |

To be of help for the Patrol Leader and the Treasurer, such a list must include remarks about the condition of the items, if they are A-1, if proper repair will put them into good shape, or if they are entirely worn out.

## The Patrol Den

Another of the Quartermaster's jobs consists in taking care of the Patrol Corner at the Troop Headquarters, or if the Patrol has its own den, to keep the furniture in the right order and the room neat looking at all times.

A Quartermaster's job is one of real responsibility; he handles valuables, and he must handle them well to be of any use for the Patrol. A Quartermaster who takes his job seriously is one of the biggest assets of any Patrol.

## HIKEMASTER

Next comes the post of what we have called Hikemaster.

If you want to take your Patrol on a day hike or an over-night trip, one of the first necessities is for you to know the best place to take them. And as you are occupied with hundreds of other things, you let your Hikemaster look after that particular task of finding a suitable place for the Patrol to go to.

The Hikemaster is the Scout who, more than any of the rest, is always supposed to be on the look-out for good c a m p sites, for interesting spots to visit. He makes his investigations at any t i m e , anywhere. P a t r o l Leaders from other Patrols, Scoutmaster,  Assistants and others are interviewed, and when he gets hints about good places, he makes visits there to see if their reputation is justified.

## Hike and Camp Places

He knows by experience and personal investigation the right places inside a radius of several miles for every kind of hike and he always has his information ready for others.

It is obviously impossible for him to keep all these details in his head. Therefore he owns a notebook in which he lists all the different points. Each site or place has its own page in his notebook. For example:

## CAMP SITE NO. 4

Place: Newton Hills.
Character: Sloping grassfield close to woods.
How Far Away: Eight miles.
Permission for Use: Apply Mr. James Willard. Address Pax Hill, Newton. Telephone Newton 501.
How to Get There: Trolley car from Broad Square to Newton. Hike 2½ miles. Fare 15¢.
Water Supply: Good well, 300 feet northwest.
Wood: Plenty of fuel and wood for projects.
Food Supply: Grocery at Newton; milk, eggs and potatoes Jack Miller's farm.
Bathing: Lake 1,200 feet west.
Points of Interest: Revolutionary battlefield, Indian burial place nearby.
Other Remarks: Fire-building in gravel pit only, no mosquitoes.
Dates of Hikes: 5-12. 6-3. 8-26.

## The Hike File

The Hikemaster has a special file in which he keeps timetables and price lists for the different bus lines and railroads leading out of the city. He has his notebook and this file ready every time the Patrol is planning a hike, so that all arrangements can be made at once. He suggests trips for the Patrol to undertake.

### Preparing for Hikes

When day and place are fixed, with the consent of the Scoutmaster, he telephones or writes to the owner of the camp site for permission to use it and next he confers with the Treasurer who has received the hike (or camp) fees for the boys. From the Treasurer he receives the necessary amount of money for purchasing tickets for the whole Patrol, and he has everything ready the minute the Patrol is supposed to start.

### And Afterward—

As soon as the Patrol returns from the camping trip, the Hikemaster sits down and writes a postcard or letter to the owner of the place they visited, thanking him for his willingness to let the Patrol use his property; by doing so, he can be assured that the Patrol will always be welcomed to the site.

As is easily seen, the Hikemaster's job is of great importance for the Patrol's outdoor life, and it is therefore necessary to have it filled by the boy who best knows the surroundings and who is interested in geography and history. A boy of this type isn't always found in a Patrol but he can be developed out of any one of the members if only the entire responsibility is placed on one single head.

## GRUBMASTER

While the Hikemaster is in charge of the finding of new camp sites and of transportation to them, the Grubmaster is responsible for that important feature of camp life—the eats.

In the early stages of a Patrol's life each Scout will usually bring his own provisions, a chop to fry, a couple of potatoes to bake, just enough butter and bread for his own purposes. And by doing so, each is initiated into the art of cooking.

But in a few months or so the Scouts will find that it is less expensive and more interesting to purchase the foodstuffs for the whole Patrol at one time and to establish a real Patrol cookery that could go in for more complicated dishes. After having had chops every weekend for a number of months you get tired of them, and then comes the psychological moment for a Grubmaster to bring variety to the menu.

There isn't any reason why a Patrol should always stick to Hunter's Stew and Rice Pudding. There are other good eats for the camper, though without making them in quantities they are not so successful.

## The Patrol's Own Recipes

The Grubmaster's first job is to hunt around for recipes and thereby prepare the Patrol's own private cookery book. He will find out which dishes seem to be suitable for camp purposes and adapt others to the same use. As he goes

along he will find that Boston Brown Bread can be cooked while other sorts of bread are baked, that hot stones and sea weeds and clams at the seashore make cooking utensils unnecessary, that planking is just the way to prepare fish, and that beans soak faster if a little bicarbonate of soda is added to the water.

And while he collects recipes, he figures out at the same time what quantities are needed to appease the hunger of eight starving boys.

He always has his recipes in readiness when the Patrol discusses camping trips and the boys have only to decide upon the dishes he suggests.

## Prices of Food Stuff

If the Grubmaster is very clever, he will also have a price list for the different ingredients which go into his recipes and that will enable him to figure out immediately what the price for the eats will be, so that he can tell his Patrol how much money each boy has to lay out for the trip.

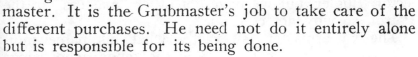

If such a list isn't in his possession he will have to get the prices together and figure out the sum in time for the boys to pay in their money before the day of the trip.

The money is paid to the Patrol Treasurer who in turn gives it to the Grubmaster. It is the Grubmaster's job to take care of the different purchases. He need not do it entirely alone but is responsible for its being done.

## Buying the Provisions

He is busy the day before the camp trip getting the materials together at the Patrol headquarters except for the perishables which are bought at the last moment before the boys arrive. He divides the provisions up in different groups for the different Scouts to carry and he checks up with one of his friends on the stuff to see if everything is there. If milk, eggs and vegetables can be secured near the camp site, he will naturally make his arrangements for getting them there instead of bringing them the whole way from the city.

## Left-overs

When the Patrol returns from the trip, he collects the foodstuff which has been left over; disposes of the things which can't be kept for another trip, as bread, butter, meat and keeps the things that can be used later, as sugar, tea, canned goods, flour, etc., in a special box at headquarters. Incidentally, with a keen Grubmaster on the task, there will be few if any perishable left-overs. It is his responsibility to provide always enough but not too much.

In almost every case you will choose for the Grubmaster the boy who is most interested in cooking. He has to have some knowledge about camp cookery to be able to collect the necessary recipes, he has to have some sense for purchasing, to buy the things at the right places, at the right prices, to get the best kind of meat from the butcher, the best kind of vegetables from the gardener.

## CHEERMASTER

Now at last we come to the eighth boy on our list. The Cheermaster. You may use any other name for him, calling him Cheer-leader, Song-leader, Stunt-collector, Bugler, but we have got other "masters" in the Patrol, so why not continue?

The Cheermaster is exactly what his name indicates. He is the fellow who brings the cheer into the Patrol, who puts pep into your yells, harmony into your songs (if possible). In other words, the one you look for any time a stunt has to be put over.

### The Patrol Bugler

Every Patrol ought to have its own Bugler, therefore, why not let the Cheermaster take the position as maker of the brass-songs. The boy with musical sense, who can sing, usually has an easy job learning to play the bugle.

But you will even sometimes find that a boy, who hasn't a note in himself can be taught to master the bugle with eminent skill.

## Leading the Cheers

Let bugling be the Cheermaster's first duty and let cheer-leading come next. As a cheer-leader he must try to learn the technique of real cheer-leaders, learn to do their acrobatic stunts (or what have you?), learn to yell without getting hoarse. He must make a collection of cheers in order to put variety into his business and he must be able with just a few minutes' reflection to invent a new cheer to fit a situation that makes a yell desirable.

## Singing and Stunting

He is the song-leader too. He has a big repertoire of Scout songs, funny songs, serious songs, patriotic songs. And he knows exactly when his pals want to sing and which songs they like the best.

Stunts are under his leadership too. He has always a recitation ready when it is wished for and he encourages his friends to take up dramatics and find playlets suitable for Patrol use, which the Patrol can put over at Troop meeting nights or at other times when they are called for.

He helps his Patrol Leader to make the right thing out of the Patrol camp fires and at the end of the twenty-mile hikes he is always the one who makes the last miles seem the easiest. He is *cheerful* in every sense.

This is a job that doesn't require m u c h

work but it does require full interest and much enthusiasm on the part of the boy who fills it. His pals must
like him well enough to be willing to follow him in his
ideas, let him run away with their natural reserve when
it comes to public appearance. He needs to be a boy of
personality plus.

It might be that it would be the youngest of their
number that a Patrol would want for their Cheermaster, and if he has the abilities, why not let him try?
A real Cheermaster will mean a tremendous lot for
the development of Patrol Spirit.

## ALL FOR ONE, ONE FOR ALL

We have now been through the different positions
of which your Patrol organization might consist and
if you look them over, you will see that they all catch
into each other like the wheels of a watch.

You, as the Patrol Leader are the spring that starts
the work, but as one wheel begins to go, all the others
follow, dependent on each other for the whole thing's
success.

The Treasurer would get nowhere without working
together with the Scribe and the Assistant Patrol
Leader, the Hikemaster and the Grubmaster both have
to confer with the Treasurer to do his own job. The
Cheermaster will need the Scribe's help for the making
up of songs and stunts. And all of them will wait for
your word to go.

Somebody will offer to help the Hikemaster find
new camp sites. Some will help the Quartermaster in
getting the equipment in order or the Grubmaster
in getting the provisions together. Everybody helps the
Scribe in the collection of material for log and scrap-
book and tells the Cheermaster about new ideas for
stunts.

The organization is for the whole Patrol.

A Patrol organized this way can get a great deal accomplished. Sixteen eyes see more than two, eight

brains get more ideas for the benefit of the Patrol than only the Patrol Leader's one set would ever be able to catch, and by working together, every one of them as a necessary part of the organization, the boys all feel their responsibility and in trying to live up to their leader's trust they will develop their own character and abilities at the same time.

## But—

If somebody ever tells you that an organization like the one mentioned on the preceding pages is absolutely necessary in order to make a Patrol run, then tell him that he is all wrong! Every Patrol Leader, worthy of his name will want to work out his own system, fitting it to his needs, as said earlier in this chapter. The plan here outlined isn't to frighten you off, but to help you on.

You will naturally begin on a small scale, with the most important jobs filled first, and even these jobs during the first months won't be as complicated as described.

Remember, too, that our organization plan isn't for a Patrol to put over the first day it is in existence. It is the work of many weeks of planning, many months of work.

The Scribe will start with his Log and as he works along he will suddenly one day discover that he can't be without a scrapbook and a letter file. The Hikemaster will have the details of the first few camp sites in his head, but he will find after the Patrol has visited

PATROL ORGANIZATION (A LITTLE EXERCISE WILL MAKE HIM GROW THIS AND THIS — THEN →    OH! BOY    PATROL ORGANIZATION

fifteen other places that he simply has to make notes about them. And it is the same way with all the other jobs. The thing grows.

The whole idea in the organization plan is to provide work for every boy in the Patrol, to make them all feel that they are moving in the midst of activities and helping things to go ahead.

You will start your organization by asking certain boys to do certain tasks. You will ask the same boys again the next time the same task has to be done. And before you know it, you have simplified your own work and your organization is right there.

The whole secret in organizing a Patrol is to always ask the same boy to do the same job, until you discover that he does it without the asking.

The Patrol may have been running several months seemingly without an organization. Then one day you will find that it is there, started as a small seed, grown up into a big and strong tree, which the winds can hardly shake.

That day you may count yourself a leader!

# CHAPTER V.

## PATROL MEETINGS

IF YOU will study any good set of Troop Meeting Programs, you will find that nearly all of them allow for a certain part of the Troop meeting period to be spent in separate Patrol meeting groups. Very likely your Scoutmaster follows this plan in your Troop. If so you will know what a splendid thing it is for your Patrol and the others to get off by themselves in their own den or corner and work on some special Patrol project or test or discuss some matters of importance. This kind of Patrol meeting has its real value and use, especially in making the Patrol feel itself a unit in its relation to the Troop as a whole.

### Real Patrol Meetings

But there is another kind of Patrol meeting which, for you as a Patrol Leader, is of even greater importance, and that is the Patrol meeting, held on your own, in between the Troop meetings. Fifteen or twenty minutes at Troop meeting isn't enough for a group of boys to get together in and build up a real Patrol. You will want to have your own special meetings besides and make them a very definite part of the life of the Patrol.

Troop life and Troop spirit are created at Troop meetings and hikes, but it is mostly at individual Patrol meetings and hikes, that Patrol Spirit is formed, that the boys are molded together as one solid, indivisible gang.

The Scoutmaster's individuality reigns at the Troop meetings, but it is at the Patrol meetings, that the Patrol Leader gets his chance to put his ideals up to his boys, to be to them, so far as he can, what the Scoutmaster stands for to the group as a whole.

At the Troop meeting the Patrol Leader is a follower, at Patrol meetings he tests himself out as a Leader.

Those are the reasons why Patrol meetings mean so much in the life of every Boy Scout.

## Making the Best of Them

And it is for you to make the very best out of these meetings. It is at the Patrol meeting that you instruct

your boys in the different Scout Tests, where you all discuss the ideals of Scouting to find the right understanding of them, where you plan for big undertakings in the future, Good Turns, hikes, camp trips, handicraft, where you bring to execution many of your plans that need manual labor. It is at the Patrol meetings that your boys learn to feel the spirit of the Patrol, the stick-together-spirit of a gang.

*All this if you are able to make the meetings contain the right things!*

You can't get more out of a Patrol meeting than you put into it. It is your spirit that runs the whole affair, and if you are not able to do it right you are liable to break down more than you build up.

By understanding the principles of such a meeting and by the planning for it in advance, you will be able to make each meeting into a happy event for your boys and you will lead them forward in Scouting, and those two things are all that you need to expect.

## Let's Plan

Suppose you are making plans for your first Patrol meeting. From the very beginning you have decided to show the boys what a real, honest-to-goodness Patrol meeting is like, and therefore you are trying to find out how it can best be planned.

There are many things to be taken into consideration. You have to find a place for the meeting, you have to fix a time, you must prepare for something to happen at the meeting, and you must arrange for it to happen in the right way.

That gives us these divisions for your consideration:

*Where?*
*When?*
*What?*
*How?*

You may have seen this formula before. In fact, it is the formula used when preparing a report of an incident, but as you see it fits just as well here.

Let us look at the four points in the right order:

## WHERE?

First of all there is the possibility of using the Troop meeting room. Maybe you could get permission to use it. But no. The room is all right when thirty-two lively fellows want a big place for a game, or when the Scoutmaster wants to say a few words to the Troop, or for large group instruction, but it doesn't fit for such an intimate thing as a Patrol meeting.

If the Patrol had its own den, there would be no doubt about where the Patrol meeting would be held. But if it hasn't any yet and at this stage it probably hasn't, you will have to find another way out.

## Meetings in the Homes

The next thing that would naturally occur to you is to invite the boys to your own home for the first meeting and later on arrange the meetings in the homes of some of the other boys of the Patrol.

Now this plan is really the very best way for a new Patrol for several reasons.

By having a meeting, say in Bill's home, you will be able to learn much more about Bill than if you held the meetings in the Troop meeting room or even used your own home right along for them. You know Bill as a boy in the Patrol but you don't know why he is as he is. By visiting his home you might find out. You will learn about his attitude toward his mother and his father; you will meet them and get a knowledge of their attitude toward Scouting, a knowledge that might help you later when you plan for meetings and hikes. By learning to know about the homes of your boys you might find that you ought not to plan for an

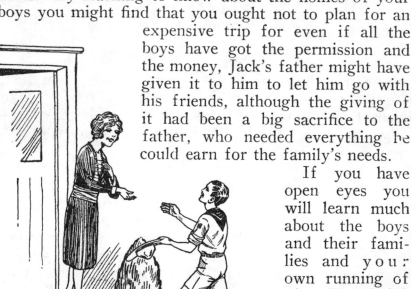

expensive trip for even if all the boys have got the permission and the money, Jack's father might have given it to him to let him go with his friends, although the giving of it had been a big sacrifice to the father, who needed everything he could earn for the family's needs.

If you have open eyes you will learn much about the boys and their families and your own running of the Patrol by coming into the different homes.

In almost all cases the parents,

too, will be happy to have the Patrol come. If there are eight boys in the Patrol it will only mean a visit every other month, and that isn't much of an inconvenience. The parents want to see whom their boy has for friends, and a meeting at their home will not only tell them that, but might also increase their interest for Scouting.

The boy himself might be happy to have the Patrol meet at his home. There might be things he would like to show his comrades; he might want them to feel how he loves his home, want to have them like it too.

Which means altogether that the right and very best thing for the new Patrol to do is to have its meetings at the homes of the different boys.

Incidentally it may be noted that at these meetings in the boys' homes you may find that the mothers may want to make it something extra. It is far from uncommon that tea or ice cream is served, or other refreshments offered the Patrols. As a rule, it is best to ask that this be not done as it establishes a kind of precedent which other mothers and boys may think they must follow. In any case, none of you will, for one minute, imagine that it is the duty of the homes to serve refreshments. Such a thing should be treated as a rare privilege and not a regular arrangement.

## A Patrol Den or Corner

When the Patrol has got acquainted with all the different homes, and when the parents have met their boys' friends, then another form of meeting place may be looked for but it ought not to be before.

Then comes the period when the Patrol would like

to have something all its own, a room it can make into
a real home for itself.

In some cases, a Patrol is happy enough to secure
the permanent use of a room suitable for the purpose
in the home of one of the Scouts.  It might be a real
room ready for occupation, or a part of a loft or of a
basement or barn that has to be fixed by the Patrol
itself before it can move in.

If such a place can't be secured, the Patrol may
have to rent one and pay the rent with money which
the Scouts are able to earn.

As a last resort there is the place, which we mentioned at the start, the Troop meeting room.  The
Patrol might get permission to use one corner of the
room and decorate it according to their own taste.  But
at its best it would only be considered a temporary substitute for a real Patrol home which should be every
Patrol's objective.

## To Sum Up

In considering your *Where,* start by having the
meetings at the homes of the boys until the day has
come when the Patrol can move into its own quarters.

The above refers to indoor meetings only.  In the
summer months the boys would no doubt prefer to

have the Patrol meetings out of doors and the meeting
place would then be the public park, the woods near
the city, at the old swimming hole, or some other well-
suited place.  This arrangement is, of course, specially
suitable for practice on outdoor tests, and ideal for a
camp fire get-together, with songs, stunts and stories.

## WHEN?

After the meeting place has been decided upon, the
next thing is to fix the time for the meeting.

## How Often?

One Patrol meeting ought to be held every week to give the boys an opportunity to live together and understand each other, but where this is impossible, meetings should be held at least every fortnight. Less than two meetings a month will mean great difficulties in building Patrol Spirit, in advancing the boys in Scouting. It might even mean that the Patrol would never grow into the real kind of a Scout Unit.

When the question about the frequency of the meetings has been settled you will have to find the day of the week and the hour of the day which is most convenient for all the boys.

If the Patrol consists wholly of schoolboys, Friday, or Saturday, will immediately come into your thought. Friday afternoon and the whole day Saturday.

If Troop meetings aren't held Friday·night, that particular night might be the best for Patrol meetings. Saturday would most often be used for hikes out in the country! But if Friday is occupied by Troop activities, any other satisfactory week day may be used for the Patrol.

If there are elementary school boys in the Patrol who do not get home from school before 4 o'clock in the afternoon, the Patrol meeting must probably be set for the evening, but if it consists of high school boys, who are free in the late afternoon, this time might be found best for the meetings.

## Special Considerations

Of course you will not let meetings interfere with

BEFORE
TROOP
MEETING

AT
BOY'S
HOME

FRIDAY
AFTERNOON

SATURDAY
OUTDOORS

BY VOTE
OF
PATROL

NOTE: PATROL MEETINGS NEVER TAKE PRECEDENCE

school work ever or, indeed, with any of your boys' other obligations. Some of the boys may have music or other special lessons or practice to attend to; others may be on the school team or have after school jobs, or even full time. All these things must be taken into consideration.

Think the whole thing out carefully yourself, have a conference with the boys and settle the day and the hour when all are able to attend with their parents' permission and without conflict with other duties.

Naturally meetings ought never to be held on Sundays, because that might conflict with the religious practice of your boys. Moreover it would be against the policies of the Boy Scouts of America to use that day (see chapter on Patrol Hikes, page 191).

When the best time for the meeting has been found, stick to it. If it is 7 o'clock Friday night, then try to keep it 7 o'clock every Friday night in the future. It is always confusing to change the meeting time from week to week. The boys are likely to forget about it that way, whereas an absolutely fixed day will soon brand itself into their minds, and they will be able to change other plans, always knowing that they are engaged for that particular night and how.

Only in very rare cases and for very good reasons should the meeting night be changed. Make such variations an exception instead of a rule.

## Be Punctual

But without regard to the date and hour, one rule is entirely fixed: Start and close the meeting at the appointed minute. One of the most important of a Scout's virtues is that he is punctual in everything he does, and the Patrol meeting must be no exception. Expect the boys to be at the meeting place precisely when the meeting is supposed to begin, and expect them to go directly home from it. If you can make the boys live up to that expectation, you will have created a habit which their parents will know how to appreciate.

# WHAT AND HOW?

Place and time for the Patrol meeting are things you have to plan with all of the members in your Patrol, a thing everybody has to agree upon before they can be put into effect.

But on the other hand, *what* is to happen at the selected place and hour, and *how,* is entirely up to you as a Patrol Leader to plan. You may have your Assistant or some of your other boys help you in the planning, but it is your job to make the decision.

How you prepare and lead your Patrol meetings is a test that will show if you have leader abilities or not.

## What Is Your Objective?

To be able to prepare the meetings you must have an objective in mind for them. Why have these Patrol meetings? What are they going to do for the Patrol?

Look ahead! You want your Patrol to be the best in the Troop in regard to Scout knowledge. That means instruction at the meetings. You want it to be the one with the best Scout Spirit. That makes it necessary for you to use some of the Patrol meeting in firing the imagination, inspiring, in molding the Patrol into a real Scout unit. But besides you want your Scouts to learn to do things, to work hard, when work has to be done, to play when play is the thing.

If you have a Patrol of Tenderfoot Scouts, you will
want the Patrol meetings to bring them along towards
the passing of the Second Class tests. If they are Second Class Scouts, the First Class tests will be your
goal, while you would want to lead a Patrol of First
Classers towards Star, Life and Eagle Awards.

*Always Forward*—that is the spirit of the Patrol
meetings.

And that is what requires your biggest work—the
instruction of your boys—an instruction undertaken
only after you have gone into the subject fully with
your Scoutmaster.

## Other Considerations

But there are a few other things that also go into
the making of a Patrol meeting, so we might just as
well consider them systematically.

At one time or another during the meeting, the
Patrol business has to be attended to; dues have to be
collected by the Treasurer, reports made by the Scribe.
There must be a period in which to plan for future
meetings and hikes, one for recreation and maybe one
for real work.

Which altogether gives us the following list of
ingredients:

1. *Business.* Collecting dues, making of records.
   Reports of last meetings in Patrol and Troop.
2. *Instruction* in Scout Tests, Merit Badges, New
   Songs, Stunts, etc.
3. *Work.* On Patrol equipment, on the den, for
   Good Turns, for the earning of money, for the
   Patrol or Troop funds.
4. *Planning* of Hikes, Camps, Good Turns, Work,
   etc.
5. *Recreation Period* of Fellowship and Fun. Discussions, singing, the telling or reading of stories,
   relation of incidents from school life, hikes,
   games.
6. *Ceremonies.* For opening and closing.

All of these things will make any meeting interesting if the Patrol Leader knows how to put them up to the boys in the right way, i.e., if he has planned for all the details in advance.

When you plan, don't make the mistake of thinking that you can easily remember what you are going to do when you get to the meeting. Don't fool yourself. You can't. And it isn't much trouble to jot the details down on a small piece of paper so that you can keep them in front of you the whole time. You might forget something if you depend wholly on your mind, but a piece of paper with the entire plan won't permit you to forget.

## Plan Ahead

Make your plans for some time ahead, not just from one meeting to the next. You need a broader outlook in order to get ahead. Divide your Patrol's future into periods, for example, consisting of three months each. Decide what the Patrol is going to do inside that period and find out how much work that will mean. Then divide the work between the Patrol meetings to be held in the same period and you have something real as a basis for the meetings.

Variety helps. If you expect your boys to be interested in one thing for more than twenty minutes at a time you will be disappointed. It makes  boys tired having to concentrate upon the same thing for a considerable amount of time. They get restless, don't listen, and all your work is thrown away. Give them instead plenty of variety. They should never be kept at a thing till they get tired of it. Get away from it and on to the next before that disastrous moment occurs. We only succeed in that in which we are interested.

And now let us treat the details of our list separately.

## Period of Business

The business is the first thing that has to be attended to but there isn't any reason why it should take up much of the time designated for the meeting. In fact, if the Patrol Treasurer and the Scribe are up to their jobs, they will have the business part attended to even before the meeting starts. As soon as the boys arrive at the Patrol Headquarters, the Scribe will make a record of it in his book, and if dues have to be paid the Treasurer will be at his victims even before they get a chance to take their hats off. The remaining part of the business, report of the things inside Patrol and Troop might be finished in a few minutes and if that can't be done you will usually find it more profitable to put it off until later in the program. Reports aren't action, and it is action with which you ought to start out.

## Instruction Period

Action is precisely what the instruction period ought to be. It is by doing things that boys learn about them,—not by just having them explained to them.

And there isn't any reason why every bit of your Patrol instruction shouldn't be action on your Scouts' part.

A Patrol meeting shouldn't be just "some more stuff to learn." It must be something *to do* if it is to hold the boys.

And the different Scout tests offer all the action a boy can desire, if the action isn't killed by making everything into dry book knowledge. Scouting is drama, and if the Patrol Leader gets that idea, he's sure to have a live and active Patrol.

A special chapter elsewhere in this book will give you

more detailed assistance. Here we are just mentioning instruction as a part of a Patrol meeting.

But whatever method you use for the instruction, don't forget that you are the one who has the responsibility for its success. You are the leader, and it is up to you to interest *all* your boys in the subjects.

One difficulty arises here. Maybe there are both Tenderfoot Scouts and Second Class Scouts in your Patrol. The Tenderfoot Scouts want instruction in the Second Class tests and the Second Class Scouts want to be taught the First Class requirements. Even so, don't make the mistake of dividing the Patrol up into small groups. It is distracting to have groups working in different corners on *different* subjects. It takes something of the feeling of co-hesion away from the meeting.

If you know your stuff, it is quite easy to have Scouts of different advancement working together. While, for example, the Tenderfoot Scouts work on signaling for perfection, the Second Class Scouts work on it for speed. The first mentioned use the last as victims for first aid, and they in turn come back to the Tenderfoot Scouts. Cooking goes together the same way,— use of axe and hatchet likewise.

It is a mistake to believe that boys of different stages of advancement cannot work together. It all depends upon the Patrol Leader.

**Work Period**

A live Patrol will always have a project suitable for work at the Patrol meetings.

Perhaps a locker has to be made for the Patrol equipment, a knot board is wanted for the Troop meeting room, a table for the Patrol den. One day a big project such as the sewing of a Patrol tent,—another day the making of book marks or linoleum cuts for sale or gifts.

But whatever you do, work while you work. If you are able to make the boys concentrate upon what they are doing, you will get it done much faster than when you let them flitter around from one thing to another leaving everything half done. Let it be a rule in your Patrol that whatever you start has to be finished, and

make the boys stick to that rule.

In some periods of the Patrol's life there might come times where it is neces-sary for the Patrol to use all of the meetings inside a certain time for work, and forget about other things for the minute. The fixing up of a Patrol meeting place might be one of these special objectives. If you have been lucky enough to secure a place for the Patrol, all the boys are certain to want to help make it into a real den. They will be willing to give their work. Plan what has to be done and stick to the work until it is finished, even if it has to take a number of Patrol meetings and maybe even extra days' work. If you don't take it seriously you will never get it done. The making of a Patrol den is a big job, and you will often be tempted to loosen up and say, "We will do this or that some other time!" The boys may seem tired of what they think is perpetual work and it may be only your bulldog-spirit that makes them finish it. But the day it is finished! Oh Boy! Won't they be happy, and what a stick-together spirit will have been created—a spirit that will live on in the future.

Another big project is the manufacture of the Patrol's camping equipment. Instead of buying it the Patrol ought to make it itself, but if for one reason or another that is impossible, the equipment ought at least to be bought with money the Patrol has earned for that purpose. You will find that a tent which has cost the boys gallons of perspiration and hard work will mean much more to them and be treated much better than one that has "just" been given to them.

Work is what makes a man. You will find, too, that it is what makes a Patrol.

## The Patrol's Planning

An important part of the meeting is the time occupied by planning the future of the Patrol.

The future must be just as much of a concern for your boys as it is for yourself if you want the Patrol to be a success. If you try to plan everything by yourself without taking the trouble to consult the Patrol you will soon find you get nowhere, indeed you may find yourself without a Patrol.

The boys want to help in the planning, but if you are the right kind of a leader, you will see that it is your plans of which they want to be a part.

Before each meeting it is your duty to consider this point of it very carefully. You must have your own ideas and plans worked out in advance and be entirely sure that your ideas are worth while. At the meeting you put your plans up to the Patrol, get your boys' suggestions and then, together,  you work out the final form for the project on hand.

Your Patrol is not supposed to be a kingdom with you as the absolute monarch. You are just a part of the Patrol, and Lincoln's famous words about a government "of the people, by the people, for the people" apply to your Patrol as well.

## Recreation Period

A Patrol has to work. It has to be instructed. But without something else to enliven the meetings, you will have a dull Patrol.

The recreation period is supposed to open up that bag of concentrated energy the boys have collected while doing their share of work. The work might have been a kind of expression for the energy inside them, but boys want sidetracks too, where they can enjoy themselves in good earnest. The recreation period is the safety-valve for their bubbling spirits.

Maybe they will want a vigorous game. It can be arranged either in the meeting room or outside. If they feel like singing, let them sing. If they want to tell their friends what happened at school the other day, let them do it. Maybe they want to listen to a story from BOYS' LIFE. Maybe they want to discuss something that is on their minds. Feel their pulse and let them do just the thing they desire.

It is unnecessary to mention that this has to be done inside the borders of good Scouting. But Scout-ing certainly doesn't want to restrain the boys in their joy of life.

It is a foolish boy who never did anything foolish. It is a foolish Patrol Leader who doesn't understand that boys' twaddling and chattering is a natural thing, which instead of being repressed needs to be led into the right channels.

## Other Features of the Patrol Meeting

We have discussed the most important parts of the Patrol meeting, but there are other features which can be brought into it with advantage.

As the Patrol works along, it will invent its own ceremonies, its own way of starting the meeting, its own way of closing it.

If the Scouts have been used at the Troop meeting to a Flag ceremony or a prayer at the start, it will be natural to start the Patrol meetings the same way.

The Flag might be hung on one of the walls in the den. A pledge of allegiance to it and a Scout Salute would be an appropriate way of starting the meeting.

The Patrol might develop a short opening prayer which is said by all the boys in unison, or the meeting might start with a short silence in which the boys can make their thoughts occupy themselves with the same ideals.

Here again it is the Patrol Leader who must lead the way. If the boys feel that the opening ceremony is artificial, it will be a far better thing to eliminate it and start in immediately on the business. On the other hand, if it is treated entirely naturally and with sincerity by the Patrol Leader, such a ceremony might mean everything in the world to the Patrol.

The same may be said in regard to a closing ceremony.

That might consist of the "Great Scoutmaster's Benediction": "May the Great Scoutmaster (all make gesture toward heaven) of all Scouts (inclusive gesture from right to left at height of shoulder) be with us till we meet again (right hands being brought to hearts and heads bowed)", or a repeating of the Scout Law ("A Scout is trustworthy, loyal, helpful, friendly," etc.), or the singing of "Taps" followed by the Patrol's private yell.

Do whatever you want to if you only do it with sincerity.

Inspection may also be made a feature every once in a while at Patrol meetings. Look your boys over carefully, have them look each other over carefully and be sure that all incorrect positions of badges on uniform, any parts of it that need repairing are brought to the attention of the wearer. Even a Patrol competition on "Who has the smartest appearance?" may be started.

## PREPARING THE MEETINGS

The meeting itself isn't always the most difficult part for the Patrol Leader. Very often the preparations for it will need more work, and work that has to be done to make the meeting run right.

Every minute of the meeting must be occupied, there must be no unnecessary pauses, and that can only be effected by having everything ready in advance.

We have mentioned before, that you ought to make an outline in writing of what you are going to do so that you won't forget anything of what you had in mind. But before you can put it down on a piece of paper, you have to work it out carefully in your mind, and these are what you must think of:

(a) *What do I want the meeting to contain?*

(b) *How will I arrange it so that every minute of the meeting is occupied and so that I know what to do in every minute?*

(c) *What materials do I need to put the meeting across?*

In order to give you the right understanding of the preparing, let us take a definite example:

### A Meeting for Beginners

Let us suppose that your Patrol consists of you and seven boys who have just been enrolled in the Troop pending their passing of the Tenderfoot requirements.

You have to plan your first meeting and will probably think the thing through something like this.

"First (a) *What will the meeting contain?*

"Well, we ought to be able to master all those requirements in good shape in three meetings. That means dividing the whole business up into three comparatively equal parts. Suppose at this first meeting, then, we work up the Scout Salute, study the Scout Law, trying to see what is behind it all, find out all we can about the composition of The Flag and practice on three  of the nine knots the boys will have to know before they can be Tenderfoot Scouts.

"Here is our list then:

> *Scout Salute*
> *Scout Law*
> *Flag*
> *Three Knots*

"It's up to me as leader," you decide, "to know exactly what I am doing. The fellows have really to be taught these Tenderfoot requirements, not just listen to a lot of hot air about them. Better mix up teaching with actually doing something. They'll get the idea better that way and it will stick in their heads longer, too."

You stop here and think a moment, perhaps scratch your head trying to remember things your Scoutmaster told you about "getting across" that first meeting with the boys. Recreation, for instance—something to work off steam! Dues! Got to have a little money to go on with. Be business like. Start off right.

You add to your list then:

> *Fun*
> *Business*

"Now then," you think with some satisfaction,

"Here's the makings of our WHAT. What about the time part?   There is (b) to consider.   *How will I arrange it so that every minute of the meeting is occupied?   How will I know what to do every minute?*  Mighty important too.   Never get through with all there is to get through with if you don't plan sharp for every minute and what's to go into it.   There's got to be some way to begin and end, too.   And some time for talking over plans."

You think again, make notes.   Perhaps scratch some of them out, begin all over again.   In the end the program looks something like this:

| | | | |
|---|---|---|---|
| 1. | *Opening ceremony* | 2 | minutes |
| 2. | *Business* | 3 | " |
| 3. | *Scout Salute* | 10 | " |
| 4. | *Scout Law* | 15 | " |
| 5. | *Stars and Stripes* | 20 | " |
| 6. | *Yells* | 10 | " |
| 7. | *Tenderfoot Knots* | 15 | " |
| 8. | *Discussion—Planning* | 12 | " |
| 9. | *Closing Ceremony* | 3 | " |

90 minutes—1½ hours

All very nice on paper but how does it actually get across?   You have to think and think hard, remember what boys like and what they don't like, suggestions your Scoutmaster made.   Decide on what seems the best way of getting in all the necessary details.

Perhaps it will go something like this in your mind.

"(1) Tell the boys that we might try starting our meetings always with a short silence, to give them an opportunity in their own thoughts to give thanks for what the day has given to them.

"(2) Ask one of the boys to act as temporary Treasurer and collect dues.   Ask another to act as Scribe to make a record in our Patrol Record Book as to the boys present and the dues received by the Treasurer.   Tell boys regular officers will be appointed shortly when we get under way.

"(3) Show boys Scout Salute. Be sure I can do it myself first, just right. Tell them what it stands for. Ask boys to stand in row. Appoint somebody to see that line is straight, everybody at "attention." Do Salute again. Have them make it after me, till they know how to do it—four or five times, perhaps. Then give the order to stand at salute. If anybody still doesn't get it, help him later, alone. Don't worry him now before the others. Explain that it is important to give the salute correctly, if we're going to be real Scouts.

"(4) Tell the boys a little about the Scout Law and what it means to a Boy Scout. Show them where they can find it in the Handbook. Have a few copies of the Law on hand to give to the boys who haven't got the Handbook. Get Joe to help me type or write them out longhand before meeting if I can't get hold of printed copies. Go through the first four parts of Law. Have a newspaper with me. Ask boys to look at the news from a Boy Scout point of view. Find examples in it illustrating trustworthiness, loyalty, helpfulness, friendliness. I must have read newspaper carefully before meeting in order to help point out examples without too much delay. Ask them to see if they can't find more to bring in next meeting. Let them ask questions about the Law, talk over what it means. Awfully important and only fifteen minutes to give to it. Have to make it all count, keep their interest lively.

"(5) Have everybody make a drawing of our Flag from memory. Afterward produce a real Flag. Compare the drawings with the Flag to see if they are correct. Notice who has best one. Tell him so. Teach them how to draw a five pointed star with one line. Show them the Betsy Ross trick of making a star of a piece of paper with one cut of the scissors.

"(6) Now for the fun. Use Scout Yell:
A-M-E-R-I-C-A,
Boy Scouts, Boy Scouts,
U. S. A.

Tell the boys to try to make up a yell we can use for our own Patrol, suggest one, practice it.

"(7) Have rope ready and show the boys how to tie the Square Knot, the Sheet Bend and the Fisherman's Knot. Have them tie them until they can do it correctly, if possible. Tell them to practice a lot during the week, promise to help anybody who needs help. Talk over the uses of the knots. Tell them how some Patrols make knot boards, with fifty or seventy-five different kinds of knots. Get 'em interested. This leads up to discussion period.

"(8) Let them ask me all the questions they want to and try to answer them. Remind them again to practice the knots, ask them to learn the whole Scout Law before next meeting if possible. Learn first four parts anyway. Tell them it's expected of them. Fix the place for the next meeting.

"(9) Close meeting by reciting the Scout Law. Give it slowly, part by part, have the boys repeat every section after me. Dismissal."

Not so bad for a beginning, if it goes anything like the way it is planned.

In regard to (c), *Necessary Equipment,* your notes will show the following:

Patrol Record Book and pencil (2)
Handbook, extra copies of the Law, newspaper (4)
Paper, pencils, The Flag, scissors (5)
Ropes for knots (7)

So much for preparations. At the meeting you will bring your list of activities, your program, and the material listed above. You will need also plenty of common sense, patience and enthusiasm, as well as a certain degree of assurance that you yourself "know your stuff."

## Other Meetings

The meeting above was prepared for the beginners' period. Some other suggestions follow, allowing for the planning of Patrol meetings inside other periods, as the Tenderfoot stage (Tenderfoot Scouts working on Second Class Requirements), the Second Class stage (Second Class Scouts passing First Class tests) and the First Class stage (First Class Scouts working for further advancements). An example is also given of meeting of mixed stages.

Such programs might go somewhat like this:

## Tenderfoot Stage Meeting

| | | | |
|---|---|---|---|
| (1) | *Opening Ceremony* | 2 | minutes |
| (2) | *Business* | 3 | " |
| (3) | *First Aid* | 20 | " |
| (4) | *Good Turns* | 10 | " |
| (5) | *Kim's Game* | 15 | " |
| (6) | *Signaling* | 15 | " |
| (7) | *Song* | 10 | " |
| (8) | *Discussion, Planning* | 12 | " |
| (9) | *Closing Ceremony* | 3 | " |

90 minutes—1½ hours

*Suggestions for Details*

(1) Silence as opening ceremony.

(2) Receiving of dues by Treasurer, checking up on Scouts present and absent by Scribe.

(3) Divide the boys into groups of two. Send the number twos outside the room. Tell the number ones: "Some boys outside this room have cut the arteries on their right feet just above the ankle. What will you

do?" The number ones rush out, each of them brings in a patient and starts the treatment. When it is ended the number twos are asked: "What do you suppose your case was? And do you consider the treatment you received correct?" The next time the number ones are sent outside and the number twos are ordered to render First Aid.

(4) Good Turns. How can we train ourselves in the habit of rendering service to others? What do we consider Good Turns? Discussion. Find in the newspapers Good Turns performed by others. Analyze them.

(5) Kim's Game varied using articles from boys'

pockets, Scout Badges, etc. Or have a visitor come to the meeting, have him leave just before this period and ask the boys to put down from memory a description of him.

(6) Signaling by sound. Use a nail to give the sound of a dot, a penholder to give the sound of a dash. While one boy is sending, the rest are receiving. Give every boy a chance to send a message.

(7) Song period. Interest the boys in getting a special Patrol song. Get someone from the outside to help you make a song, if necessary.

(8) Planning the future, discussing Troop work, etc.

(9) Scout Law as closing ceremony.

*The Necessary Material:*

Newspaper (4)

Articles from boys' pockets, Scout Badges; or arrange with an acquaintance to interrupt at an exact minute (5)

Nail and penholder (6).

## Second Class Stage Meeting

| (1) | Opening ceremony | 2 | minutes |
|---|---|---|---|
| (2) | Business | 3 | " |
| (3) | Signaling | 10 | " |
| (4) | Good Turns | 10 | " |
| (5) | Map Making | 15 | " |
| (6) | Play | 20 | " |
| (7) | First Aid | 15 | " |
| (8) | Discussion, Planning | 12 | " |
| (9) | Closing ceremony | 3 | " |

90 minutes—1½ hours.

*Suggestions for Details.*

(1) and (2) as described under Tenderfoot stage meeting.

(3) Using an electric buzzer or a flashlight. Sound and light signaling.

(4) Discussion of Patrol Good Turns and planning of one to take place in the near future.

(5) From field notes the most important outlines of a map are dictated by the Patrol Leader while the boys put them down on paper in the conventional signs. Example: "Start at the lower corner of the paper on the right hand side. Use 1 inch as a 100 foot measure. A road runs  200 feet in West North West direction, turns, 350 feet direct North, 100 feet Norh North West, etc. When you start on that road from the point where

we began and walk up 100 feet you will find a church exactly 350 feet to the North, 400 feet further up on the same road you will find a school house on the West side of the road, etc." The boys follow the dictation on the paper and afterwards the maps are compared.

(6) The Patrol is to perform a small play or special stunt at the next Troop meeting and therefore uses the Patrol meeting for the instruction.

(7) First Aid for the First Class tests may be taught as in the Second Class tests. (See Tenderfoot meeting.)

(8) Planning hikes, competitions. Discussion of how to get recruits and how they can be trained for the Patrol.

(9) Closing with the Scout Law or Great Scoutmaster's Benediction.

*Necessary Material.*

Buzzer, electric bell or a couple of flashlights (3)

Paper and pencils. Make a list of field notes (5)

If necessary have just as many copies of play as there are players to take part in it (6).

Bandages for First Aid (7)

## First Class Stage Meeting

| | | | |
|---|---|---|---|
| (1) | *Opening Ceremony* | 2 | minutes |
| (2) | *Business* | 3 | " |
| (3) | *First Aid, Signaling* | 15 | " |
| (4) | *Our Constitution* | 10 | " |
| (5) | *Merit Badge Work* | 25 | " |
| (6) | *Game* | 10 | " |
| (7) | *Songs, yells* | 10 | " |
| (8) | *Discussion* | 12 | " |
| (9) | *Closing Ceremony* | 3 | " |

90 minutes—1½ hours.

*Suggestions for Details:*

(1) and (2) as described under Tenderfoot stage meetings.

(3) Review of the Patrol's specialty—first aid, signaling, etc. Training to keep the boys in practice.

(4) A short review of the Constitution, the duties of government officials, legislative bodies, etc.

(5) The Patrol as a whole wants to pass certain Merit Badge tests. It has an instructor and now uses a part of the Patrol meeting for training.

(6) Example: Intelligence tests. The Patrol Leader has chosen 30 questions from Quiz Books, or has made them himself. The questions are numbered and given to the boys. They write the answers and results are checked with the correct answers.

(7) New songs are learned, new yells invented to be used at coming Troop events.

(8) Planning advance work, hikes, discussing Troop work, how to help the Scoutmaster in his work, etc.

(9) Close with Scout Laws.

*Necessary Material*:

First Aid bandages, buzzer or light for signaling (3).
A copy of the Constitution of the United States (4).
Arrange for having an instructor present (5).
Copy of Quizzes for each boy. Paper, pencils (6).

## Meeting for Mixed Stages

| | | |
|---|---|---|
| (1) *Opening Ceremony* | 2 | minutes |
| (2) *Business* | 3 | " |
| (3) *Signaling* | 15 | " |
| (4) *Use of knife and axe* | 15 | " |
| (5) *Games* | 15 | " |
| (6) *First Aid* | 20 | " |
| (7) *Yells, Songs* | 9 | " |
| (8) *Discussion* | 8 | " |
| (9) *Closing Ceremony* | 3 | " |

90 minutes—1½ hours

*Suggestions for Details:*

(1) and (2). See Tenderfoot stage meetings.

(3) Start messages slowly, increase speed. Find out at which speed boys go out.

(4) Scout Question Ball, or "Spell Down" (H. B. for Boys, 560 and 563) on Use of Axe and Knife.

(5) Buzz-Buzz, Rooster Fight, Tractor (H. B. for Boys, 557 and 558).

(6) Second Classers treating Tenderfoot Scouts and vice versa.

(7) and (8) Around artificial camp fire.

(9) Close with Scout Law.

*Necessary Material:*

Buzzer or flashlight (3).

First Aid bandages (6).

Artificial camp fire (7-8).

## It's An Art

The preparing and running of Patrol meetings is an art all by itself, but fortunately it is an art which can be acquired by any Patrol Leader if he will take the trouble to train himself for it.

# CHAPTER VI

## PATROL INSTRUCTION

ONE of the most important functions of a Patrol Leader is to help his boys ahead in the passing of their tests, in advancing in Scoutcraft.

It isn't Scoutlike to stand still. Scouting is "Forward." If a goal has been reached, immediately another is beckoning in the distance.

The real Patrol Leader will have his boys go through the Tenderfoot, Second Class and First Class stages as fast as is consistent with thoroughness. He will have them move along all the time. That naturally means that he himself must be advancing too.

You can't teach your boys the requirements if they are entirely new to you. You can't expect them to be interested in the Scout tests if you show them your own ignorance in regard to them.

As in all other cases inside the Patrol, it is your example, the Patrol Leader's example, that helps the boys to work. If you are in front of them in advancement, it gives you authority to lead them ahead. If you aren't, not a soul can blame them if they stagger behind.

If you want to teach your boys the Scout requirements, you must know them thoroughly in advance.

You must have studied them yourself, have gotten all the help possible from your Scoutmaster and other Troop leaders, from experts outside the Troop, and you must have passed your requirements with distinction yourself.

But a real Patrol Leader will seek help wherever it is found. He will also try to get as much information as possible from books on the different subjects.

In the "Boy Scout Service Library" several valuable pamphlets are found. But naturally one of your best helps is the Handbook for Boys. Your instruction must, as a matter of course, follow the procedure as laid down in the Handbook.

### Boys Want to Do Things

The minute the boy enters the Patrol and wants to pass the different tests he finds things *to do*. There are knots to tie, salutes to learn to make just right, first aid to demonstrate, signaling to perform, cooking to practice, and a host of other things.

And still there are people who act as if all these things could be taught a boy by words, words, words.

*Words ought never to be used, if a picture can illustrate the point; a picture never, if the point can be demonstrated to the boy, and a demonstration never, if the boy himself can be put into action doing the thing.*

This naturally does not imply that words should never be used. There are many cases where you will find the use of oral explanation all important. But it means that words alone won't drive the works. Action is the main feature of Scouting.

### Methods of Instruction

Action on your part as a demonstration, action on the boys' part as training. And when new points have to be taught, your demonstration and your boys' following it with their own actions is the right way of putting the thing across.

You will have to use your imagination to turn all the Scout requirements into action, but it can be done.

You might do it *directly,* by simply asking the Scouts to go ahead and do a thing. Let them use their own brains. You will help them best by letting them help themselves. Take for example fire-building at an outdoor meeting. Suppose you have told them just how it is done, even demonstrated it for them. Still they haven't really learned anything about the thing, first hand. It is only by making a fire that a boy learns to build one. Let them start making the fire themselves, after telling them a little about how to do it. Let them blow their faces red, get their eyes filled with smoke. When they have tried and maybe invented their own way of doing it, you can help them further along by giving them advice, show the why of their failure, if they don't succeed.

If a direct method can't be applied, try the *combination of demonstration and action.* Knot-tying, signaling and many other Scout activities are learned most easily that way. You simply lead the boys along in doing a thing. In knot-tying, for example, let them have the ropes in their hands, and let them follow your actions while you are tying the knot on your own rope.

By doing the things the boys learn them, but if you want them to be really well trained, you must let them make use of their newly acquired knowledge time and again.

*Competitions* inside the Patrol interest them in improving their abilities. Let them test each other's skill to try to find out who is best.

Also *games* will help to improve the boys' technique and skill. Plenty of interesting dramatic games can be invented covering the different Scout subjects.

The above only gives you general suggestions as to methods of Patrol Instruction. More detailed help will be found in the following pages.

# THE TENDERFOOT REQUIREMENTS

At the very first Patrol meeting you may gather your fellows around you and say something like this to them.

"You have asked to become Scouts in the Patrol and Troop to which I belong, and the Troop has decided to try you out and to give you your first training. As you know, you cannot become a Scout without having shown that you are willing to work and work hard to get the privilege, and the first work which is in front of you is the passing of the Tenderfoot tests."

Then ask the boys to open their Handbooks at page 28 where they will find the Tenderfoot Requirements. Ask one of the boys to start reading aloud what the Handbook says about the tests.

When the requirements have been read, ask questions to see if the boys actually understand them, and explain that the passing of these tests is the first thing that is expected of them if they want to join the Boy Scouts of America and also, thereby, the World Brotherhood of Scouts.

Then take up the different points separately.

## Tenderfoot Requirement No. 1

*Know the Scout Oath and Law, Motto, Sign, Salute and Significance of the Badge*

Make your boys realize from the very beginning that of all the requirements necessary to pass from ordinary boy to First Class Scout this is the most important, for the simple reason that if the boy doesn't know his Oath and Law and doesn't try to live up to them, *he isn't a Scout,* even if he has his shirt sleeve covered with all the Merit Badges obtainable.

You must do your best to impress upon the minds of your boys the significance of this requirement, and even after they have successfully passed the test it must perpetually be held up to them.

## Projects in Oath, Law and Motto

(1) Have a *discussion* on the meaning of the different points of Oath and Law.

(2) Have the boys *write down the Oath and Law* on first page of their notebook, to be carried with them always.

(3) Make sure that the boys *know the Oath and Law* in full by heart, and try to live up to them.

(4) Plan *Patrol Good Turns* and bring them to execution.

(5) Use Law occasionally for *opening or closing ceremony* of Patrol meetings.

(6) Use *Oath for recital* at specially solemn occasions, as for example when initiating new members into Patrol, at first and last camp fire in camp, at Patrol birthday party, and particularly the evening of February 8th, at 8:15 P. M., on the Birthday Anniversary of the Boy Scouts of America, when all American Scouts recommit themselves to the Scout Oath.

(7) Have a discussion of the Scout Law in people's daily life based on *clippings* from current newspapers. Discuss especially striking Good Turns.

(8) *Read or tell stories* of real things Scouts have done, illustrating Oath and Law. Every Patrol library ought to contain for this purpose "The Boy Scout and His Law," by Barry Chalmers.

(9) *Dramatize* the different points of the Law and put them on as Patrol stunt at a Troop meeting.

(10) Conduct a *contest* every once in a while to see how many of the boys can write down the Oath and the Law correctly.

(11) Have a Patrol *"Oath and Law Hike."* See Hiking chapter.

(12) Earn money and purchase from National Supply Department the big *Oath and Law poster* for Patrol Den or Troop meeting room, or make one yourselves.

(13) Show the boys the *Motto* "Be Prepared" on the Scout Badge. Discuss with them the meaning of the Motto.

## Projects in Sign, Salute and Significance of Badge

(14) Demonstrate to the boys the difference between the *rendition of Sign and Salute*.

(15) Have a *Sign and Salute drill* with whole Patrol.

(16) Make the boys understand that you expect them to *use Sign and Salute* at all proper occasions.

(17) Have a *discussion* to make sure that the boys

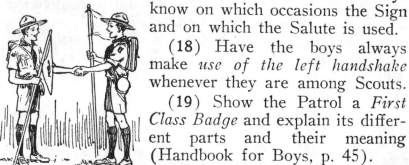

know on which occasions the Sign and on which the Salute is used.

(18) Have the boys always make *use of the left handshake* whenever they are among Scouts.

(19) Show the Patrol a *First Class Badge* and explain its different parts and their meaning (Handbook for Boys, p. 45).

(20) Be sure that your boys always *wear their badges* and insignia correctly.

(21) Show and explain to your boys at Troop meeting the *insignia* of your Scoutmaster, Assistant Scoutmaster, Junior Assistant Scoutmaster, Senior Patrol Leader, Committeemen, and other officers of the Troop.

## Tenderfoot Requirement No. 2

*Know the composition and history of The Flag of the United States of America and the customary forms of respect due to it*

The Flag of the United States of America! Our Flag!! Naturally every boy in our country ought to know all about it, its dimensions, its history, how to respect it. It is the symbol of our land, of its past and its future, and it would be a queer American boy who wasn't interested in everything that had to do with The Flag.

The history of The Flag is full of romance, but also the building up of The Flag from red, white and blue pieces of cloth into our National Emblem can be filled with interest. Looking at the figures and decimals of the proportions of the stripes, the stars, the blue field and the seemingly endless rules of respect may scare many boys away. And yet these details may be simplified and made vivid to them if they are only treated the right way.

## Projects

(1) Have the boys draw rough *sketches of The Flag* from memory. Produce The Flag or a correct drawing of it and have the boys compare.

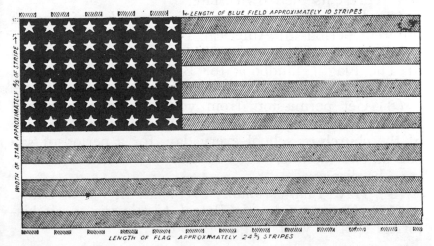

(2) Discuss the correct *proportions of The Flag* with the Patrol and try to find a way of simplifying them, using the width of one stripe as unit. (You may find these figures: width of Flag, 13 stripes, length of Flag twice thirteen minus 1-1/3 stripes, width of blue field, 7 stripes, length of field almost correctly 10 stripes, diameter of stars almost exactly 4/5 stripe).

(3) Show and teach your Patrol the *Betsy Ross trick* of making a 5-pointed star from a piece of

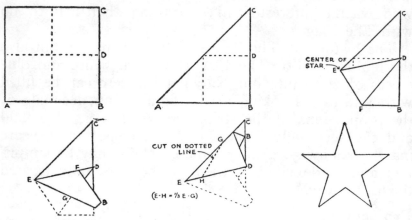

paper with just one cut of the scissors (see illustration).

(4) Have the boys find out for themselves which *star* represents their own State.

(5) Have the boys make *colored sketches* of flags of different periods of American History.

(6) Have a *quiz competition* based on the history of The Flag (Handbook for Boys).

(7) Teach the correct way of *folding The Flag*.

(8) Get permission from your minister or school principal for your Patrol to *hoist and lower The Flag* of the church or school every day, for a period of say one or two months, or on special days when The Flag is to be displayed.

(9) Have *Flag ceremony* every day in Patrol Camp.

(10) Have a patriotic *Patrol pilgrimage* to an historical spot in your neighborhood.

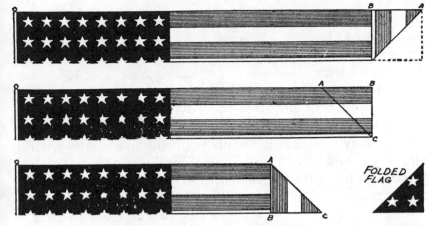

FOLDED FLAG

(11) Use an actual Flag in going through the different *forms of respect* until you are sure your boys get them. Let them learn this simplified rule: "(a) Consider yourself the Flag. (b) Consider your right hand the blue field (the Union). (c) *Always* face people."

(12) Teach your Patrol the words of *"The Star-Spangled Banner,"* its history and how to sing it.

## Tenderfoot Requirement No. 3

*Tie the Square Knot and any eight of the following knots: Sheet Bend, Bowline, Fisherman's Knot, Sheepshank, Slip Knot, Clove Hitch, Timber Hitch, Two Half Hitches, Carrick Bend, Miller's Knot, Rope Halters, Pipe Hitch, Stevedore Knot, Barrel Hitch, Girth Hitch, Binder Twine Bend, Lariat Loop, Hitching Tie.*

It may be difficult for your boys to understand why knots have been considered so important that they have been placed alongside knowledge of the Scout Oath and Law and of The Flag of our country.

Make it clear to them that knot-tying is just one of the things that helps a Scout to live up to his motto, "Be Prepared." Bring to their attention the many cases where human lives depend upon whether a knot holds or not. Have them think of the painters suspended in mid-air on a thin board while they are painting a house; of engineers building temporary bridges over rivers; of mountain climbers on their dangerous trail.

And then have them think of all the daily uses of knots. You tie your shoe laces with a kind of a square knot; you fasten your mother's clothesline to its posts with a clove hitch; make up your big packages with a slip knot and a couple of half hitches. Your mother repairs your buttonholes with clove hitches. The fisherman repairs his nets with sheet bends. The doctor fast-

ens his bandages with square knots. The archer uses the timber hitch to put the string on the bow, and the angler a fisherman's knot to connect his catgut with his line. The sailor uses a number of knots in his everyday life, so do the farmer, the engineer, the carpenter and a lot of others. You may be able to increase this list considerably, but the main point is to give the boys a vivid and real picture of the uses of knots.

## Projects

(1) Have the Patrol *decide upon* which *nine knots* out of the nineteen it wants for the Patrol knot requirement. Provided, of course, that this has not been decided by the Troop or Council, in which case you will naturally follow the local requirements. If you choose your own be sure to have knots for following uses included (a) end knots, (b) for tying two ropes together, (c) for tying rope to something else, (d) for making permanent loops, (e) for shortening rope.

(2) Develop a *knot-tying equipment*: 8 rope pieces 4-5 feet long (old clothesline, or 2/5 inch diameter rope), a few sticks for hitches.

(3) Discuss practical *uses of knots.*

(4) Teach *parts of rope.* (H. B. for Boys, page 69.)

(5) Teach *requirements of a good knot.* (H. B. for Boys, page 69.)

(6) *Demonstrate knots* and teach boys to tie them.

(7) Have *quiz competition* on uses of different knots.

(8) Have Patrol *knot-tying competitions for speed* (based on the "champ-nit" principle, Handbook for Boys, page 564) to see who is the fastest in the following: (a) Tie single knot, (b) tie all nine knots, (c) tie single knot with eyes shut, (d) tie knots behind back, (e) biggest number in one minute.

(9) Have Patrol *knot-tying competitions for carefulness,* as for example : (a) by the help of a string carry a glass filled with water without spilling; (b) find out who is the Patrol package wrapper champion.

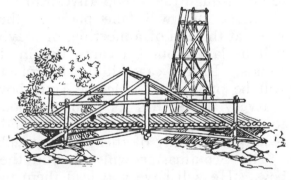

(10) Go on a *Knot Hike* : Mend that broken gate, fasten that boat more securely to dock, etc.

(11) Teach the boys *lashings* and build bridges, signal towers, camp implements, also miniature models.

(12) Introduce *rope-spinning* and *lasso-throwing* to Patrol.

(13) Make *Patrol knot board.*

(14) *Dramatize* knot-tying for a stunt at Troop meeting.

## The Tenderfoot Investiture Ceremony

Your Patrol has been through all of the Tenderfoot

Requirements. You have examined your boys in all the details. You have been a strict examiner, and you know that your boys know their stuff. The moment has come when they may become members of the Boy Scouts of America,—when they are ready to join the World Brotherhood of Scouts.

According to the national regulations it is the Scoutmaster who actually examines candidates for Tenderfoot tests; but it is *your* job to see that they are really "prepared," thoroughly, through and through. When you are sure your boys are ready, tell your Scoutmaster and ask him to arrange the time for the examination. If he is satisfied that the boys are really prepared in their Tenderfoot Requirements he will arrange for them to go through the Troop Investiture Ceremony.

Maybe this will take place in the Troop meeting room at the end of a meeting, or maybe the scene for it will be laid around a camp fire in the middle of the woods. In any case all the Patrols from your Troop will be present to welcome your boys into Scouting.

Every Troop has its own ceremonies, but common to them all are their seriousness and dignity. There is no place in any of them for horseplay and nonsense. The Scoutmaster will ask you the names of your boys. He will have you lead them up in front of the Troop. Maybe he, or possibly one of the Troop Committee will ask them a few questions. And then the great moment has arrived when your boys will pledge their allegiance to the ideals of Scouting. Slowly they will repeat the Scout Oath. You will perhaps feel their voices tremble as they give their solemn promise as Scouts. Then your Scoutmaster will welcome them into the Troop and while the Troop yell thunders around you, you will lead the boys back to their Patrol. They are members now. *They belong.* They are permitted to wear the Scout Uniform.

They have made the first step into the wonderland of Scouting. It is for you to lead them further along the trail.

## SECOND CLASS REQUIREMENTS

As soon as the Tenderfoot Requirements have been passed and the boys have been admitted to the Troop get them started at once on the Second Class tests.

If you have been in Scouting for some time yourself and have kept your eyes open, you will have found that some Patrol Leaders let their boys go month after month, sometimes even a year, without getting them any further than through the Tenderfoot Requirements. They are not very much interested in test-passing themselves, and the result is that their boys very often "get tired of Scouting" and drop out.

"Get tired of Scouting" they say. But how could they "get tired of Scouting" when they never had seen any Scouting? Scouting isn't a thing you get tired of, but if you stay for months in a Patrol where nothing happens, and where the Patrol Leader doesn't care, you get tired of *that,* tired because you don't see any of that real Scout life you expected when you joined.

Don't disappoint your boys. They joined your Patrol with great expectations and it is for you to see that all their expectations are fulfilled. There is plenty of adventure and romance in Scouting. It is for the Patrol Leader to see that his boys find all they dream about—*and more.*

At the first Patrol meeting after the Tenderfoot Investiture Ceremony, have the boys go through the Second Class Requirements. Then ask questions to find out if they understand the requirements.

As soon as the reading and discussion part is over, start immediately on the different requirements. Di-

vide them up in such a way that you get variation
into your Patrol meetings and hikes.

## Second Class Requirement No. 1

*At least one month's service as a Tenderfoot*

Naturally this does not mean that the boys have to
wait for one month before they can start to pass any of
the Second Class Requirements.  The only reason it

has been put in
is that the au-
thorities want a
Scout to know
w h a t  Scouting
really is before
he advances to
any ranks above
that of Tender-
foot. Some boys
may join and pass straight through all of the tests and
yet they may not know what it is all about. And it is to
prevent this that we have this first requirement.

That word "service" is important.  It means that
the Scout has actually taken part in the Patrol and
Troop activities since he joined; that he has been
present at meetings and hikes, faithfully performed
the duties which were placed on him and in all ways
tried to live up to what was expected of him, and to
the satisfaction of his Scoutmaster and Patrol Leader.
In this way the boy simply cannot help beginning to
realize what Scouting really means.  He will have
made friends inside the Movement and he will have
had a chance to take part in the life they live.  And
that kind of "service" is supposed to have continued
for at least one month from the date when he was
registered by his Scoutmaster with the Boy Scouts of
America, and after he has passed his Tenderfoot Requirements and affirmed his Scout Oath.

## Second Class Requirement No. 2

*Know the general directions for First Aid; demonstrate treatment, •including dressing, where necessary, for hemorrhage, fainting, shock, bruises, injuries in which the skin is broken, burns, sprains, and demonstrate with the triangle the following bandages: head, arm (sling), hand, foot and ankle bandages, eye and jaw bandages (roller bandages may be substituted on arm and ankle); artificial respiration.    The Scout may elect to demonstrate any five requirements on animals.*

You will easily understand that the knowledge of First Aid is one of the most—if not the most—important things which is required of a Second Class Scout. By knowing how to treat a wound a Scout may be able at some time to save the life of another; by knowing artificial respiration he may be able to bring an apparently drowned person back to life again. You will therefore understand that the First Aid instruction must be given very carefully if you expect your boys' First Aid to be a real *aid*. You can't go through this requirement with them too often. It should be repeated again and again until you are sure that the knowledge sticks.

## Projects

(1) Bring in *newspaper clippings* describing accidents. Have a boy as the victim. Ask the others, "What would you have done in this case?" Have boys demonstrate.

(2) Try to get a *Doctor* or *Red Cross expert* to teach your Patrol the fundamentals of First Aid.

(3) Use the *"buddy system"* in your training. One

boy as the victim, another the bandager—change about.

(4) *Dramatize* First Aid. On hikes or at meetings

have a boy play wounded, have the rest treat him.

(5) Divide Patrol up in two teams. Try *"Patrol First Aid Race."* (Handbook for Boys, page 553.)

(6) Earn money and purchase official *First Aid kit*. To be taken along whenever Patrol undertakes a hike or camp.

(7) Get together a *training kit,* containing a few bandages, some compresses and a couple of bottles with colored water to represent mercurochrome and iodine. Also include a few safety pins and a pair of scissors. To be used for practice purposes only.

(8) Have a *First Aid contest* with the other Patrols of your Troop to find out which is best.

(9) Have a *First Aid quiz* or spell-down inside your own Patrol.

(10) Have competition among the boys to find out who can *treat himself* most correctly in case of accident.

(11) Find out as many uses as possible for the *Scout Neckerchief* in First Aid.

(12) Train your boys in telephoning a short and clear *message* to doctor regarding an accident.

(13) Make up a *First Aid demonstration* to put on at Troop meeting night.

## Second Class Requirement No. 3

*Elementary Signaling: Know the alphabet of the Semaphore Code, or the General Service (International Morse) Code; or the elementary signs of the Indian Sign Language Code.*

As you will see, for this requirement there are three alternatives from which Scouts may choose the one in which they are most interested. Take it up with your boys. Tell them the advantages of the different systems—discuss them. Then go ahead and decide upon the system the Patrol thinks will be of most value to it. On the other hand, there is nothing to prevent your Patrol from taking up two of these alternatives. In fact, it is recommended that you take up either the Semaphore or the Morse Code, so that you may be able to send your messages for miles, should it be necessary, and also the Indian Sign Language Code for use at Patrol meetings or as a secret Patrol language. The extra work will be more than repaid by the great fun you will get from it.

## Projects

(a) *General*

(1) Use the *buddy system* in your training, the boys being divided up into pairs of which one sends while the other receives and vice versa.

(2) Make up big *chart* for Patrol Den with the two codes.

(3) Use *all-alphabet sentences* in your training. As for instance—"Quite a few brave kids enjoy camping in exhilarating zero weather." (55 letters.) "The quick brown fox jumps over the lazy dog." (35 letters.) "Whenever the black fox jumped the squirrel gazed very suspiciously." (57 letters.) Not to mention poetry:

"Under the spreading chestnut tree
The village blacksmith stood.
But he went crazy and quit his job
When a zinc box hit his foot." (103 letters.)

Make up other all-alphabet messages for use in your Patrol.

(4) Make up a *secret code* for your Patrol. Either by inventing a special way of writing the letters, or by

letting one letter sent represent another letter, as for example a-b, b-c, c-d, y-z, z-a.

(5) Have a *spell-down* inside the Patrol. Each boy in turn asking the others questions related to signaling.

(6) Try *relay signaling,* i.e., a message sent through several stations distributed over a considerable distance.

(7) Have a *Treasure Hunt* in which all messages are written down in code.

(8) Take your patrol on a *Signaling Hike* where all orders are executed by Morse or Semaphore.

(9) Divide Patrol into two *groups competing* against each other. Also challenge other Patrols of Troop to signaling competitions.

(10) *Official Morse* (or Semaphore) *Signaling Competition*: Four men. Reader, sender, receiver and writer. Stations fifty yards apart. No signs or communications other than flag signals permitted. Flags to be army standard size. A thirty word message totaling at least 150 letters will be given to reader. As soon as writer has taken down message he runs back to start with it. No abbreviations allowed. No insertions or corrections on message as received. Each letter wrong to be penalized one second. Speed event.

(11) *Official Signaling Competition* (alternative): Two stations, each four men, 200 yards apart. Each station must send and receive three ten-word messages. Speed event.

(12) *Official Signal Tower Race*: Three Scouts hold three others on their shoulders. They come

together and lock arms.  No. 7 then takes No. 8 on his shoulders from where he climbs to the top of the tower.  No. 7 then passes up two Semaphore flags to No. 8, who sends the Semaphore alphabet.  Speed event.

(b) *Projects in Semaphore*

(**13**) Make up a set of *flags for Semaphore.*

(**14**) Teach the boys *correct way of holding* Semaphore flags.

(**15**) Divide letters up in *natural groups* as indicated in Handbook for Boys, page 142, and teach them to your boys.

(**16**) Remember that Semaphore signaling is an outdoor form of signaling only.  Have the boys send *messages over* even considerable *distances,* if possible with the use of field glasses.

(c) *Projects in Morse*

(**17**) Make up two *flags for Morse,* one light, the other dark.

(**18**) Demonstrate *choice of flag* in relation to background, i.e., the use of dark flag against light background, light against dark.

(**19**) Teach boys *correct way of holding* and moving flag.

(**20**) Teach your boys the *letters* divided up into groups, either in alphabetical order or as indicated in Handbook for Boys, page 140.

(**21**) Use *different methods* of sending and receiving.  At day: by sight—flags, heliograph, smoke.  At night: by sight—flashlight, lantern, fire.  At day or night: by sound—whistle, bugle, buzzer, tapping (See Merit Badge Pamphlet on Signaling.)

(22) Make up and use special *trick system* between Patrol members: As for example, winking eyes, moving certain fingers, chewing movement of jaw.

(d) *Projects in Indian Sign Language*

(23) Divide the 42 words and numerals into four *groups* containing ten letters each, and one group containing the remaining two letters plus numerals. Teach one group at a time to your boys.

(24) When the boys master the words, get hold of William Tomkins' book on "Universal Indian Sign Language" and teach them the necessary *grammatical rules* for building up sentences.

(25) Make up *English sentences,* translate them into Sign Language words and execute them. As for

example: English— "The Patrol went camping. We went by boat up the river w i t h two tents. N i g h t came, we were hungry, ate and drank and went to sleep. S l e p t well." Indian Sign Language—"Eight Scouts go camp. We all go boat river with two tents. Night come, we all hungry, drink, go sleep. Sleep good."

(26) On a Patrol hike use *Sign Language* for all communications.

(27) Get together with other Patrol about *Sign Language.* This helps keep up interest.

## Second Class Requirement No. 4

*Track half a mile in twenty-five minutes; or if in town, describe satisfactorily the contents of one store window out of four observed for one minute each.*

The big idea of this requirement is *Observation* with

capital "O." The Boy Scout is supposed to go through life with his eyes open, always observing and storing in his memory things which may prove to be useful to him later on.

"Track half a mile in twenty-five minutes." What does that mean? Track? Yes, but what is a track? Let us define it as "any kind of a sign left by a living creature." The track of a man is not only his foot-print, but also the matches he struck and threw away; the ashes he knocked out of his pipe, the button he lost, etc.

Tracking isn't a thing you can learn in an hour. It is an art that needs great study. Of all the Second Class Requirements this one is more than any other "outdoor stuff."

Start the training for this requirement on the very first Patrol hike. As you walk along the road you may find the imprint of a man's foot or a horse's hoof. Show it to your boys. Make them interested in finding the next imprint, then the next and still the next.

There is an alternative for the tracking test which is very seldom used. That is, the ability to describe satisfactorily the contents of one store window out of four observed for one minute each. It is all right that it is seldom used in passing this fourth requirement, because a Scout's life is lived in the open, not in the street, but it ought to be used much more frequently than it is as training in observation.

## Projects

(1) Use the *"Hare and Hounds"* game for your training. One person (or two) represents the hare.

He is given material for laying a track and sent out several minutes before the hounds, runs a certain length of time, then returns by another route to starting point, all the time laying the track. After the lapse of the number of minutes' handicap given the hare, those representing the hounds start in pursuit, following the track and trying to catch the hare before he reaches the starting point in returning. The first few times the tracks must be made clearly visible. Have for example the hare throw small handfuls of corn or chicken feed every 25 to 30 feet. Then use powdered dry paint, first bright ochre, later green or brown colors. Then small pieces of different colored woolen yarn, whifflepoof, tracking irons, trail signs. (Handbook for Boys, page 156.) Then the actual footprints of the hare.

(2) Make a *whifflepoof* out of a round piece of wood in which is hammered a number of nails.

(3) On hikes, study *tracks of animals and birds*.

(4) Make *sketches* with correct measurements of tracks found on the hike.

(5) Teach your boys to make *plaster casts of tracks*. (See chapter on Patrol Handicraft.)

(6) Make a *tracking training ground*. Rake up a piece of ground. Have the boys walk, run, walk backward, walk with heavy burden over it. Compare tracks. Make notes.

(7) *Study tracks* of carts, bicycles, automobiles. Learn to recognize in which direction the vehicle has moved.

(8) For training in observation play *"Kim's Game."* Place on a tray, or on the table or floor, about twenty or thirty small articles such as two or three different kinds of buttons, pencils, coins, clips, Scout badges, nuts, stones, knives, string, photos—anything found in boy pockets, or elsewhere—and cover them over with a cloth or coat. List these and make a column opposite the list for each boy's replies. Then uncover the arti-

cles for one minute by your watch, or while you count
sixty. Then cover again. Have boys write down the
names of articles which they remember. Check up on
the list. Give one point for each article remembered.
Subtract two points each for articles mentioned which
were not on the table.

(9) *"Shop Window."* Take a Patrol down street
past four shops with one minute's stop at each window.
Then after moving them off to some distance have
each boy write down from memory what he noticed in,
say, shop No. 3. The one who sets down most articles
correctly wins.

(10) Have a *stranger* enter Patrol Den during meeting, have a few remarks with you, then disappear. Have
boys write down from memory description of person,
his height, his most important features.

(11) On hike start suddenly and ask where the last
road passed led to, how many persons were in automobile which just rolled by; how many stories the
house last seen had.

## Second Class Requirement No. 5

*Go a mile in twelve minutes at Scout's Pace—
about fifty steps running and fifty walking,
alternately; or lay out, measure by the stride
method and stake a four acre tract of land.*

Be sure that you do not misunderstand Scout's Pace,
as so many other Patrol Leaders have done when they
have wanted to know what the record for that mile
was. One could tell that his Patrol had done it in
9½ minutes. Another Patrol had used 9¾, while

still another had only used 9 and was certain that they had broken all records. They certainly had, but in quite another way than they thought. The fact is that the world record for one mile at Scout's Pace is exactly twelve minutes, not more and not less.

The Scout's Pace requirement is not a speed test. The value of Scout's Pace is that it brings you forward fast without tiring you and besides it acts as a measure of time and of distance. If the milestones tell you that you have run one mile in Scout's Pace, you will know that twelve minutes have elapsed. On the other hand if your watch tells you that twelve minutes have gone you will know that you have covered one mile. This may help your Patrol and your boys in a lot of ways. If you have an appointment at a place two and a half miles away at 8:30 you will know that if you leave in Scout's Pace at 8:00 precisely you will get there just in time. In map making you will need to know distances and you will easily see that it is faster to run for six minutes to measure half a mile than it is to walk slowly and count your strides.

## Projects

(1) Have the boys realize that the secret in Scout Pace is to keep an even *rhythm*. Change from walking to running—rather, trotting—but do not change the rhythm of your steps.

(2) Have your boys walk 50 steps and run 50 steps, altogether 100 steps. Measure out carefully with a string, say, 20 feet long. By dividing the number of feet found into 5,280 feet  (one mile) you find out how many times this dis-

tance must be covered in twelve minutes. Then figure out how long a time you are permitted to use for your 100 step course. You may find it to be, say, 30 seconds. Then train your boys until they are able time and again to run the course in 30 seconds. At next meeting double the distance, and have the boys run it in exactly 60 seconds. Then increase to ¼ mile in three minutes, ½ mile in 6 minutes, 1 mile in 12 minutes.

(3) Lay out a couple of *½ mile courses* around your favorite camp site. Keep your boys in training.

(4) Use *Scout's Pace on hikes* occasionally.

(5) Have Patrol do *Scout's Pace for 12 minutes,* stopping at a signal. The one nearest the mile mark wins.

(6) Have an automobilist measure out a *five miles' course*. See which of the boys can come nearest the goal in one hour.

(7) *Official Scout's Pace Race.* One man. Scouts do Scout's Pace on a measured mile. The one who finishes nearest to the exact twelve minutes wins. Accuracy Events.

(8) Have *surveyor* help in training the boys to lay out one acre and four acre tracts of land.

(9) Have *competition* among boys laying out four acre tract. Have surveyor present as judge.

## Second Class Requirement No. 6

*Use properly knife and hatchet*

A Scout could make himself comfortable and at home on a desert island, if he only had his knife or his hatchet along with him. They work for him as the man Friday worked for Robinson Crusoe. They constitute the most important part of his equipment. They are his most useful friends and therefore they ought to be treated kindly, always protected against bad usage, always kept sharp, dry and clean.

## Projects

(1) Have a *carpenter* teach the Patrol the correct way of sharpening knife and axe.

(2) Secure *Scout axe* and sharpening stone for Patrol equipment.

(3) *Discuss rules* for correct uses of knife and axe.

(4) Have *quiz* on rules.

(5) Teach the boys *correct way of whittling.*

(6) Have *competition* in whittling fuzz-sticks, paper knife, fork or spoon; later, more advanced whittling, as neckerchief slides, individual totem poles, chains, ball in cage, fans, bas-reliefs. (See Chapter on Patrol Handicraft).

(7) *Manufacture articles* for sale for the Patrol funds (See Handicraft chapter).

(8) Make *models* of fires, trail signs, camp furniture, complete camp, log cabins, etc. (See Handicraft chapter).

(9) Start training in use of axe by having boys cut *tent pegs.* Then demonstrate chopping on *dead timber. Never touch a living tree with an axe.*

(10) Have a *wood-chopping contest* inside the Patrol.

(11) In camp, make *rustic furniture* and other camp implements by the help of the axe.

## Second Class Requirement No. 7

*Prove ability to build a fire in the open, using not more than two matches; care for and put it out*

When you go through the woods or over the fields you may find some small round spots where no vegetation grows. Even if the grass or the moss grows in abundance everywhere around it, it is as if a curse has been put on these spots—"Thou shalt produce no life."

The solution may be that a careless camper has put the curse on it by having had a fire there. Rain has washed the ashes down in the ground, wind has spread the coals, and only the dead spot is left, and it certainly doesn't beautify the landscape. The reason that no vegetation is able to grow there is that the heat from the fire charred and destroyed the organic plant nutrition which is found in the soil and the ashes made it too alkaline, thereby adding to the impossibility of plants growing there.

A Scout will always want to leave a spot in the same condition in which he found it. He doesn't want to put ugly stains on a beautiful spot. And, therefore, before taking up fire-building he will take up the use of the hand spade.

If a square piece of sod is removed from the ground before you build the fire, and after the fire is out, the ashes are dug under and the sod replaced, you will leave the place with the satisfaction of knowing that nobody will ever be disturbed by the fact that a Scout has camped on this particular place. At the same time you would be dead sure that the last embers of the fire were out.

Therefore, every time the Patrol goes out to train for fire-making or cooking, take a small spade along with you. It isn't much of a bother, and you will find many uses for it in making fireplaces, digging ice-box, refuse pit, latrine, and so forth.

Before building any fires be absolutely positive that you are permitted to make fire on that particular spot. If it is private property you must get permis-

sion from the owner, if it is public property you must be absolutely certain that fire-making is allowed by asking the local authorities (fire wardens or guards).

## Projects

(1) Make sure that your boys are familiar with the *safety rules* regarding fire-building.

(2) Demonstrate the laying of the simplest form of a fire: *the pyramid fire*. Point out most important features of fire-building: relation to wind, tinder, necessity of reserve wood, how to shelter match from wind, the use of a fuzz stick, how to feed flame, etc.

(3) Teach boys where to find suitable *wood for fires*. Hardwood for coals, soft wood for flames. Also where to find dry tinder on rainy day.

(4) Have boys build *different kinds of fires* and fire places: Pyramid, crisscross, hunter's or trapper's, reflector, star, council fire.

(5) Have a *string-burning contest*. Stretch a string tightly between two poles 18 inches above the ground. Have the boys lay their fires under it. All fires are started at the same time. After lighting, fires must not be

touched nor extra wood added to them. The boy who has made the fire which first burns through the string is declared the winner.

(6) *Official Water Boiling Contest*. One man. Officials to furnish a one-quart water bucket with wire handle, single-ply tin, filled with water to within ½ inch of top, shaving of soap added; one stick of well-seasoned wood 3"x3"x36"; two matches. Contestants to furnish knife or axe. No preliminary preparation of fireplace or of wood permitted. Only two matches

allowed and spilling of water disqualifies. Water must boil over. Speed Event.

(7) Have each boy in Patrol make his own *fire-by-friction set* or gather material for *flint-and-steel* set.

(8) *Official Fire by Friction Contest.* One man. Apparatus must be made by Scout from natural material found in United States. Tinder to be natural material, the following materials to be barred: powder from previous attempts, chemicals, shavings, pencil sharpenings, paper cloth, cotton, string or rope. "Warming up" is not allowed, but using notch that has been used before is permissible. Speed Event.

(9) Have *competition* to see who can clean up best after fire.

(10) Make fire-making an *all-weather proposition.* Have contests on rainy days or on days following periods of drenching rain.

## Second Class Requirement No. 8

*Cook a quarter of a pound of meat and two potatoes in the open without any cooking utensils*

After having trained in fire-making on one of your Patrol hikes, you may take up cooking without utensils on the next.

In all matters of cooking or handling food, insist that your boys keep their hands clean. No touching of food with dirty hands should ever be permitted.

## Projects

(1) Teach the Patrol the making of a hole under the fire for *roasting potatoes.*

(2) Teach your Patrol the *"count-to-eight" rule*: Put your hand close to the fire, so near that you are just able to keep it there while you slowly count to eight and will want to snatch your hand away in order not to burn it when you arrive at count eight. If you are able to count to ten before feeling that you must

take your hand away, it has been held too far from the fire, if you are able to count to six only, you are too close. When the boys have found the right distance have them put their meat there on a spit supported by a couple of forked sticks. Have them check up every once in a while to see if the heat is just right. Move the steak according to the heat. By following the "count-to-eight" rule it is not necessary to use coals only. Flames will do for the roasting. Just be sure that the meat is arranged on that side of the fire from which the wind comes.

(3) Have a *Patrol roast* (beef, chicken, etc.) following the "count-to-eight" rule closely.

(4) Try *other methods* of preparing meals without

utensils: Frying bacon on hot rocks, planking of fish, clay baking of fowl, clam bakes, kabobs.

(5) Teach your Patrol *bread-baking* without utensils, as twist; in the ashes; in dug-in-a-bank oven.

## Second Class Requirement No. 9

*Earn and deposit at least one dollar in a public bank (premiums paid on life insurance, are accepted, if earned); or earn, own, and raise some farm animal*

This part of the Second Class Requirements isn't a thing in which you ought to train your boys. It is purely a personal matter, each boy going out on his own and pursuing his own business.

The only thing you ought to do is to inspire your Scouts to get the work done, and the money earned, by bringing to their attention the Ninth Scout Law. You may give them suggestions as to work they might take up, but let the boys themselves hunt for the jobs. If they really want to, it won't be difficult for them to get an opportunity to earn some money by undertaking simple jobs, or by making handicraft articles.

Somebody said "Jobs do not turn up in this world unless somebody turns them up." Have your boys remember that and have them go out hunting.

As soon as the first dollar is earned and put in the bank, encourage them to go ahead and earn another. If you can get them into the habit of looking around for work and doing odd jobs, thereby earning a little money, you will have accomplished something to be proud of. Remember to keep clearly before them all the time that this earning money on jobs is a totally different thing from their Good Turns for which, of course, no pay is expected or taken.

## Projects

(1) Suggest to your boys that they earn their money by taking over such *jobs* as delivering goods, caddying for golfers, soliciting for magazines, carrying newspapers around, chopping wood, mowing lawns, or anything else you may think of. In this connection have it clearly in mind that the boy does this work as a boy, not as a Scout, for which reason the Scout Uniform should not be worn.

(2) If any of your boys live on a *farm* they may take up raising rabbits, squabs, chickens, growing vegetables or doing regular farm work.

(3) Make it a Patrol project to make *handicraft articles* by which the boys may earn the money for this requirement. (See chapter on Patrol Handicraft.)

(4) Have a *Patrol entertainment* (in camp, or in Troop meeting room) to which parents and people interested are invited. Charge a nominal entry fee. Put

on a real Scoutcraft demonstration together with a few amusing stunts and Patrol singing.

(5) Get permission to *collect junk* from junk rooms of friends of the Patrol. Repair articles and put them in shape for sale.

## Second Class Requirement No. 10
*Know the sixteen principal points of the compass*

Don't start teaching your boys the compass points at a Patrol meeting. The compass has nothing to do with a meeting room. You are able to find the door without knowing in which corner of the globe it is.

Start teaching the compass on a hike. It is there in the open that you will find the greatest advantage in knowing the use of the compass. Take up compass study time and again. Make perfectly sure that your boys are always able to orient themselves.

## Projects

(1) Have the boy on the *hike* face the sun at twelve noon sharp, (beware of Daylight Saving Time; in that case it must be one o'clock sharp). Ask them, "Where is South?" Be sure that they realize that the sun is straight South at twelve noon, and demonstrate the other compass directions to them.

(2) Have the Scouts gather a number of sticks and place them on the ground forming a *compass*. Teach them the different points.

(3) Have each Scout make a *drawing of the compass* with the sixteen points indicated.

(4) Make a *compass chart* for the Patrol den.

(5) Have a *"compass facing game"* arranged as a "champ-nit" contest. Tell the boys to face Northeast, West, Northwest, and so forth. The one first to get into right position goes out and the game is continued until only one boy is left.

(6) Have a *"Treasure Hunt,"* all the messages giving distance and a compass direction to follow to arrive at the treasure.

(7) Undertake a *"Bee-Line hike."* Follow a compass direction cross-country, through, over or under all obstacles.

(8) Have a *compass spell-down* at a Patrol meeting or on a hike.

(9) Teach the boys the actual *use of a compass.* Make them understand the difference between "true" and "magnetic" North.

(10) On a hike, show the boys how to use a compass to *orient a map.*

(11) Teach the boys to find the *compass direction* in the open by the help of the sun (and a watch), stars at night, moss on trees, prevailing winds, etc.

## Second Class Requirement No. 11

*Demonstrate his practice of at least five rules*
*of safety at home, or work, or school, or on*
*the street, or road, or farm*

A Scout is supposed to "Be Prepared" to meet any emergency. But it is of equal importance for him to help in seeing that nothing is done or left undone which might endanger the safety of others. He knows that "an ounce of prevention is worth a pound of cure."

## Projects

(1) Before a Patrol meeting, arrange in den different *violations of safety,* as for example, thumb tacks on the floor, an opened knife on the table, a gasoline bottle (with water for gasoline) without cork, and other offenses against safety. When the boys arrive, have

them look around, see what is wrong and write it down on a piece of paper stating why they think it is wrong. Then have them correct all points, remove thumb tacks, close knife, find a cork for the bottle, etc.

(2) Have a *discussion on Safety* based on reports of actual accidents which might have been prevented by carefulness.

(3) Have the boys *study* section on Safety in Handbook for Boys, page 173. Discuss the different points.

(4) When Patrol is out hiking, or in camp, *practice rules* of safety. Don't do any jay-walking. Walk on correct side of country road (facing oncoming traffic). Be very careful in bathing. Use knives and axes correctly.

(5) Have the Scouts *co-operate with* their *school* in regard to safety devices.

(6) Try to have a *policeman* demonstrate to the Patrol important points of traffic safety.

(7) Make sure that the boys *practice safety rules* in their homes.

## Second Class Requirement No. 12

*Furnish satisfactory evidence that he has put into practice in his daily life the principles of the Scout Oath and Law*

Living the Scout Oath and Law! The last and most important of the Second Class Requirements.

A boy may know how to build fire with one match, or even without a match at all, know how to treat the most complicated injuries and signal the most difficult messages without being a Scout. It is the living up to the ideals of the Movement which makes a boy into a Scout.

Take the Oath and the Law up with your boys again. By this time they ought to have a deeper understanding of them than they had when they first joined. Talk them over seriously, if possible some night on a hike around a camp fire. Ask your fellows to measure themselves in order to find out for themselves if they have really "done their best."

Your example during these last months has meant everything in the world to the behavior of your boys. If they have found in you the leader they wanted to follow they will have been trying to do things in such a way that you might be satisfied with them. If you have succeeded in putting an ideal in front of them, they will have been doing all they could to follow it.

But the "satisfactory evidence" they have to furnish isn't only in regard to their behavior in the Patrol. The parents, the teachers, the Scoutmaster must be satisfied too. The boy must show to all that he has really tried to live the life of a Scout.

You can give your boys no instruction in this important part of the requirements. It is not a knowledge which they can acquire. It is a state of mind, and that can only be developed from the inside, from the boys' own hearts. But your spirit, and the spirit of the Patrol will have helped immensely in building it.

## The Second Class Examinations

After having gone through all the Second Class Requirements with them, your boys are now ready to appear before the Court of Honor or the specially authorized examiners of your Council or city.

But before they do, you will go on a hike with them and have them review their knowledge. You wouldn't think of sending them to the examiners before you had examined them yourself.

Go through every one of the requirements very care-

fully on that hike, and have the boys understand that the day they appear before the Court of Honor they are to show the right Scouting spirit, prove that they really are prepared.

But not only that. Have them understand that the honor and reputation of the Patrol is at stake. The way they pass the examinations will prove what kind of a Patrol they belong to.

Let them realise that at the Court of Honor they are not only trying to pass some tests. They are representing their Patrol, too, and the other boys of their Patrol expect them to make a fine showing. The Patrol's good wishes and anticipation go with them. It is up to them to prove that the faith which is put in them is deserved.

And the day they pass, Oh, boy! what a great feeling in the Patrol! Maybe the Scoutmaster will present the badges to the boys in front of the Troop during a meeting. Maybe he will come to one of your Patrol meetings and perform the ceremony there. But whatever the procedure is, the Patrol ought to be proud of its members and have them really feel it. Something special must be done to celebrate. Use your imagination. You are the Patrol Leader. You know your boys. You know what they like and are able to make them feel happy. But do something. Make the occasion a red-letter one.

## THE FIRST CLASS REQUIREMENTS

The first really important step in the advancement of your Scouts has been reached the day they pass the Second Class Requirements.

But you won't want the words Second Class to stick to your Patrol for very long. You don't want your

Patrol to be considered Second Class, and First Class it will never be until quite a big percentage of your Scouts have advanced into First Class, Star, Life or Eagle rank. Don't be satisfied with the next best when you know that by steady work the best may be reached.

Your boys have learned to work during your bringing them through their Second Class tests. Don't let them stop now. Start in immediately on the First Class instruction. A delay may prove dangerous.

As you go along you may find that instructing your boys has become easier; that giving First Class and Second Class instruction differs quite a bit. The reason is obvious. As Tenderfoot Scouts your boys didn't know much about Scouting. They had to be led along very carefully. Now, however, they have got a real insight into it, they have grasped the meaning of Scouting, and instead of actually leading them forward you will realize that in many cases all that is necessary for you to do is simply to show them the road to follow, and they will be able to go ahead without your having to point out every step.

## Starting the Training

Quite a few of the First Class Requirements have their root in what the boys already have learned as Second Class Scouts. By actually using their Second Class Signaling, for example, they are training themselves for the advanced test. By going on hikes they will not only prepare themselves for the 14-mile hike, but they will also improve their cooking and their ability to use an axe. In fact, the only First Class Requirements which are entirely new to them are Swimming, Map Reading and Making, Judging and Nature Study. Just four out of the twelve. The others only consist of improving what they have already learned.

If you bring this to their attention, the First Class Requirements won't seem so terribly difficult to them as they may have done at the beginning.

The requirements may be passed as soon as the boys have had two months' service as Second Class Scouts, though you will very probably find that they will need far more time. You may find too that the Swimming test may upset your plans of having the boys pass quickly. Swimming is usually a summer activity. Not all Scouts have access to a swimming pool. That means that the Patrol sometimes will have to wait about a year to pass all First Class Requirements if it hasn't been fortunate enough to start its training in the spring months. If the Patrol has to wait, the best thing to do will be to have it pass all requirements except Swimming and then interest the boys in the Merit Badges which are open to Second Class Scouts. This way there

won't be any halt in their work. They will be advancing steadily, a thing which will prove a success to the Patrol. But whatever way you have to follow, be sure to get your Second Class Scouts started right away on their advancement.

At the meeting following the Court of Honor session go through the First Class Requirements with your boys in the same way in which you went through the Tenderfoot and Second Class Requirements (Handbook for Boys, page 194) until you have been through them all. Then ask them questions to find out if they understand the requirements.

As soon as the reading and discussion is over with, start immediately on the different requirements. Divide them up in such a way that you get variety into your Patrol meetings and hikes.

### First Class Requirement No. 1

*At least two months' service as a*
*Second Class Scout*

What was said in regard to one month's service as

part of the Second Class Requirements naturally refers to these two months' service also.

But as First Class Scouts you will expect your boys to be familiar with all phases of Scouting, not only the things which go into the requirements but the background for them as well, and to have taken their full share of Troop life and community service.

By now your boys will know about all functions of the Patrol and Troop to which they belong. They will have taken part in several meetings, hikes, camps and community Good Turns and by so doing they will have gotten a wider outlook of Scouting. They will have found out what is expected of them as Scouts.

At the same time they ought to have learned to know all the officers of the Troops, its Scoutmaster and his helpers. They ought to have become acquainted with the other Patrols and their leaders. And they ought to have learned the history of the Troop so that they will know when it was started, who have been its leaders, what honors have been bestowed upon it, what important things it has undertaken and brought to a finish. By teaching your boys the story of your Troop you will make them feel proud of belonging to it and you will be doing your part to develop Troop spirit in them.

But the knowledge of the organization ought to be brought even further. Naturally you will want your boys to know which institution stands behind the Troop and sponsors it, and you will give them an opportunity to meet the members of the Troop Committee and explain their work. And you will also want them to know about their Council and the National Organization to which they belong.

In order that your Scouts may get the fullest insight into the organization you will encourage them to study the chapter in the Handbook for Boys (pages 582-596) which deals with the Scout Movement in America.

There will be no examination in the above mentioned things when your boys appear before the Court of Honor to pass their tests, but you will easily see that without knowing about the organization to which they belong and its functions they can't really be considered First Class Scouts.

### First Class Requirement No. 2

*Swim fifty yards—The Scout must jump over-board, feet first, in water slightly over his head, swim 25 yards, make a sharp turn about and return to the starting point.*

The swimming test is by many considered the most difficult of the First Class Requirements, but in reality it is far easier to learn to swim than it is to learn to signal correctly or to get the knowledge of first aid into your head—*provided you have the right kind of teacher.*

Even if you are the most perfect swimmer possible and a wonderful life-saver, you mustn't think of teaching your Patrol to swim all by yourself. The risk and your responsibility is too tremendous. But if you are a life-saver you are certain to know other swimmers who would be willing to help your boys and you would know where to find safe swimming facilities. If you can't swim well yourself you will have to try to find somebody who can give the Patrol the opportunity to learn swimming. In the bigger cities you may find that the American Red Cross, Y. M. C. A., the Y. M. H. A., the Knights of Columbus, and a number of clubs have swimming pools and regular teachers and would be happy to help you give the Patrol the desired training. Naturally you will have your Scoutmaster's approval before you go to these places. If no pool is available, swimming must be taught your boys during the summer months and the place for them to learn it would be at the Council camp or at the Troop camp if these have the necessary instructors.

As mentioned above: *Don't ever undertake alone to teach your boys to swim, and don't ever forget that under no circumstances should swimming be undertaken on Patrol hike or in Patrol camp except under leadership of Senior Life Saver approved by your Local Council.*

## Projects

(1) *Secure teacher* and swimming facilities for Patrol in cooperation with your Scoutmaster.

(2) When the boys have passed their swimming test, make sure that they *follow up* on their swimming by improving their stroke. Also by learning new strokes and training in life saving.

(3) Have the boys realize that *correct breathing* is a prominent part of swimming, and train them in this.

(4) Make your Patrol a group of *divers*. Not only for style, but also for accuracy (diving through inflated inner tube, etc.).

(5) Try to have Patrol represented in *life saving guard* at Troop or Council Camp.

## First Class Requirement No. 3

*Earn and deposit at least two dollars in a public bank (premiums on life insurance are accepted, if earned); or plant, raise and market a farm crop*

This requirement is in fact simply an expansion of the ninth requirement for Second Class Scouts and therefore what is said about that on page 152 in this book applies to the First Class Requirement as well.

## Projects

See Second Class Requirements No. 9.

## First Class Requirement No. 4

*Send and receive a message by Semaphore Code, including conventional signs, thirty letters per minute; or by the General Service Code (International Morse), sixteen letters per minute, including conventional signs; or by the Indian Sign Language Code, thirty signs per minute*

The way to teach your boys First Class Signaling is simply by having them continue the Second Class Training, adding to their "vocabulary" by including the conventional signs (and in Indian Sign Language new words) in the messages and forcing them to send and thereby also receive faster.

·Note the wording carefully:

It says "thirty letters *per* minute", "sixteen letters *per* minute", "thirty signs *per* minute" and *not* "thirty letters *in a* minute", "sixteen letters *in a* minute", "thirty signs *in a* minute." That means that it's *not how many* letters or signs a boy is able to send and receive in one minute that counts, what is called for is his *average speed* in a minute. Your boys are not supposed to be able to send say thirty Semaphore letters in one minute. No, they are asked to send ninety letters in three minutes, hundred and fifty in five, two hundred and forty in eight, and so forth. Thirty letters in one minute isn't much, but to continue with that average in several minutes is a real test and that is what all the First Class Requirements ought to be.

But it is not enough that your boys are able to send the letters with a certain speed, they must also know how to get their messages through. They must know how to call another station, how to send the message in such a way that the receiver can really receive it, how to execute requests which may be made by the receiver in regard to speed and to background, how to erase and correct misspelled words and so forth. They are not only supposed to know the conventional signs but also how to make use of them. If a First Class Scout can't do this his signaling test means nothing.

## Projects

See Second Class Requirement No. 3.

### First Class Requirement No. 5

*Make a round trip alone (or with another Scout) to a point at least seven miles away (fourteen miles in all), going on foot, or rowing boat, and write a satisfactory account of the trip and things observed*

The Fourteen Mile Hike is the fifth of the First Class Requirements, but if you try to analyze it to see how many things are involved in it, you will find that you certainly don't want your boys to pass it as Test No. 5. In fact, you may come to the point that you want them to take it up as one of the very last of the First Class Requirements.

They may be able to pass it as soon as they have become Second Class Scouts if you don't put too much into the wording of the requirement, but if you want the try-outs to prove that your boys are actually going to be First Class, you will find that the Fourteen Mile Hike becomes one of the most difficult tests.

The fourteen miles itself isn't the hardest part of the test, though even that is rather hard, especially for an untrained boy. It is the observation and report parts of the requirement which really count most.

The best way of training your boys for this requirement would be to have them realize that every Patrol hike or Troop hike they undertake is a part of their training. By taking them out in the country, by following all the bypaths that lead away from the main road, by telling them about good camp sites, about places of historical or other interest in the neighborhood of their town, you will be able to make these hikes mean something real to them, and the day they appear for the examiner to pass the hiking requirements, they will know exactly what they ought to look out for, where they ought to go, and what they ought to see.

## Projects

(1) Start the training by having the Patrol undertake *short Saturday hikes.*

(2) Later go in for *over-night camping,* in connection with hiking.

(3) Try several of the hikes mentioned in chapter on *Patrol hikes.*

(4) Teach your boys *hiking technique,* i.e., knowledge of necessary equipment, right clothing, the correct way of walking, how to rest, care of feet, safety on the

road, right way of eating and drinking on the hike, hiking courtesies, observation.

(5) After a Patrol hike have a *discussion* with the boys to find out what they have seen and learned.

(6) Have all members of the Patrol make short *reports* of every Patrol hike, the reports to contain these four features: (a) description of hike, things observed, incidents which occurred, (b) hour of start, return, important happenings, when certain land marks were passed, (c) mileage covered, (d) rough sketch (or sketches) of country covered.

(7) Have *competition* in report making, the best report to be included in the Patrol log.

(8) Before the boys go up for the Court of Honor, have a *"dress rehearsal" hike,* as far as possible under the same conditions under which the real hike will take place.

### First Class Requirement No. 6

*(I) Review Second Class First Aid Requirements; (II) Describe methods of panic prevention, what to do in case of (III) fire, (IV) ice, (V) electric and (VI) gas accidents; (VII) what to do in case of a mad dog bite, or snake bite. Demonstrate the treatment, including dressing where necessary, (VIII) for a fracture, (IX) poisoning, (X) apoplexy, (XI) heat exhaustion, (XII) sunstroke, (XIII) frost bite and freezing; also demonstrate the treatment for (XIV) sunburn, (XV) ivy poisoning, (XVI) bee stings, (XVII) nose-bleed, (XVIII) ear-ache, (XIX) grit or cinder in the eye, (XX) stomach-ache; (XXI) demonstrate transportation of the injured; (XXII) demonstrate the triangular bandage on the head, eye, jaw, arm (sling), chest, fractured rib, hand, hip, knee, ankle and foot. (Roller bandages may be sub-*

*stituted on arm and ankle). (XXIII) Demonstrate how to make and apply a tourniquet.*

While simple First Aid was a very important part of the Second Class Requirements, advanced First Aid forms an even more significant part of the First Class Requirements. A thorough knowledge of First Aid will—probably more than any of the other requirements—help you to live up to the Scout Motto "Be Prepared."

In order to teach your boys, naturally you must have the necessary correct knowledge yourself. If you haven't, you should not attempt to teach it by the help of textbooks. You should try to get hold of somebody who actually knows the stuff by training and experience and have him take your Patrol through this important requirement.

If your boys get the wrong slant on cooking, signaling, judging, etc., it is bad enough, but it is not likely to hurt anybody else. But if they get a wrong slant on First Aid, it may mean serious damage to somebody else, maybe even imperil life. Therefore be perfectly, absolutely, positively dead sure that they learn to do things right.

Don't let your boys think that they can learn their First Aid by the help of the Handbook alone. The Handbook tells the treatment, but it is *practise,* PRACTISE, PRACTISE, *and common sense*—just as frequently—that teaches First Aid.

## Projects
See Second Class Requirement No. **2.**

## First Class Requirement No. 7

*Prepare and cook satisfactorily, in the open, using camp cooking utensils, two of the following articles as may be directed: Eggs and bacon, hunter's stew, fish, fowl, game, pancakes, hoecake, biscuit, hardtack, or a "twist", baked on a stick, and give an exact statement of the cost of materials used; explain to another boy the method followed*

The training for this requirement was started the day your boys built their first Second Class fire. If you have been taking them on Patrol hikes, or Troop hikes, where individual cooking was done, or if they have been in camp, they will have had the opportunity to increase their knowledge in regard to outdoor cooking and they will have had plenty of time to make the different dishes mentioned in the First Class Requirement. The greatest secret of success in cooking consists in regulating the fire correctly so that it burns evenly the whole time while the meal is being prepared. A good fire is all important, but it takes time and patience to learn to build the right kind of a fire and to keep it going.

Therefore during the first part of the training for this First Class Requirement put more emphasis on the fire than on the actual cooking. See to it that the boys learn the trick of keeping the fire burning steadily, very hot when speed is called for, subdued when slow cooking is desired. Also insist that they have plenty of fire-wood collected before they start cooking so that they won't have to go out looking for more when the boiling or frying is at its height. So much about the fire. The different recipes are explained thoroughly in the Handbook for Boys, pages 251–259.

## Projects

(1) Have the *mother* of one of your Scouts help the Patrol in its training for this requirement.

(2) Save money for and get together a complete *Patrol cooking outfit* (see chapter on Patrol Camping).

(3) Have a *competition* running over several Patrol hikes to find out which boy can best prepare all recipes mentioned in requirement.

(4) *Official Flapjack Contest:* Competitors must furnish their own material and utensils. Each Scout may use such ingredients as he wishes. Quality of flapjacks rather than speed to be considered first.

(5) Divide Patrol up in pairs. Have pairs take turn preparing meal on hikes for complete Patrol. Start *competition* on this basis.

(6) When Patrol has developed expert cooks invite parents to visit Patrol camp for an *outdoor feast.*

(7) Develop a special *Patrol cook book*. Let boys contribute their favorite recipes. Provide them with fancy names, specially for your Patrol.

(8) Have the boys do their own *shopping* and keep exact account of amount involved.

(9) Have each Scout put down in *writing methods* followed in preparing meals.

(10) Other projects under Second Class Req. 8.

## First Class Requirement No. 8

*Read a map correctly, and draw, from field notes made on the spot, an intelligible rough sketch map, indicating by their proper marks important buildings, roads, trolley lines, main landmarks, principal elevations, etc. Point out a compass direction without the help of the compass*

When hiking through unknown territory without a guide, it is necessary to be able to read a map and thereby follow the route you want to take. This is the most important function of a map and the prime reason why Scouts should learn map reading and making. But your map can tell you many other things besides. It helps you in judging distances. If you, for example, want to know the distance from the crossroad where you are standing to the church you see in front of you, the map gives you the correct distance by a simple measurement. Your map may even function as a time-piece. If you are standing on a road, for example, which is indicated on the map, you may turn the map, so that you get it oriented correctly. The map will then give you the northerly direction. And from the north direction, plus the sun, you are able to figure out the time.

## Projects

(1) Earn money and secure *Topographical Maps* made by the United States Geological Survey over your particular section of the country. Maybe you are able to get them through a local book store. If not, write to the Director, United States Geological Survey, Washington, D. C.

(2) Teach boys on blackboard or paper the most important *conventional signs*. Have them draw them in their note-books. Find the signs on the map.

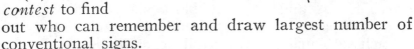

(3) Make up a *chart* of conventional signs for Patrol Den.

(4) Have *contest* to find out who can remember and draw largest number of conventional signs.

(5) Have a *map-reading hike*. Take Patrol to high place with view of surrounding landscape. Spread out map. Show "magnetic north" line and "true north" line and explain difference. Orient map with the help of (a) compass, (b) watch and sun, (c) surrounding

landscape. Find points found on map in terrain and vice versa. Estimate distances and check up on map.

(6) At Patrol meeting take Patrol along on *imaginary hike* on map, asking questions as "What kind of road is it?," "What is that over there?," "Where is that crossroad leading?" Have the boys take turns answering.

(7) On a hike let boys successively take over *leadership of Patrol* and follow route laid out on map. Change leader after every one mile or 15-20 minutes hiked.

(8) At a Patrol meeting have boys make *imaginary maps* containing all the conventional signs which they remember.

(9) Lay out *landscape on floor* or on table covered with paper, using ribbons for roads and rivers, blue paper for lakes, sand for hills, small green sponges on stands for trees, wooden blocks for houses. Have boys make map sketches true to scale.

(10) Make sure that your boys remember *the four important features* of every map made (a) line indicating magnetic north, also true north, (b) scale, (c) name of locality, (d) name of boy who made it.

(11) Have boys find out length of their *pace* for help in map making.

(12) In map-making training follow closely instruction given in *Handbook for Boys*, pages 266-274.

(13) Make mountain of clay. Slice horizontally to demonstrate principle of *contour lines.*

(14) Have Scouts make *maps of increasing difficulty:* House and lot, city block showing all houses, section of park, camp site, ¼ mile of road and 100 feet to each side, map showing hill (contour lines), stream or lake, and woods.

(15) Have *competitions* in making sketch maps of country covered on Patrol hike.

(16) Make *large map* of Patrol's favorite camp site and its surroundings for Patrol den.

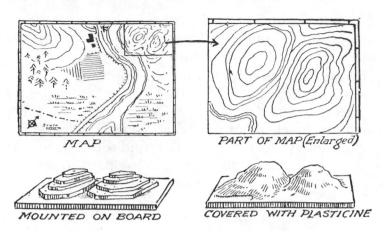

MAP

PART OF MAP (Enlarged)

MOUNTED ON BOARD

COVERED WITH PLASTICINE

(17) Make a *relief map* of country surrounding camp site.

(18) Have *mounted topographical map* in den on which all Patrol and Troop hikes are indicated with colored lines or thread fastened on with glue or small pins.

(19) *Enlarge topographical map* and find out which changes have taken place since map was made.

### First Class Requirement No. 9

*Use properly an axe for felling or trimming light timber; or produce an article of carpentry, cabinet-making, or metal work made by himself; or demonstrate repair of a decaying or damaged tree. Explain the method followed*

The elementary use of an axe (or hatchet) was learned by your boys when they passed their Second Class tests, and before you start training them for the First Class Requirement you ought to review what they have already been taught.

In very many cases it proves necessary to substitute the axe test with the manufacture of a handicraft object. But the use of an axe in the woods is far more fascinating to boys than the mere handling of tools in making a household article. The spirit of the pioneers and the backwoodsmen is in their blood, and the chopping down of a couple of trees gives them a satisfaction which they can't derive from anything else.

If you can, therefore, find an opportunity for your boys to do the real thing. But remember, never think of cutting down live trees. Dead trees and the permission to touch them are what you should go hunting for. In every forest you will find dead trees, from  thin saplings to giant trees. They are useless as they stand, but still more so when felled because rain and the wet ground soon will decay and destroy them. But don't touch them without permission. Maybe you can find a tract of land where the chestnut blight has left the chestnut trees with a dried-out trunk and dead branches stretching toward the sky. The cutting down of such trees may be considered a Good Turn to the owner of the land. The clearing of trees after a forest fire is another project and then again your Patrol might get a chance to practise on stumps which have been cut too high above the ground.

If you succeed in getting permission to chop down trees, don't forget that the whole procedure is not entirely without danger. *There are rules which you must have your boys understand before you start out and they must be followed carefully.*

The most important rule is always to clear away underbrush and vines within the reach of the extended axe, overhead as well as around you. If the axe should be caught by a vine, it might easily be torn out of your hand or be given a wrong direction, and a bad injury to yourself or somebody else might result.

By watching a good chopper your boys may learn

Do        Don't

something about axemanship, but naturally it is only by practising themselves that they become experts.

In regard to the alternative for using an axe—the production of an article of carpentry, cabinet-making, or metal work, this ought to be taken up by your boys themselves in their own homes or maybe in the school workshop. It can hardly be considered right to make Patrol instruction out of this, because ideas, necessary material, tools and space, will vary so much that no general instruction can take place. Encourage your boys to go ahead and get their work over with, but insist that the final product be a thing worthy of the Patrol, completed in a real workmanlike manner. No half-done work to be accepted.

Another alternative for the axe test is the repairing of a decaying or damaged tree. This part is of particular interest to rural Scouts, but even so the chance of learning and training for this requirement is very small. If some of your boys are interested in this, it is certain that they will try to get an opportunity to demonstrate their skill. The treating of tree wounds isn't difficult and may easily be learned from the Handbook for Boys. Fillings and bracings are, on the contrary, very hard to handle. They can only be learned from actual practise.

If your town has a regular tree surgeon, it would be a fine thing if you could persuade him to give your boys a few lessons. If it hasn't, write to U. S. Department of Agriculture, Washington, D. C., for bulletins on the subject, or to The Davey Tree Surgeons, Kent, Ohio.

Do           Don't

## Projects

The Merit Badge pamphlets in Carpentry, Wood Work and Metal Work may give your boys suggestions; also in the public libraries they will find a great number of books from which to get ideas and instruction. See also chapter on Patrol Handicraft and Second Class Requirement No. 6.

## First Class Requirement No. 10

*Judge distance, size, number, height and weight within 25 per cent*

The judging part of the First Class Requirements is by many considered one of the most difficult tests and your boys will need considerable training before they are able to judge things within the allowed limit of 25 per cent on either side.

For training purposes the sequence mentioned above isn't the best. It will be better to group the different items in another order and, starting with distance judging, continue with height, size, number and weight.

The judging test is a *judging* test. It may sound unnecessary and absurd to mention this. Nevertheless the requirement is often misunderstood and Scouts are permitted to use simple methods of measurements.

This is naturally wrong. Distances, sizes, numbers, heights must be judged by the eyes alone, weights by the eyes or by the feel. No extra help may be used.

Another thing: measuring is absolutely necessary during the training in judging. It is by checking up to see if your estimates are correct, by comparing your figures with the correct ones, that you learn to judge. Therefore, never let your boys just judge distances, numbers, and so forth. Have them measure out and count immediately afterward, in order to see how nearly right they were.

The requirement doesn't specify how great distances, heights, sizes, weights, are to be judged. It is up to you to make your own standards, and you will naturally want them to include all the items that might occur in the daily life of your boys.

## Projects

(1) Measure out on the ground 100 feet. Drive stakes down. Have boys pace distance. Have them try to get the distance fixed in their mind's eye. Arrange different objects between boys and end stake. Have them estimate the distances. Next try 200 feet, 300 feet (100 yards), 200 yards, etc.

(2) Have *competitions* in estimating distances over flat country, broken ground, over rivers, ravines, etc. Check up by pacing or, where this is impossible, by a map or by method mentioned in Handbook for Boys.

(3) Have boys estimate 12 distances, 3 between 0-100 feet, 3 from 100-300 feet, 3 from 100 yards to 300 yards, 3 from 300-500 yards. Have them write down answers and measure the distances to find out if they are within the 25 per cent limit.

(4) Let *familiar distances* help your boys in their training, as for instance: Baseball field—home plate to first base, 90 feet; basketball—foul line to below basket, 15 feet; tennis court—36 feet by 78 feet; football field—160 feet by 300 feet; normal desk—30 inches high; normal chair—18 inches high; auto tracks —about 4 feet 4 inches apart, etc.

(5) Start *judging of height* with simple objects which may be easily measured, as for example, heights in the Patrol den of chairs, table, windows, walls.

(6) Have boys judge heights of bushes, trees, flag poles, buildings, church towers, until they get an all-

round idea of height. Check up by measuring with one of methods described in Handbook for Boys (page 280).

(7) For *estimating numbers,* play "Kim's game" (see Second Class Requirement No. 4) using numbers

of different articles, also different numbers of marbles, clips, nails, etc.

(8) On hike have *competitions* in estimating number of things in shop windows, number of cars parked, number of windows on the front of a building, number of cattle in field, trees along a certain part of the road.

(9) For training in *judging weights,* make up articles of different weight, as for example, bags with sand and sawdust, packages of books, of bricks, bottles with water. Weigh them carefully, have boys estimate weight and check up with actual amount.

## First Class Requirement No. 11

*Describe fully from observation (1a) ten species of trees or plants, including poison ivy, by their bark, leaves, flowers, fruit and scent; or (1b) six species of wild birds, by their plumage, notes, tracks and habits; or (1c) six species of native wild animals, by their form, color, call, track and habits; (2) find the North Star, and name and describe at least three constellations of stars*

This nature part of the First Class Requirements ought to be far more than a test to your boys. It ought to mean a definite habit of observation.

By now your Patrol must have been on a number of hikes, maybe also in several camps, and if that hasn't made the boys interested in Nature's wonders around them they must either be very unobserving—or, something is the matter with your leadership.

Their interest in nature study may have started as mere curiosity. If you have been able to answer their questions, a great deal has been accomplished. If you haven't, it may have meant the weakening or the suppression of a budding interest.

Boys' interest in nature is very often a thing that must be developed. Some have a love for all living things from the start, while many seem to be entirely indifferent. And it is up to the Patrol Leader to a very great extent to open the eyes of his boys to the glory of nature surrounding them.

## Projects

*Trees and plants*

(1) Undertake special *Patrol nature hike* with study of trees and plants.

(2) Have boys make *tree notes,* describing bark, leaves, flowers, fruit, general shape of tree.

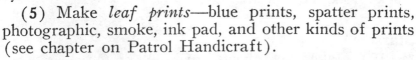

(3) Start a Patrol collection of *pressed flowers,* neatly mounted on cardboard.

(4) Make a *collection of leaves*.

(5) Make *leaf prints*—blue prints, spatter prints, photographic, smoke, ink pad, and other kinds of prints (see chapter on Patrol Handicraft).

(6) Make a collection of *wood specimens* (see Handicraft).

(7) Make *census* of trees in your locality.

(8) Every Scout in the Patrol to *plant* at least one *tree* yearly.

(9) Learn about *edible wild plants* and make use of them on Patrol hikes in the cooking.

(10) On hikes have *competitions* in finding certain leaves or plants, biggest number of different leaves, biggest number of plants identified and named.

## Birds and Animals

(11) Visit local *natural history museum* and study birds and animals for help in identifying them in the open.

(12) Have early morning *Patrol bird hike,* starting from camp just before sunrise. Make list of birds identified.

(13) Make collection of different *bird feathers* mounted on sheets of paper.

(14) Build *bird houses* and hang them up in suitable places.

(15) Build *bird bath and feeding stations* and keep them provided with water and food the year round.

(16) Visit local *Zoo* and study the appearance and habits of its animals.

(17) Make *photographs of animals* encountered on hikes.

(18) Teach your boys to make *plaster casts* of animal tracks (see Handicraft chapter).

## Stars

(19) Make up charts of most important *constellations* for Patrol den.

(20) Go on a *star study hike.* Point out constella-

tions by the help of a flashlight. Have boys show you that they have actually identified the star groups.

(21) At Patrol meeting have boys arrange checkers or small pieces of white paper in the shape of the various *constellations* shown them on hike.

(22) Have a *night map hike*, using stars only for orientation.

(23) Tell the boys the ancient *legends* of the most important constellations.

## First Class Requirement No. 12

*Furnish satisfactory evidence that he has put into practice in his daily life, the principles of the Scout Oath and Law*

When we treated the Twelfth Requirement of a Second Class Scout we spoke about what was expected of him in regard to this "satisfactory evidence."

Every word we spoke there holds good in regard to this First Class Requirement, but in increased degree. After all, the Second Class Scout has only been in our Movement for a short while. Even if he has used his eyes and mind well, he can hardly have appreciated in full what the Movement stands for.

But a First Class Scout can and must!

He has been a part of a Patrol and a Troop for months. He has lived the life of his Brother Scouts. He has caught their spirit, the spirit of the Scout Law. He is a Scout.

His "satisfactory evidence" must mean "really satisfactory." He must have shown that he wants to be a real member of the great brotherhood.

Again, as we have said already, you can not teach him this. *It must develop from his own heart.* But your example has a tremendous effect on each of your boys. Not directly, but indirectly, you teach them to live up to the Scout Law.

And the day a boy is able to furnish the evidence

from his Scoutmaster, his parents, his teachers, that he has put into practice in his daily life, the principles of the Oath and Law, you may feel yourself just a wee bit proud that he is one of your boys, that you may have been one of the tools to help this boy live the life of a real Scout.

## The First Class Examination

Here again every word said about Second Class Examinations holds good.

It is the honor of the Patrol which is at stake when your boys appear before the Court of Honor or the specially authorized examiners.

You want your boys to pass and with as many points as possible. Therefore you try them out in a strict examination before you consider them ready or let them consider themselves so.

If you can inspire your boys to live up to a high standard in regard to test passing, their First Class pin will mean far more to them, not only at the moment they get it, but in all the future.

# CHAPTER VII

## PATROL HIKES

AT one of the very first Patrol meetings you have with your Scouts, one of them will ask: "When do we go on a hike?" and in a moment the rest will join him in a multi-voiced chorus.

Boys, and especially Scouts, want to go hiking. The out-of-doors fascinates them. The woods, the rivers, the "wide open spaces" call them. And they obey.

As soon as you are able you will want to take your boys on Patrol Hikes. You want your Patrol to be a real one, and only a hiking Patrol is a real Patrol.

Before you start taking your boys along on a hike, you must realize that there is a difference—and a big one—between a Patrol meeting and a Patrol hike. You may be in possession of all the leadership and knowledge to run successful Patrol meetings and yet be without any ability to get something real out of a Patrol hike.

### Degree of Responsibility

The most conspicuous difference between the two is the different degree of responsibility that goes with each.

There are usually not very many dangers in running

an indoor meeting. It is when you start to take the group out in the open that the danger moment may creep in. There is traffic to be encountered, cliffs and rivers and swamps to be avoided; there is the danger that an innocent camp fire will blow up into a forest fire if care is not taken. And a lot of other unforeseen things might happen which would put you to a severe test.

And, let it be said immediately, you will certainly not think of taking your Patrol on a hike if you aren't honestly, absolutely sure that you will be able to pass that test with flying colors.

It is too dangerous to make experiments with a first Patrol hike. Everything must be planned and supervised so that nothing can possibly go wrong and you can only be sure of that if your preliminary training in the Troop under the Scoutmaster has taken in all details of hiking.

On Troop hikes you will naturally have used your eyes to see how everything is made to run smoothly. But even more helpful has been the Patrol Leader's Hikes in which you have taken part and which have been an important part of your training as a leader.

These Patrol Leader's Hikes have become a fixed procedure in almost all Troops throughout the country. Just as the Scoutmaster, his Assistants, his Patrol Leaders will come together for Leaders' Councils ("Cornertooth" meetings) to discuss the work in the Troop and to train the Leaders in Scout requirements, in the same way the Leaders will go on hikes together to get this intensive training in hiking technique.

## The Word "Hike"

Before we go any further we will have to get to an understanding of what is really meant by the word "hike."

Originally a hike was just a long trip undertaken on foot. But nowadays any trip that brings you out in the open is considered a hike, even if hardly any walking is done. People go even as far as to speak of trips to a museum or zoo as educational hikes, of visits to factories as industrial hikes, etc. We aren't going into that kind of hike here. When in the following pages we speak of hikes we are thinking of trips, short ones or long ones, which bring the Patrol from the monotonous life in the streets out into nature, the kind that can give to the boys that feeling of liberty and of room for expanding the lungs and using the limbs, which they hunger for in the city.

## Different Groups

We shall not here treat the so-called overnight hike which is really a matter of camping rather than hiking, though it may include hiking. You will find that in the "Patrol Camping" chapter. Here we shall speak only of the one day hike, that is a hike which brings your boys back home before dark.

For convenience' sake we will divide one day hikes into two separate groups like this:

*(a) The Sandwich Hike*
*(b) The Chop Hike*

These titles speak fairly clearly for themselves, still a brief explanation may be useful.

## Sandwich Hikes

A *Sandwich Hike* is a hike on which the Patrol doesn't want to be tied up by fire-making and cooking. This may be because it has other special training on hand such as: signaling, judging, nature study, etc., and it wants to use every minute of its time for that purpose. Maybe again the Patrol knows that the hike will bring it through territory where fire building isn't permitted or there may be other really good reasons for making short work of the eating business. Anyway, on a "Sandwich Hike" it will be necessary to bring along ready prepared food or food which can be quickly gotten ready and eaten and requiring little clean-up afterward. This needn't, of course, be sandwiches. An inventive Patrol, particularly a Patrol with a clever "Grubmaster," will think of other, more interesting substitutes and variations. But the point is, plan for and be satisfied with a simple, quick meal.

## Chop Hikes

A *Chop Hike* is a hike where fire building and cooking is to take a prominent place in the program. Firemaking immediately increases the Patrol Leader's responsibilities and the cooking means more preparations before the Patrol is ready to start. On the first Chop Hikes, the boys will prepare their own individual meals. This will serve as training for the Second and First Class Requirements. Later the Patrol wants to go in for real Patrol cookery, i.e., a few of the boys alternately making the meals for the whole Patrol.

## Hiking Technique

The first thing you will do when hiking is mentioned in your Patrol is to check up on your own leadership ability. In fact you may have done so even before you became a Patrol Leader in order to "Be Prepared."

Ask yourself this important question: "If I take these boys along on a hike can I be sure that I can meet any obstacles and difficulties which may arise with a cool head and enough knowledge and presence of mind to overcome them?"

It is about the same question that your Scoutmaster will ask himself when you ask him for permission to take your boys along on your first hike: "Am I sure that this Patrol Leader of mine is able to undertake this job and bring it to a successful finish?" After all, it is your Scoutmaster that has the greatest responsibility for everything that happens in the Troop. And if he isn't perfectly sure that you can tackle the job yet, he won't give his permission—for your sake. If he doesn't it is up to you to work all the harder to be ready next time, beyond the shadow of doubt.

## Leadership Requirements

Your Scoutmaster will not make an unreasonable decision in this matter.. There are tests he will apply to make sure of your fitness. He will doubtless consider the following points and insist that you measure up to them as a minimum of Scouting knowledge before giving his consent to your taking out your Patrol alone.

(1) *You must have earned your First Class Badge.*

(2) *You must have had hiking experience on at least 3 Troop hikes and 2 Patrol Leaders' hikes ("Cornertooth"–hikes.)*

(3) *You must have had at least one month's experience as a successful Patrol Leader.*

And furthermore before you start on any hike the Scoutmaster will insist that:

(4) *You must have the written consent of the parents of each boy.*

(5) *You must have a reasonable familiarity with the country to be covered.*

(6) *You must have the permission of the property owner to build fires and cook (if going on a Chop Hike).*

By looking through this list yourself, you will understand why every single one of the requirements is necessary. If anything should happen, you and the Scoutmaster and everybody else concerned will be able to say that all precautions were taken beforehand. But a word to the wise is sufficient. If you have the right feeling as to your responsibility and make the boys live up to your expectations, it is 999 to 1000 that nothing will happen.

It would be well (in fact it is the custom in most Troops) for the Scoutmaster or an Assistant to go along with you and your Patrol on the first Patrol Hike. It will be understood that he won't do anything, will not interfere in your leadership in any way, not even give any suggestions. He will just *be* there. This will prove to be a great help to you. Maybe you will feel a little awkward about it. Maybe his presence will make you a little nervous. Never mind. It will make you see where you are acting right and where wrong without being told. The presence of the Scoutmaster or other adult leader will be as a second conscience to you. You will feel intuitively if all details are as well worked out as they ought to be, if you are giving adequate leadership.

So much in regard to what is expected of you. Now we will go through the planning and the hike itself systematically.

In planning for Patrol meetings we put together a sort of a formula:

*Where?*
*When?*
*What?*
*How?*

This applies to hikes as well, though perhaps in a somewhat changed order:

*What?*
*Where?*
*When?*
*How?*

## PLANNING THE HIKE

**You** will first take up the question of a **Patrol** hike with your Scouts at a regular meeting.

The instruction part of the meeting is over with, you have had your fun, now the future has to be planned.

Somebody urges a hike, and immediately questions fly through the room, *"When do we go?"*, *"Where do we go?"*. But the question which must be answered first is *"What kind of hike is it to be?"*

### What?

For every hike you must have an objective clearly in mind. Is the hike supposed to advance the group in Scoutcraft? In signaling, tracking, Scout's pace, compass work, cooking, map making, for example? Or is it going to be a nature hike, an exploration, a pilgrimage to a historical spot? Or what?

If some of your boys are still Tenderfoot Scouts, you will very likely want the hike to be a Scoutcraft hike. The rest may always follow when your boys are more advanced in Scouting.

Very well then. What does the Patrol need most by way of Scoutcraft training?

Signaling? In that case you will want to take them to rather open places where signaling over distance may be effectively carried on.

Tracking? Then wooded country is best.

Cooking? Permission, firewood, water, all these have to be considered.

Different tests require different country. So we get to the *Where?*

## Where?

If your Patrol organization is working already (see Chapter 4), you will turn to the Hikemaster for suggestions. What he has to propose will form the basis for further discussion. If you haven't any Hikemaster as yet, you will put the same question anyway, ask all the boys in the Patrol for suggestions.

If there are several plans proposed, make sure to weigh each of them carefully before deciding upon a route and a place which fits the particular object of the Patrol.

A few general hints may be helpful here:

To start with, the hikes ought to be short. Boys without walking training soon get tired. And tired boys don't see the funny side of things. If there is trolley-car or bus service available make use of them, ride to a stop from which point a mile or two of hiking may bring you to a place suited to your purposes. Later on you may increase the amount of walking. The whole thing is a matter of training. If you can get your boys enthusiastic about walking—which, by the way, is one of the finest of exercises—you will soon find them themselves suggesting far-away places to which to hike.

Another good rule to follow is: Keep as far as possible away from the main road. On the main road you have to look out for the traffic the whole time. Usually there aren't many beauty spots to be found and the hiking itself is far more tiring than if you choose the by-paths.

In a short time you ought to have found some suitable favorite hiking places. Stick to them for a time but don't forget to find others before the fellows start to tire of the first ones. Here is where your Hike-master will come in strong, when you've got him on the job. Let everybody keep their eyes open, too, for good hiking objectives and places.

## When?

If your boys are school boys, there can be no doubt about the *When?* Saturday or some holiday will be the answer. Then you are able to start out early in the morning and need not return before night. No lessons are waiting for you. Everybody's mind is quite free; ready for a good time and an adventure.

Even if your boys have jobs they may still get their week-ends off—Saturday afternoons and evenings are excellent for hikes even if you naturally do not get as far on them as the full days. And working boys get an extra lot of fun out of hikes.

The question of a Sunday hike may come up here, in cases where your boys cannot get them in on other days.

In this matter every Patrol Leader ought to know about and faithfully conform to the resolution adopted by the National Council of the Boy Scouts of America (March, 1922).

*"WHEREAS, the Boy Scouts of America is specifically pledged to encourage reverence and faithfulness to religious obligations;*

*"AND WHEREAS, the attention of the National Council has been called to the fact that in some cases, Scouts have been permitted to neglect church attendance while at week-end camp or on week-end hikes,*

*"BE IT RESOLVED, that the National Council records its disapproval of programs for the week-end hikes or camps which preclude the attendance of Scouts from religious services, or which cause loss of credits for the individual or Patrol, or Troop if the Scout elects to remain at home to attend church."*

But if you are certain that your boys have fulfilled their obligations in this direction and if your Scoutmaster and your boys' parents fully approve you may undertake a Sunday afternoon hike. Such a hike may even prove of more value than a hike undertaken at any other time. At church you and your boys have heard of God's mighty handiwork and going out into nature afterward where every leaf, every insect, every bird tells of that work is almost certain to be a thing of real inspiration to you and your boys.

The day being decided upon, the hour has to be fixed.

If a trolley car or bus ride precedes the actual hiking, be sure to figure on enough time for it so that all boys can reach the destination in time. Eight o'clock in the morning would be about the best time for the boys to

leave their homes for an all day hike. Certainly don't start later than nine. No time for sleepy heads when a hike is on. For an afternoon hike an hour must be fixed which is satisfactory to all.

Just as important as the starting hour is a definite hour for the return. The boys must be able to tell the parents precisely when they may be expected home and that hour must be strictly adhered to. We spoke about this in regard to Patrol meetings and we repeat it here: One of the most important of a Scout's virtues is that he is punctual and trustworthy in everything he does. If the parents of your boys find out that their boys actually return at the hour fixed, they will learn to rely upon you and respect the work that is being done in the Patrol, and they will have no objections to letting you take their boys along on other hikes.

## How?

The *How* side of the question is the one which has to be worked out in more detail than any of the others. While the others were all a matter of planning, this can more appropriately be considered a matter of actual preparation.

Permissions from parents must be acquired, transportation arranged for, eats gotten together, equipment considered, expenditures decided on and provided for.

## Permissions

Permissions are a necessity, especially for the first Patrol hikes you undertake. This provision isn't put up in order to try to shift a part of the responsibilities

over on the homes. It is to make perfectly sure that the parents really and fully agree to have their boys go on the hike, a sort of a proof that they are willing to support the Patrol in its endeavor to put the "out" into "Scouting."

If you have been accustomed to have Patrol meetings in the different homes and thereby have made the parents acquainted with you (also with your leadership abilities) and the rest of the members of the gang, you will find no difficulty in getting the permissions. The difficulty comes when the homes aren't familiar with you or with any other members of the Patrol. In this case the best thing for you to do would be to visit the homes, have a talk with the parents of your boys and explain to them what it is all about.

The permission ought to be as short as possible, just a "I give my son (name) permission to go on the hike of the Wolf Patrol, Saturday, May 5, 8 a. m. to 6 p. m. (signed)".

The permissions may be collected by the Patrol Scribe just before the Patrol starts on the hike. But it would be far better if the whole thing were planned far enough in advance so that the permissions can be brought by the boys to the Patrol meeting preceding the hike and delivered there.

Naturally the Scoutmaster must also know of and approve of the hike, as said on page 187.

### Transportation

Transportation is the next thing to be considered. As mentioned above, trolley cars or bus lines may be

of use. Or you may take a short railway journey to bring you and your Patrol to the starting point of the actual hiking. In many places a simple walk over a few miles will bring you out of town and you will arrive at a point fit for your purposes.

### Meeting Place

If the Patrol headquarters is situated at a convenient place, you may want to use that as your starting place. From there the group will use any method of transportation it has decided upon. Or maybe the home of one of the Scouts will prove to be the best place for assembling. Naturally the Patrol will only meet this way if the boys live fairly close together. If the members live far apart and have to use trolley or bus to get to such a place, the most reasonable procedure to follow would be to make the trolley or bus terminal the meeting place. On the other hand, if the Patrol is going by train, it will meet at the railroad station, the Patrol treasurer having previously bought tickets for the whole Patrol with money paid him by the boys at the preceding meeting.

## Expenses

Transportation costs money. Therefore before any extensive hikes are decided upon, the Patrol Leader must be perfectly sure that all the boys can afford the trip. Naturally this is not done by asking them tactless, embarrassing questions, but by visiting their homes and using eyes and ears. If you have the least bit of a feeling that some trip may be too expensive for some of the Scouts, don't undertake it. Parents are willing to sacrifice much for their boys, but if they once get to feeling that Scouting is a thing that is always requiring money, even small sums, it may scare them.

If you and your Patrol want to go on elaborate hikes, which take a considerable sum of money, the way out will be to have the Patrol earn its own money (see Chapter on Handicraft), which is, after all, decidedly the best way.

## Eats

On Sandwich Hikes and also on the first Chop Hike, the question of eats will be decided by the boys themselves. From home they will bring material enough out of which to prepare an easy lunch.

For the so-called Sandwich Hikes ready made sandwiches *may* be taken, but it is far better to have the boys bring the different ingredients and prepare them in the open. At the same time, as has been said, there are many other ways of preparing a meal, and from the following you may get suggestions to pass on to your boys.

We have divided the different materials in groups. The point is that if one thing is chosen from each group and put together a fine combination will result.

### Breadstuffs

| | |
|---|---|
| White Bread | Rolls |
| Whole Wheat | Bran Rolls |
| Rye Bread | Corn Muffins |
| Raisin Bread | Oatmeal Cookies |

### "Spreads"

| | |
|---|---|
| Butter | Orange Marmalade |
| Margarine | Strawberry Jam |
| Peanut Butter | Raspberry Jam |
| Cream Cheese | Grape Jelly |

### "Fillings"

| | |
|---|---|
| Sardines (canned) | Cheese (Am., Swiss) |
| Salmon (canned) | Cold Cuts—Meats |
| Tuna Fish (canned) | Bologna |
| Hard Boiled Eggs | Tomatoes |

### Fruit in Season

| | |
|---|---|
| Apples | Bananas |
| Pears | Dates |
| Oranges | Figs |
| Peaches | Raisins |

For the Chop Hikes any of the following things may be considered. The material is brought from home in its raw form (except possibly bread) and prepared without utensils.

### Breadstuffs (or substitutes)

Any of the breads mentioned on page 196
Twist

Bread baked in ashes
Potatoes baked in ashes
Roast Sweet Corn

### Meats

Kabob
Broiled Pork Chop
Broiled Veal Cutlet
Bacon or Ham

Eggs, fried on stone
Planked Fish
Fowl, clay baked

### Dessert

Any of the fruits mentioned on page 196

Baked Apple.
Baked Banana

The boys will collect their material individually at home and wrap it into strong brown paper. Show them how to fix the string around it in such a way that the finished package may be suspended from the belt when on the hike. A still better method consists of taking two haversacks along. Put all the foodstuff in these and have the boys take turns carrying them.

## Clothing and Equipment

For hiking in the summer time the very best clothing you can get is the Boy Scout Service Uniform, i.e., the shorts and sleeveless shirt. This particular uniform is created for comfort.

When on a hike it is of importance that the blood circulation be free and unhampered. Any tight clothing spells discomfort. But not only in this direction are shorts and sleeveless shirts of value. They also permit the air to flow freely around the limbs, hardening the skin and stimulating the pores.

It is sometimes objected that underbrush treats the bare knees roughly. The facts prove that this seldom causes any serious difficulty. Thousands of Scouts spend their summer vacation in camp in shorts and very few inconveniences are reported. In fact, their advantages seem to far outweigh any possible disadvantages in their use. Our climate (at least not in the Northern States) isn't always fit for an all-year use of shorts. The result is that boys who have to choose between breeches and shorts generally prefer breeches. But shorts are less expensive and their use should certainly be encouraged wherever possible.

For short hikes the costume isn't so important, but care should always be taken to see that the boys are wearing the right kind of shoes and stockings.

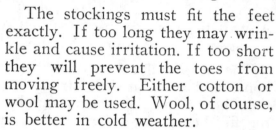

The stockings must fit the feet exactly. If too long they may wrinkle and cause irritation. If too short they will prevent the toes from moving freely. Either cotton or wool may be used. Wool, of course, is better in cold weather.

There is a saying that "on a hike your shoes as well as your companions ought to be good old friends." It is a great mistake to go on a hike in new shoes. They ought to be "broken in" at home. If this has to be done in a hurry, the Scout may stand in about three inches of water with the shoes on for five minutes and then go for a brisk walk until they have dried on his feet. But let him ask permission before he goes in for a stunt of this kind. His parents might possibly object to such a procedure. Before the shoes are quite dry it is a good plan to rub a little oil (neatsfoot oil is recommended) into them. That keeps the leather smooth.

The best kind of shoes to wear is thus described in the Hiking Merit Badge Pamphlet: ". . . straight on the inside, so that the big toe can point straight ahead, as nature intended. The front is broad enough to give all the toes free play. It has a single sole, and it is flexible—a prime desideratum for good walking. The heel is low and broad . . ."

It is worth considering that all these features are found in the Official Boy Scout Shoe.

If the shoes get wet, they may be dried by filling them with scraps of news-papers and put aside. Also a frying pan may be filled with clean pebbles, heated a little over the fire (not too hot), the pebbles then put in the shoes and sha-ken around for a while.

STYLE SHOES AND SMILE SHOES

If it looks like rain, a raincoat or a poncho must be added to the outfit. If it is very cold, naturally the Scouts must clothe themselves more warmly than above indicated. The correct way of wearing a sweater or a pull-over, is to put it on *under the uniform*. You want to show the world that you are Scouts—not look like a miscellaneous assortment of camouflaged tramps.

So much about clothing. Other equipment may be wanted. The most expedient way to decide upon that is to get together with your boys, make a complete list of items, then choose those which seem really necessary.

## Personal Equipment

Necessary:

Uniform
Raincoat or Poncho (if it is raining or threatens rain)

Lunch                          Knife
Cup                            String

*Personal Equipment (continued)*

If wanted:

Haversack
Notebook and Pencil
Matches
Compass
Camera
Canteen (if you aren't sure of drinking water)
Cooking Utensils—Individual Outfit—Plate, Fork,
    Knife, Spoon.

## *Necessary Equipment*

The *uniform* is mentioned above as necessary equipment. *Poncho* is given as a possible substitute for *raincoat*. Now wearing a poncho certainly has its advantages in a lot of cases. Nothing is more inconvenient, however, than to stoop down to build a fire or to turn the pork chops in the pan if you have a poncho draped about you. The flap in front of you will be in the way the whole time and you won't have your arms free. This difficulty may be remedied a bit by taking along an extra belt, to wear outside the poncho when special work has to be done. For the actual hiking you will often find a poncho more convenient than a raincoat. It makes your movements freer, and when the weather clears a poncho can be rolled up to fill far less space than a raincoat. It is also handier to sit on, if eating lunch, after a shower.

Your *lunch* and *cup* you may want to put in one of the haversacks which the Patrol brings along on the trip, and which are carried in turn by the different boys. If no haversacks are taken it is advisable to make up the lunch in a small individual packet, tie a string around it and fix it to the belt. The cup may also be hung in the belt. When buying the cup be sure to get a durable one, preferably of enamel ware and one of sufficient size. Beware of aluminum. Hot tea in an aluminum cup requires lips of leather and fingers like pliers.

# PERSONAL HIKE EQUIPMENT

A good, *sharp knife* will always come in handy. And be sure always to keep its edge keen and clean.

A *piece of string* belongs in every boy's pocket. Therefore its merits and possibilities need not be listed here. They are numerous and varied as every boy knows.

In regard to the *haversack* you are almost sure to find that several of the boys have them already. Maybe not models suited for real camping trips but good enough to carry a little duffle and equipment on a one-day hike. At this stage of the game it isn't wise to go in for buying of new stuff. With more hiking experience you will learn what you actually need and when you buy your real Patrol equipment you will get things that afterwards you will not regret having bought. Notice what other Patrol Leaders use. Get tried and proved good suggestions from campers generally before you procure your permanent outfit.

*Notebook and pencil* should be carried in the shirt pocket. Have the boys make notes on every hike you undertake as training for the fourteen-mile hike for passing the First Class requirements. The habit also serves to sharpen their powers of observation and deduction.

*Matches* are necessary, if possible in waterproof container. A small medicine bottle is often recommended for the purpose. But if you adopt the idea don't carry the bottle in the pocket. It may be smashed with serious results. Keep it in the haversack. A shaving soap screw-top tin is excellent. Another tip is to melt some solid paraffin, remove from fire, cool a little, then immerse the matches in the paraffin for a moment, take them out and let them cool. The paraffin layer around the match will keep it perfectly dry and doesn't affect the ease with which it may be lighted.

A *compass* in the pocket is important, especially if you are going on discovery hikes through country unknown to you. Usually a compass is unnecessary if you know your First Class requirements, yet it sometimes happens that one may lose his head at the same time as he loses his way. So take a compass, and recommend to each boy that he has one along. Recommend also that somewhere on the back of it be scratched "N—B," meaning "north part of the needle is the black part of it" (if that is the way north is indicated on your compass). In their bewilderment people often forget this point and walk south when they think they are walking north.

The *camera* should be packed in top of haversack where it can easily be found. Though if it is a small one, it may be hung in the belt for quick use, you will soon find out that the haversack is the best place for it. Whoever is responsible for picture taking should be sure to bring along enough films, also an extra empty roll. There isn't any fun in having to sacrifice a perfectly good film if in changing you happen to lose the empty roll in the ravine or the river.

# PATROL HIKE EQUIPMENT

As for the *canteen* recommend to your boys a felt-covered aluminum one carried in a strap over one shoulder. But don't let the canteen tempt anyone to drink the whole time on a hike (See discussion of the whole subject of drinking water on the hike on Page 214).

And so we get to the *individual cooking utensils.* The National Supply Department puts out an excellent individual cooking kit which is recommended. Yet you may find that on this point in the game a less expensive kit ought to be considered. All any boy needs just now is a pan, a pot, a plate, fork, knife and spoon. In a number of cases mothers will let their boys borrow the equipment from the kitchen. If it has to be bought, the nearest five and ten cent store is the place to seek. Here you can buy a small pot and a pan that will answer the purpose as well as any expensive kit. A

cheap enamel, tin or aluminum plate will be all right,
also a set consisting of an ordinary strong fork, spoon
and knife need not cost more than thirty or even
twenty cents.   At all events keep as far as possible
away from "collapsible" eating sets.  They will get your
goat sooner or later.

## Patrol Equipment for One-Day Hike

Necessary:
    First Aid Kit
If wanted:
    Maps
    Axes, Spades (for fire building)
    Cooking Utensils
    Dish Towels
    Signaling Flags, Tracking Irons, etc.
    Rope

A *first aid kit* ought to go with your Patrol always
wherever it goes, not any elaborate kit necessarily, but
one which will assure your being prepared for possible
accidents.  A few sterilized bandages, a few mercurochrome swabs, some adhesive tape, an ointment for
burns will answer most purposes.   An excellent and
Official Boy Scout First Aid Belt Kit that contains
what you need is for sale at the National Supply Department (75c).

*Maps* are put into the "If wanted" list.   Even so a
map of the country which you are traversing ought
always to go along with you on your trips.   It is by
using a map that your boys will learn map reading and
you ought to give them this chance on all trips.  The
best maps to get are the Topographical Maps of the
United States Geological Survey (see Page 171). Keep
the map where you can easily get at it, in a breast
pocket or in an outside pocket of a haversack.

*Axes* and *spades* you may want if the Patrol goes
in for fire making on the hike.  And in that case the
spades are really more necessary than the axes (see

Page 149). Many Scouts have the curious belief that it is impossible to build a fire without the use of an axe. This is a dangerous mistake. In nine cases out of ten the axe is entirely uncalled for. Enough branches are generally found on the ground to keep a Patrol fire going. And if any of them are so tough that they can't be broken by the help of a knee or a foot and a strong arm they won't serve the purpose of fire making anyway, so it isn't necessary to have an axe to chop them up with. Try to persuade your boys to use the axe as seldom as possible. If they absolutely have to use it be sure that all safety measures be taken.

*Cooking utensils* necessary for Patrol cooking are described in full on Page 250.

*Dish towels* must not be forgotten. Use the least expensive ones you can get hold of. Two will suffice. Be sure to dry them thoroughly if possible before packing them. If that can't be done have them taken out immediately after the return from the trip and washed and dried, ready for the next trip.

For special activities, special equipment is required. For example, *signaling flags* if you want to go in for signaling, *tracking irons* or *whiffle poof* or corn or chicken feed if you want your boys to train in tracking. In other words bring along with you whatever equipment is necessary for the training in Scout requirements you are working on.

*Rope* may often come in handy. A couple of Boy Scout Guard Ropes or a couple of 10-15-foot clothes lines will supply your need.

## GETTING READY FOR THE HIKE

Taking it for granted that the details described above have been discussed at a Patrol meeting, or maybe at two meetings and you have come to your decisions as to plans and equipment. The time has now come for you, as a Patrol Leader, to sum up what has been decided upon and make out the final orders.

Be sure that all the boys get everything straight—

when to meet, where to meet, what to bring. It doesn't help the success of an undertaking if you start out with misunderstandings. Don't depend on the boys remembering everything. Have them write down in advance on a piece of paper or in a notebook the different facts.

Then everything is all set. There is just one little detail more for you to attend to. Before starting on the hike make up a short outline of the program for the day. This will help you in getting the most possible results out of the hike.

Put down the time of starting and returning. Decide upon the meal hour and fill the time before and after this with the approximate number of minutes used for trolley car or bus rides, actual hiking and such Scoutcraft activities as are going to form a part of the hike.

Such an outline program may look somewhat like this:

## PATROL HIKE TO MORTON HOLLOW
### SATURDAY, SEPTEMBER 28th.

8:20—Meet at Den. Check up on equipment.

8:40—Start for trolley car ride.

9:30—Arrive at Atwater Ave. Terminal. Start hike. Follow west shore of river up to Green Lake. Nature study. Trees, plants, birds, animal tracks.

10:40—Arrive at camp site at Morton Hollow. Training in signaling over distance, then fire building and preparing of meal.

12:20—Lunch. Cleaning up after meal. Packing. Rest.

1:20—Games for fun from Handbook for Boys.

2:00—Making camp site trackless. Ready to leave.

2:20—Hike to the new bridge at Hartford, then proceed to trolley car.

4:40—Leave Atwater Ave. on trolley.

5:20—Arrival at Patrol Den.. Dismissal.

6:00—Boys home at hour promised.

## Starting the Hike

Every preparation is made, all plans worked out. At last the day for the hike is here. Whether it rains or shines you proceed to your meeting place. Any weather is Scouting weather.

You, as leader, arrive at the Patrol Den a little before the time set. Already some of the boys are probably there discussing the prospects of the hike. You are greeted by a loud "Hello" and get into the conversation immediately. "Harry hasn't showed up." "There is still time!" "Do you think Joe's coming?" "Certainly. He promised to!" And slowly the time creeps by until the watches say 8:20. All the boys are there now, properly dressed. Equipment packed. A short check-up is made to be sure that no matter of importance has been neglected. Then the Patrol is ready to start for the day's adventure.

The trolley car or bus or railroad which is to bring the Patrol outside of town is reached and the boys are soon "all aboard."

## "A Scout Is Courteous"

Too often criticisms are heard of Scouts not behaving properly while traveling in public vehicles. The excitement of the minute makes them talk loud, run up and down in the cars, behave as if they were wild animals just broken loose from the Zoo. Sometimes this behavior is due to nervous excitement. Very often, however, it is the boys' instinct to show off that makes them behave this way. Some-

times it is because they think people like to see a group of real live boys. As a matter of fact, people generally do. But the "real liveliness" may sometimes become nothing but impertinent nuisance and nobody ever admires that.

You can't keep a Patrol of boys quiet on a long trolley ride. But there isn't any reason why you shouldn't expect them to behave like gentlemen. A Scout is courteous. And one way of making people realize this is by showing the right conduct when the Patrol travels as a group.

Naturally it goes without saying that no member of the Patrol will remain in his seat if a lady or an elderly man is standing. But there are many other ways of showing courtesies. Refrain from too audible talking, singing, and other noises. Keep in your seats and don't run all over the place. When getting on and off don't crowd; do everything as quietly as possible.

It is not only on the trolley ride that courtesy is expected of a Patrol. Wherever it goes courtesy must go with it. And neither must any of the other Scout Laws be forgotten.

If a sign on the route says "Keep off" or "Private" or "No Trespassing," it means "Keep off," "Private" and "No Trespassing." Likewise you will remember that a gate is of no value if it isn't closed, that the owner of a piece of property has a reason for putting a fence or barbed wire around it, that cultivated fields aren't public highways and private fruit trees not for everybody's rifling.

By using common sense you can keep away from doing things which the general public may consider a breach of good behavior.

## Getting on the Road

At last the ride is ended and the boys swarm out of the trolley. The actual hiking begins.

Right here is a point to be definitely noted. Whatever kind of hike you are on, be sure it isn't a hitch hike. You and your Patrol aren't traveling country roads just for the sake of being picked up and carried along by some friendly motorist. You are hiking, to *hike*—not to see how fast you can get there. You are hiking to enjoy the trail and the exercise and fresh air, the things of interest and beauty around you. Discourage hitch hiking. It isn't hiking at all.

And let it also be said right here: A hike is not a race. You are not out to break any world records. You are out to have a joyous walk through beautiful country, to observe nature around you, to feel the freedom that only a group of live boys can feel. You are out to seek adventures and not to rush through a part of the country at top speed.

But even so, set your pace at the beginning. A steady pace that can be kept up throughout, only interrupted by interesting pauses. It is a mistake to stroll along in too leisurely fashion. Sauntering is the most tiring form of walking. A free, easy stride that will bring you forward about three miles an hour is what you ought to adopt. This is a good average speed. It won't tire you out and you feel that you 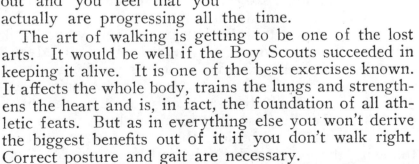 actually are progressing all the time.

The art of walking is getting to be one of the lost arts. It would be well if the Boy Scouts succeeded in keeping it alive. It is one of the best exercises known. It affects the whole body, trains the lungs and strengthens the heart and is, in fact, the foundation of all athletic feats. But as in everything else you won't derive the biggest benefits out of it if you don't walk right. Correct posture and gait are necessary.

In "The Boy Scout's Hike Book," Edward Cave says in regard to walking: "There is a technique in walking which distinguishes the pedestrian from the mere stroller. And every Scout should aspire to master it. . . . It is very simple. No study or hard practice is required. You do nothing more than eliminate a few faults and pay attention to a couple of details—and commence to walk with your head as well as with your feet. . . . The thing to do is seriously to take up pedestrianism, say once a week at the outside, and at that time give almost *your whole attention* to it. Simply start the practice of taking a walk, regularly, and invariably make this walk *like a pedestrian*. . . . Get into a habit of 'hitting it up.' . . . You will find that if you walk fast you naturally keep your shoulders down and chest up, and look straight ahead of you, instead of at the ground. You put your feet down almost flat, heel first, toes pointed straight ahead, and you keep your hands out of your pockets, because you have to swing your arms to make speed. . . . By walking 'against the watch' you are compelled to walk properly. And—the first thing you know you have formed a regular habit of walking correctly."

Take this point up with your boys. Have them train themselves at home in learning the right way of walking and everything will be easier for them when they get on the road.

## Don't Follow the Main Road

And by saying road, we do not mean the concrete main road that leads from town to town. It may be necessary for you to follow it for a short while until you get to a place where a by-path leads off to adventures, but get away from it as soon as possible.

There isn't much to see or learn on the main road. The automobiles are the same as you see in the city; the billboards advertise the same products as do the shop windows. And besides there is a danger point in following the main road which must be considered. The traffic is usually heavy and you must be on the lookout all the time.

If you must, for a time, follow the main road, keep always to the *left*. In several states there are laws which compel a pedestrian on all highways to walk facing the oncoming traffic. It ought to be considered the rule always. It is only by doing so that you are able to see and avoid possible dangers.

Beware of side roads where trucks constantly swing into or off the side road without signaling. Look out, also, at cross-roads. In approaching a cross-road always look to the left first, then to the right in crossing it.

## Starting the Adventure

The actual hike does not start before you have left the main road, before you get into the by-paths which, by the way, do not necessarily have to be paths.

The bank of a river, the shore of a lake, the ocean beach, the ridge of a hill, the old overgrown trail through the underbrush, even just a compass direction that will lead you cross country and through trying obstacles — all are inviting trails from which to choose.

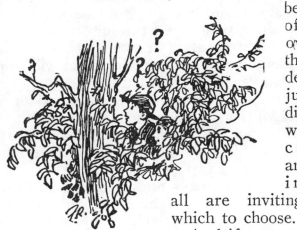

And if you are the right kind of a Patrol Leader your program of activities will start right there. Up to this point, the mere tramping part was the chief object but now you will put the emphasis on something else.

## Nature Study

Nature study will come first to your mind. Some Patrols go through forests with eyes that do not see. Your Patrol will be a seeing Patrol. The boys will discover trees they haven't identified before and renew their knowledge of old friends. They will notice the plants as they walk along, find animal tracks to follow, and maybe even see the birds and the animals themselves. It is for you to start them along these stimulating lines of discovery. Once started they will continue to make discoveries for themselves, unprompted.

## Scoutcraft Training

Also training for the Scout requirements has its place on the hike.

A lot of fun can be had out of signaling if the Patrol is divided in two groups that proceed at some distance from each other. Messages from one group to another will describe what is being discovered.

The compass directions can be explained and learned by the boys as they go along. Map-reading and map-making can be taught and judging may be taken up. And this is not all. By looking through the chapter on teaching the requirements (Chapter VI) you will find plenty of ideas to work in on the hike that will help your boys to advance in Scoutcraft.

If some of your boys are preparing for Merit Badges the Patrol hikes will bring them many opportunities for training and boys with special hobbies may satisfy them at will. Such hobbies may include sketching and photography, collecting of plants or making of leaf prints, plaster casting of tracks and gathering of minerals, to mention a few only of these possibilities. Be sure that all of the boys are actively occupied and interested on the hike.

## Beauty Along the Way

There are people who believe that boys do not have any appreciation of beauty. Quite the contrary. They have a keen appreciation of it but being boys, they just do not speak about it very often. A quiet spot near a babbling brook, a group of wind-lashed trees, a glorious sunset, fantastic cloud formations, a starlit sky may influence their moods deeply, even bring them to silent awe. Don't be afraid of bringing these things to their attention on the hike. But do not defeat your aims by declaiming: "Isn't that beautiful!" It must be done in a quiet natural way.

## Rests

After having hiked for some time you will find that your boys get tired. Some of them may start lagging behind, a little out of breath, yet dragging on as best they can. They do not want to ask for a rest for fear of being considered weaklings. As soon as you see signs of weariness, call a halt. Even better it will be if you call for the rest before the definite signs show.

For untrained hikers it may be necessary to stop after about every half hour of hiking, to have them get back their breath and relax. Trained hikers can walk longer distances without feeling tired.

A good rule to follow is to let a short rest period follow each hour of steady hiking. And let them *be really short*—three to five minutes, seldom more. Too long rests stiffen the leg muscles which have been limbered up during the walking and make it difficult to get started again. Also if the boys are hot and perspiring a long rest period will cool them too much and may result in somebody's getting a chill. Get going again before anybody is cold. As a general rule it may be said that you get farther and with less effort if you walk steadily and with short rests than if you travel by quick spurts and long rests.

During the rests have the boys lie down. The best position for them to take is with the back on the ground and the legs vertically against a tree, a stump, a fence or other object. Then try to have them move the legs slowly for a few minutes as though pedaling an imaginary bicycle. On getting up  again they will be surprised to find how easy it is now to go on.

"The theory is that the blood gets down into the legs and the heart is taxed to the limit to keep up u good flow while walking. Lying on the back and moving the legs causes the blood to flow back easily, be re-vitalized in the lungs and thus refresh the fatigued muscles." (J. W. Benson in The "How" Book of Scouting.)

## Drinking Water

If water is near at hand during the rest periods you will see the boys swarm toward it to get their thirst quenched. Stop them, for several reasons.

One reason is that if they start drinking they will get thirsty very soon again and continue to be in a state of thirstiness throughout the hike. Instead of drinking, it is far better to suck a small pebble. This stimulates the salivary glands and keeps the mouth moist all the time.

Another reason, and a more important one, is that the water may be contaminated by decayed organic matter or by germs related to different diseases such as typhoid fever, diarrhoea and dysentary. The looks of the water doesn't prove anything as to its purity. It may look like the purest crystal clear spring water and yet contain poisonous matter. *Don't ever touch water when you aren't perfectly sure that it is fit for drinking.*

If the water from a certain well is used by the people living in the vicinity you may feel assured that it is all right, also if you can secure information about its purity from the local health authorities. If you can't, be on your guard. Don't take any chances.

If you absolutely need water and aren't sure as to its purity you will have to sterilize it.

One way of doing this is by boiling it hard for *twenty* minutes to kill the germs. After cooling it, it is fit for drinking even if the boiling of it has also taken away the biggest part of its refreshing quality.

Another way and an easier way is by treating the water with certain chemicals that destroy the impurities. A few of these treatments are described as follows:

1—*Calcium Hypochlorite* (Chloride of Lime).

    a. Powdered *Calcium hypochlorite* may be had at any drugstore in small cans. Mix one level teaspoonful of the powder with a little water into a paste and dissolve this in one quart of water. Stir every once in a while for an hour. Let the undissolved part settle and pour the clear liquid off into bottles. Bring a small bottle of this along and put *one* teaspoonful of the solution into *two* gallons of water for disinfection. Let it stand *at least* 30 *minutes* before using.

    b. Powdered *Calcium hypochlorite* in small glass ampules containing one gram (15 grains) may be had from camping outfit stores or chemical supply firms. Break one ampule and dissolve its contents in one quart of water. Use two teaspoonfuls of this strong solution for disinfecting *quart* of drinking water. Allow it to *stand at least* 30 *minutes before using.*

2—*"Zonite,"* a liquid manufactured by "Zonite" Co., New York City. May be had at any drug store. Mix one teaspoonful of "Zonite" with nine teaspoonfuls of water and use one teaspoonful of this solution to disinfect one gallon of drinking water. Let it stand *at least* 30 *minutes before using.*

3—*"Halazone"* tablets manufactured by Abbott Laboratories, Chicago, Ill. May be had at any drug store. Dissolve one tablet in one quart of drinking water to be disinfected. Allow it to stand *at least* 30 *minutes before using.*

All of these processes require at least half an hour's halt.

If you aren't sure of the water in the part of the country through which the hike will bring you and if you don't want to use your time waiting for water to be disinfected, it would be a good idea to bring along from the city a couple of canteens with drinking water to be used on the road. As soon as you get to your camp site you will find time to prepare bigger quantities of drinking water if necessary.

Whichever way you obtain your drinking water explain to your boys that the way to drink on a hike is by drinking just a little at a time and as slowly as possible. This gives the maximum of refreshment. Many hikers recommend the using of the first mouthful for filling the mouth only and by shaking the head getting the water into all corners of the mouth. Later they drink two or three mouthfuls and are ready to continue.

If refreshment is necessary, stick to water. Do not allow any stopping to buy soda water or to bombard every roadside shop for ice cream. These things have no place on a Scout hike. They only serve to make the boys so much more thirsty afterwards.

## Arriving at the Lunch Spot

The road having been properly covered, the Patrol arrives at the spot decided upon for lunch.

As soon as they get there, have the boys take off their haversacks and arrange them in a line on the ground close together, the so-called "duffel-line." Keep

the haversacks there as long as the Patrol stays on the spot. This is the first point of orderliness and orderliness must be insisted upon in everything the Patrol does. Don't let anything be spread around on the ground. No paper, no axes, no eating utensils. Everything must be kept together. Make somebody responsible for seeing that this is strictly followed.

If this is a Sandwich Hike the boys will now unpack their foodstuff and start eating. If it is a Chop Hike, the first thing to do is to get fires going before the preparing of the meal takes place.

The first few Chop Hikes will provide training in the Second Class requirements for fire making and cooking without utensils. Suggestions as to how this training may take place are discussed in the chapter on "Patrol Instruction", while menu ideas are provided on page 197. Therefore here we shall only touch a few of the high spots.

## Preparing the Meal

Before the boys start fire-making, have them decide upon a spot. (Don't permit them to spread themselves over a too big area). Have them clear the ground and use the spade to dig up the sods in order not to kill the vegetation (see Page 149) and be perfectly sure that all fire hazards are eliminated. You can't risk the starting of a forest fire that may destroy valuable timber. Look around carefully. Have water within easy reach and have also present a few leafy branches with which to beat down any fire which might begin to spread in the grass. Let the boys be sure that they have collected enough wood before they start the fire.

Insist that they clean their hands before touching any foodstuff.

Then just let them go ahead having their fun in preparing their primitive meal.

After having passed the Second Class Requirement in cooking the boys will start on their First Class test. They will bring along in their equipment the necessary utensils (Page 203) and will start preparing regular meals. This is the most favored way of making a lunch on a one-day hike and by sticking to this kind of cooking for a few months you may expect your Scouts to develop themselves into real cooks. Be sure, though, that they don't stick to the same recipes the whole time. Have them try as many different things as possible because only in this way will they develop a general cooking ability.

The next step will be to go in for regular Patrol cooking on the one-day hikes. This constitutes actual training for the Patrol camping and until it is mastered, Patrol camps will not be the successes which they ought to be.

By Patrol cooking is meant the preparing of a complete meal for the complete Patrol by means of the Patrol cooking utensils.

This naturally necessitates the getting hold of the necessary equipment but it also necessitates the development of a special Patrol organization in order to do it in the most efficient way. The organization will consist in dividing the Patrol up into groups of which one will do the actual cooking while others will take care of getting the water and firewood, keeping the fire going and looking out for other details.

This organization is created on one-day hikes where training for camp takes place. Since this is a matter of special value for the camp it will be discussed fully in the Patrol Camping Chapter.

In Patrol cooking the whole Patrol will naturally be served at one time. In individual cooking the boys will eat their meal as they get it ready. Yet the boys ought to follow the same scheme in order to try to have the different meals ready at the same time. It will increase the fun of the hike if the Scouts can have their meal together instead of eating separately. The latter rather too much suggests a dog gnawing his solitary bone. Scouting is social and companionable.

As soon as the eating is over the boys will clear up their fire sites, put out the fires and replace the sods so that no trace is left.

The washing of the dishes may take place with cold water, the bottom side of a sod being used for scouring. On the other hand the boys may be told to heat a little water in their pots before putting out the fire and clean their dishes and the pot itself with the hot water.

### Rest After the Meal.

When everything has been cleared up a rest period will follow. A rest after each meal before starting to exercise again is a great help for the digestion and ought to be lived up to in the Patrol.

Get the crowd started as they rest on a discussion of the hike, of the afternoon's program or plans for the future, just a sort of a friendly chattering.

You will tell by the boys themselves when this rest period has lasted long enough. One gets up, another follows. A general signal for starting something.

### Patrol Games

Try a couple of lively games. Any kind of a tag will do, especially if the camp site presents a number of natural obstacles. Any game in which the Patrol is divided up into two groups each of which tries to become the winner is good. You will probably remember some from school, besides those which you will find in your Handbook for Boys.

An hour will easily run by in fun and laughter and before you know it, it will be time to start the return trip.

## Check up on Camp Site

Before starting for home there is one very important thing which must be done. You must make sure that the camp site has been cleaned perfectly.

Have the boys form a line spread out across the site. They must just be close enough together to be able to observe every square inch of the ground. Give a signal and have them move slowly forward picking up anything no matter how small it may be, that could tell that human beings had been on the spot. After having gone over the camp site in this thorough manner you and the Patrol may rest assured that all is shipshape. Then you are ready for the home trip.

## Returning

Do not use for your return trip the same route which you covered on the way out. Try to leave a way open for fresh discoveries and adventure.

In returning much depends upon the surroundings. You will usually find that it is difficult to get the boys going again on nature study or training for requirements, unless something special turns up. The climax of the day has been reached in the preparing and eating of the meal. From the dish washing to the minute you reach home enthusiasm is likely to slacken. Therefore, it is necessary to stimulate it by trying to put some extra interesting features into the return trip.

This may be done by laying the route through interesting places. It may be done by getting the boys started telling of their school experiences, or of their favorite sports, their baseball team, anything they like to talk about. But it may also be done by trying to get a song under way. Maybe the good old ones like "Clementine," "Old McDonald," "Three Good Turns"; maybe some of the latest song hits. Here's where your "Cheermaster," if you have one, will be useful. Get the crowd started on something and the road will be shortened, everything will proceed smoothly and the boys will be getting home in high spirits.

Maybe you will want them to come to the Patrol Den for the dismissal. Maybe you will just say "good-bye" and leave them at the trolley. It doesn't make any difference what plan you follow as long as they get home in the time that was set for their return.

And if they get home happy and tired, but not exhausted, you may count the day as a success.

## OTHER KINDS OF HIKES

The hike described above is a typical one-day Patrol hike. It includes a number of activities and will prove of general interest to the boys.

But naturally the same program for a hike can't be used indefinitely. Variety is needed to keep up interest and very much depends upon the ingenuity of the Patrol Leader in inventing new kinds of hikes and putting new ideas into every one of them.

In the Handbook for Scoutmasters, Scout Executive, F. F. Gray, of Montclair, N. J., has given a number of hike ideas. Some of them are best fitted for Troop purposes. Others can be used equally well by a Patrol as by a larger group. Here are some of the most suitable.

*Nature Study Hikes.* Careful preparation is necessary. Try, if possible, to have an expert accompany the

Patrol on the hike. Note-taking, observation and comparison, specimen collecting, sketching, and the camera are the usual methods of study.

*Compass Hikes.* Conducted entirely by compass. It can be combined with the map, night, storm, adventure, exploration and other hikes. In a strictly compass hike, the course should be carefully laid out in advance on paper.

*Tracking and Trailing Hikes.* Requires one or two Scouts to lay the trail or make the tracks, the rest of the Patrol to follow. The exercise of much ingenuity is possible on this hike in developing surprises, novelties and interesting problems.

*Map Hikes.* Map reading should precede map making. The hike is made entirely by map, and preferably cross country. Map reading along a straight road requires little skill. Map making hikes should be short, and careful notes should be taken. Later on, this hike can be supplemented by the camera.

*Signal Hikes.* Are conducted entirely by signals. This hike can be combined, later on, with a night hike or a compass hike. Of course, signaling can be made useful on almost any kind of hike, but this particular kind of hike is one of specialization.

*Night Hikes* are novel. The night world is so different from that of the day that the strangeness lends interest and romance to the hike.

*Storm Hikes,* of course, require special opportunity and necessitate careful preparation. Learning to travel under adverse conditions happily and safely is the important feature.

*Adventure Hikes* afford abundant opportunity to cultivate common sense and good judgment. The hikers

may separate into groups of two, and come together at some prearranged place and time, to exchange stories around the camp fire. This style of hike is especially useful in driving home the fact that life is full of interesting situations if we but look for them.

*The Good Turn Hikes* take the boys out singly, or in pairs, for a definite time, looking specifically for opportunities to do Good Turns. They should return and report at a given time. A variety of experience will be encountered. Interesting and novel matters on the subject of the Good Turn is sure to come up. The boys' reports should be written, not oral.

*The Exploration Hike* is taken over country new to the Scouts. A cave, a mountain, or a lake furnishes interesting objectives. It should be as full of surprises as possible and may be either cross-country or along back roads, trails, water courses, paths, a canal or other unusual routes. This type of hike often develops many unsuspected points of beauty or interest in near-by places. It can also be combined with the travel or the compass hike.

*The Game Hike* is made with the intention of spending the greater part of the day in playing Flag Raiding or similar games. The games should be arranged in advance, although the hikers need not be acquainted with the details until the play begins.

*The Treasure Hunt* is similar in many ways to the tracking and trailing hike, with an objective—the treasure—added. At the end may be not only the "Treasure" but a lunch or some other pleasant surprise. To be classed as a hike the Treasure Hunt must be at least a mile in length and should cover as great a variety of territory as possible.

*The Fourteen Mile Hike* comes under the First Class requirements. The ideal hike of this kind is, in as large a measure as possible, a review of the chief features of Scouting practice. Few can take this hike properly without considerable experience in hiking.

*A Starvation Hike* requires previous experience and

practical knowledge concerning edible plants, roots, berries, nuts, fruits, etc., to be found growing wild along the probable course of the hike. Mushrooms should be entirely avoided, in fact they have but little food value. The annual death toll of mushrooms mounts beyond that of hunting.

*History Hikes* are taken to points of particular historical interest. Where practical, the hikers often enjoy attempting to re-enact some feature.

*Camera Hikes* teach choice of subjects, methods and general practice. The conservation of films also demands thought. There should be a good reason behind the taking of any picture. Of course, the Scouts should learn to develop their own pictures when possible.

*Fathers' and Sons' Hikes* deserve particular mention. When the Patrol has had some hiking experience invite the fathers to go along with their boys on a real Scouting Hike. Go exploring, show the fathers some of your Scout dexterities, make them a real outdoor dinner. You will find that the fathers as well as the boys will enjoy such a hike immensely.

# CHAPTER VIII.

## PATROL CAMPING

THE outdoor part of Scouting fascinates the boys. The hikes that bring them out into nature have their absolute approval, but after all the experience which they are most looking forward to from the day you start the Patrol is—*Camp*.

Camp is a world that is filled with adventure to every real boy. It stands for freedom, fun and adventure. Unlucky is the Scout who hasn't had his taste of camp life.

One of your greatest services as a Patrol Leader is to try to make your Patrol into a *Camping Patrol,* trained in the ways of the experienced *campers*. This takes time. It takes also patience and perseverance. But it can be done, and you are well under way toward doing it, the day you have made your boys into real *hikers* as described in the previous chapter.

Camping is really just an advanced form of hiking. The planning has to be more elaborate. The amount of equipment necessary is increased. Sleeping out under primitive conditions enters into it, making things more complicated. Yet the general plan and purpose are the same. In camping as well as in hiking you must follow the same safety precautions, you must decide upon your time and your place, means of getting there, ways of filling the day with a varied program and the like.

The Patrol hikes are all training for the greater adventure—the Patrol Camp.

## When to Start Patrol Camping

Two things are required before the Patrol starts its camping.

1. The Patrol must be in possession of the *equipment* necessary.

2. You, as the Patrol Leader, must be in possession of the *experience* necessary.

Equipment is specially necessary for the inexperienced camper. An old camper may go out in the wilderness, build his own shelters of material found on the spot and spend the night in comfort. But it wouldn't be wise to take out beginners on an adventure of this kind. It might forever set them against camp life.

However, it isn't necessary that much new equipment be purchased for the first few camping trips. Cooking

 utensils may be taken from the homes. Most families have extra blankets that the boys may bring along. Just one thing must be gotten: the tent. But how? That is the problem which must be solved.

A certain Patrol Leader was asked by his boys: "When do we go camping?" His answer came back with a snap: "The day we have earned the money to get our own tent!"

And this is precisely the right attitude.

You may be able to borrow a tent from another Patrol or from the Troop. Maybe some well-meaning philanthropist might even think of presenting your Patrol with one. Resist the temptation. Such a tent would never be more than just a tent, while a tent earned by the Patrol itself will be a treasure in which every boy will be proud to share ownership.

In this case as in many other cases it is not the path of least resistance that takes you the farthest.

If you encourage your Patrol to earn and save its pennies and make its own equipment you will be building Patrol Spirit and traditions at the same time, which as we have said elsewhere is vitally important.

Just imagine what an incentive it is for your Scouts to know that "we go camping the day we have earned our own tent." It will make them work to achieve the

adventures. If you are the right kind of a Patrol Leader you will start the work early. If you begin your preparations for camping soon after the start of the Patrol the equipment will be there the day the Patrol is ready to go camping. Start a special equipment fund. Inspire your boys to bring pennies they earn by their own small jobs, take up Patrol Handicraft (see Chapter IX), and find other ways of earning Patrol money.

The day the tent is acquired you may go camping. Later on the Patrol will earn and get together its own cooking utensils and other things that will make the equipment complete.

## Different Types of Camping

The equipment necessary and the experience required of you as the leader depend entirely upon the type of camping which the Patrol is undertaking. So let us, before starting the more detailed description, look at the different types which we will have to consider:

*A Short-Term Camp* is a combination of hike and camping, the camp extending one or two nights. The Patrol will hike to a suitable camping site, pitch the camp, make its meals, have its camp fire, sleep in tents or under shelters through the night, and hike back to the town in the afternoon.

A *Standing Camp* is a Camp extending over more than three days and two nights, a complete camp being put up with all possible camp improvements and with a definite daily schedule, including all phases of camp life.

A *Travelling Camp* is a moving camp. Every morning or every other morning camp is broken and moved to some other place. Here the camp is again put up, one or more days are spent in exploring and real camp life, then again the whole camp moves on. This is the most difficult kind of camping. It needs well trained boys and exceedingly good leaders. While in the Standing Camp the daily varied routine constitutes the life of the campers, in the Travelling Camp the big thing is the hike, the seeing of other places, the exploring of unknown territory. Travelling Camps may be on foot, on bicycles, horseback, by automobile or in boat or canoes.

And now for the planning and the carrying out of the three types.

## THE SHORT-TERM CAMP

### Your Experience

As the Patrol works on getting its outfit together you must do all you can to increase your experience. There is a certain standard you must live up to, a certain minimum of Scouting experience which you must have before your Scoutmaster permits you to take out the Patrol on a camping hike.

1. *You must have earned your First Class Badge.*

2. (*a*) You must have taken part in at least two Troop Camping hikes and one Patrol Leaders' camping hike (conducted by the Scoutmaster) or have had the experience of at least one week in a Standard Boy Scout Camp.

(*b*) You must have undertaken at least five one day hikes with your Patrol to the satisfaction of your Scoutmaster.

3. *You must have had at least* three *months' experience as a successful Patrol Leader.*

And furthermore before starting on any Camping Hike

4. *You must have the written consent of the parents of each boy.*

5. *You must have a reasonable familiarity with the country to be covered* and the camp site to be used.

6. *You must have the permission of the property owner to* make camp, *to build fires and cook.*

By looking back on the experience necessary for you as a hike leader (page 187) and comparing with the above you will see that several points are the same while others make greater demands. The added requirements necessary for the camp leader are printed above in upright type.

As in the case of the first hikes a Patrol undertakes, the Scoutmaster or an Assistant will go along with the Patrol and help it through its first camping adventures. You will find it a tremendous help in the beginning to have an adult present to help you meet the small difficulties that will arise because of your boys' lacking experience. A good Patrol Leader is never unwilling to take the advice of others.

## Planning the Short-Term Camp

If planning was necessary in order to turn a hike into a success, planning is ten-fold more necessary to get the best out of camping. In fact the planning and preparing may be said to be two-thirds of successful camping.

The planning takes place at the Patrol meetings.

Every detail must be considered. And again we will apply our old formula:

> *What?*
> *Where?*
> *When?*
> *How?*

## What?

The what part is easily determined upon. "Camping" is the answer to that. Or in more detail: a hike to a suitable camping site, setting up the camp, sleeping on the spot, making the meals, and hiking back to town.

Signaling, tracking and other Scout activities may be put into the hike and be used for training in the camp. But those are all of less importance.

*Camping is, first of all, training in camping.*

## Where?

On the ideal camp site naturally.

You may have heard the formula. Still you may not remember it, so here goes:

In its simplest form it is:

*Shelter, water, wood!*

In fact those are the things of prime importance, things first to consider. Those three sum up the necessary requisites of a camp site, though naturally other factors enter into the choice of an *ideal* site. To elaborate the formula, the following considerations may be urged.

### The Ideal Site

The ideal site is a fairly open spot, elevated enough to avoid possible fog which may rise from waters in its neighborhood, level, or even better, a little slanting, to afford natural drainage. Grass-covered, sandy, or gravelly soils is what you will look for. Three things you will avoid—*Clay,* because the grass which covers it will soon wear off and rain will make it muddy and filled with small puddles—*Loose Sand,* because it gets in everywhere spoiling your food and filling your clothes—*Rich Vegetation of Grass,* because it indicates waterfilled, damp ground, mosquitoes a-plenty and a dew-fall that will not evaporate during the day.

Your ideal spot will have shelter against the prevailing winds. Trees will furnish this. They will cover the western and northern side of the site exposing the camp to the sun during the early hours of the day. You will want trees around your camp but you won't want to camp immediately under them, especially not in rain. They may seem to shelter you from the rain but the trouble is that dripping from the trees will continue several hours after the rain has passed and it will take hours for the tents to dry. Another disadvantage about camping under trees is that some trees have the inconvenient habit of dropping their dead branches—a trick that may prove a misfortune to a camper.

Water you will want within a reasonable distance. Not only for drinking purposes but also for bathing. But play safe in regard to water. Read again what is said in regard to drinking water in the chapter on Patrol Hikes (page 214) and insist on using the safety devices and precautions. For bathing you must test the spot to find out if any traps are lurking. Always remember: Safety First.

Wood for fuel and for camp implements must be present in sufficient quantity. A camp site can't be called ideal if wood has to be carried to it from afar.

So much about the camp site itself. Another thing that plays its part is the surrounding country.

The place should be in the midst of beauty and picturesqueness and far enough away from human beings to secure privacy. If visitors swarm over the camp grounds there will be little real camping going on, and if the site is too close to main-roads with their hot dog stands and billboards you may be sure that visitors will arrive. Also in order to be considered ideal the camp site mustn't be so far away from your home town that it is not easily accessible without too much time and too much money spent on the traveling.

## How to Find the Place

The ideal camp site is hard to find. Some people insist that it only exists in the imagination. Still you may be able to find it and *get permission to use it*. This last point is a thing which may keep even the best camping site out of your reach. If the owner puts down special restrictions for the use of his property be sure to adhere to them strictly.

By the time that the Patrol is ready to start its camping it ought to know where the best camp sites in the surrounding country are to be found. Your Hikemaster, if you have one, will help there. During the one-day hikes you are certain to have found several suitable places, and the Hikemaster will have kept notes of them to make sure that they won't be forgotten.

## When?

Again as was the case when discussing one-day outdoorings we must take into consideration whether your group consists of schoolboys or boys who work.

School boys are generally free from Friday afternoon until Monday morning, w h i l e working boys have sometimes only the Saturday evening and Sunday at their disposal, though in some cases they may have the Saturday afternoon off.

For school boys only it will therefore be seen that the answer to the When? is: From Friday afternoon to Saturday evening with one night's camping. Or in case church attendance can be arranged for (see page 191): From Friday afternoon to Sunday evening making it a two-nights' camping trip.

If the Patrol consists entirely of working boys the answer must be: From Saturday night to Sunday evening, the boys getting together and leaving for camp as early Saturday night as possible. This will usually mean that they can't arrive at the camp site before it is getting dark which is a great disadvantage especially if the Patrol consists of untrained campers. If there should happen to be boys in the Patrol who get off early in the day it ought to be arranged that they go out to the site in the afternoon, put up the tents, build the fireplace and have everything ready when the rest of the Patrol arrives in the evening.

The same will be the case if the Patrol is a mixture of school boys and boys at work. In this case the school boys may even go out Friday, spend one night in camp, make everything ready to receive the city group Saturday evening and spend the second night with their larder working comrades.

In any event a time must be fixed for the start and for the return of the boys on the camping trip, and this must be strictly followed. Sticking precisely to program is one of the things that make parents believe in Scouting.

## How?

In the preparing for camp your Patrol organization will be put to its severest test and you will have a chance to find out if the organization actually works.

As was the case with the one-day outdoorings the planning of camp is done at the Patrol meetings. Here the most important things are decided upon, but not all the details are worked out here. These are considered by the boys whose job it is to take care of special Patrol routine matters.

At the Patrol meeting you all decide upon time and place (this, after conference with Hikemaster) and personal equipment necessary. Everything else is assigned to small committees consisting of one or two boys. It cannot be too often repeated, also, that naturally the Scoutmaster must approve your plans.

What has to be done before the Patrol can start on a camping hike amounts to the following:

(a) *Consent* must be procured from the parents.
(b) *Money* for transportation and eats must be collected at meeting preceding the camping hike.
(c) *Foodstuff* must be bought and distributed among the boys.
(d) *Patrol equipment* must be gotten together and distributed among the boys.

## Organizing the Patrol for Camp

Each of these duties will be assigned to the boys that are best able to do the particular jobs. If the Patrol organization (see Chapter IV) is in action the jobs are easily distributed. If not, a special camping organization must be developed. But certainly, by the time that the Patrol is ready to go camping, the real organization ought to be fairly well worked out. Therefore in the following pages we shall develop the camping organization on the basis of the one already in action inside the Patrol.

Let us start by making up a list of the boys in your organization. This is what you have:

Patrol Leader                  Quartermaster
Assistant Patrol Leader        Hikemaster
Treasurer                      Grubmaster
Scribe                         Cheermaster

The object now is to distribute two of these boys to every one of the four points mentioned above in such a way that their natural abilities and the work they have been doing in the Patrol will insure the greatest efficiency.

By taking the four points consecutively you will arrive at the following results:

(a) *Parents' Consent.* You, as *Patrol Leader,* are the one who has had most to·do with the parents of all of your boys. Therefore the most natural thing for you to do is to personally supervise the collecting of the written forms of consent, from the boys' parents. If any difficulties arise you will be the one to straighten them out. You may also have to help the boys  getting their personal equipment together from their home. The other boy to put on the job is the *Scribe.*

He is the one to whom all written matter generally goes. So let him get the consents together in co-operation with you.

(b)  *Money*.  The *Treasurer* will take care of this. But before starting to collect he must naturally know how big the expenses are going to be.  Therefore he must consult with the Hikemaster who knows about the transportation costs and the Grubmaster who plans the menu. He needs a helper. Let him work together with the *Hikemaster* with whom he already has made his connection.

(c) *Foodstuff*.  This is the job of the *Grubmaster*. But it being a thing of prime importance for the suc-

cess of the trip he will need the very best help and advice. Have the *Assistant Patrol Leader* go to his rescue. The two of them will be able to handle the job satisfactorily. They must work in close connection with the Treasurer who provides them with the money for the necessary purchases.

(d)  *Patrol Equipment*.  This matter is managed by the *Quartermaster* in co-operation with the last boy in the Patrol, the *Cheermaster*.

In looking over the above it will be found that group (b) and (c) are very much inter-linked.  The money part enters into both of them and consequently it will be necessary for the two groups to work together. Also it will be found that the job of getting the equipment together may be a rather big one.  The two boys handling it may need the help of others.  Therefore in our final make-up of the organization we will take all of this in consideration and show the groups as they will probably work together.

| GROUP A | GROUP B |
|---|---|
| *Consents and Equipment* | *Expenditures* |
| Consents — Patrol Leader, Scribe | Collecting and Travel — Treasurer, Hikemaster |
| Equipment—Quartermaster, Cheermaster | Food—Grubmaster, Assistant Patrol Leader |

This is the organization for the preparing of the camping hike. But before we go into the necessary details of equipment, food and the rest, we must look ahead.

Preparing the camp is one thing. Establishing the camp is something entirely different, but it also necessitates an organization of the Patrol in order to be accomplished with the greatest possible efficiency. Naturally we do not want to make a number of organizations. The one we make must be able to cover the preparing for camp as well as the camp itself. If it doesn't, it is no good. This point can be easily tested.

Let us just look at the duties which have to be attended to at the arrival at the camp site. They fall into two divisions.

For convenience and brevity we will list these two groups of activities as "Tenting" and "Cooking" though there is more to Group One than merely setting up tents and more to Group Two than merely preparing "grub." Roughly, the two divisions cover the following:

(1) *Tenting,* pitching tents, preparing beds, making latrine and other sanitary measures. In other words, making the camp site habitable.

(2) *Cooking.* Building fireplace, collecting wood, getting water, making fire and the actual cooking.

These two divisions are covered perfectly by the organizations as worked out above.

The "Tenting" part will be undertaken by Group A which is already taking care of the equipment with the

Patrol Leader in charge, while the "Cooking" part is given over to Group B under the leadership of the Assistant Patrol Leader.

As soon as the different jobs are assigned to the Scouts they go ahead performing their duties.

Some of these duties, like securing the consent of the parents, collecting the money necessary and getting the equipment together, can be done some time in advance, while buying the foodstuff and purchasing transportation tickets will be done shortly before the camping hike is started.

## Parents' Consent

At one of the Patrol meetings preceding the trip you will ask the boys to be sure to bring a written permission to go camping signed by their parents along with them at the next meeting. This permission will be similar to the one required for one-day hikes (see page 193) only including sleeping out as well.

You will have your Scribe collect and file these permissions as soon as they come in. Some boys may not bring them before the day the hike is started. It doesn't make any difference when they come in. Just be sure that they are all there by the time that the Patrol starts its adventure.

## Money

The amount of money necessary is settled by a get-together of the Treasurer, the Hikemaster, the Grubmaster and the Assistant Patrol Leader. They decide upon purchases which have to be made, get the price of transportation, add all expenses together and divide it by the number of boys in the Patrol.

Is it necessary to mention that they will make it as economical as possible?

The price of the trip is announced to the boys and the Treasurer collects the money at the meeting preceding the hike in order to be able to buy the necessary material.

## Foodstuff

As soon as a menu has been decided upon the Grubmaster will work out a list of ingredients and start his purchasing.

Meat, bread, butter, eggs, and fresh vegetables will be left to be bought at the last minute, while things that keep well, such as sugar, flour, salt, beans, etc., will be bought at the earliest convenience.

The Assistant Patrol Leader will help to purchase the foodstuff, putting it into the Patrol provision bags and distribute these to the Scouts of the Patrol.

## Equipment

The equipment for a camping trip must be given some real thought especially if the trip includes any amount of hiking. Tents, cooking utensils, foodstuffs together with the personal equipment for a comfortable night in the open weigh, and often weigh heavily. The art of equipping the Patrol consists in taking just *enough* along with you and not one piece of unnecessary equipment.

In the following are described both a personal and a Patrol equipment which have stood their tests. By experimenting you may find out that you do not use certain of the things on the hikes which you undertake. Then leave them at home. On the other hand, you may find that weather conditions at the place where the camp site is situated necessitate things being added to the list. Go ahead and do so. But do not forget that every ounce feels like a pound if you have to carry it for hours.

Neither the personal nor the Patrol equipment mentioned below are gotten together in one day. They are the result of working and saving on the part of every member of the Patrol. They constitute the goal toward which every Patrol will work thereby developing the spirit and the stick-togetherness of the Patrol as a unit. Not only will the Patrol try to earn its own money to be able to buy its own equipment, but it will also try its hand at the actual making of equipment. Help in this direction is given in the chapter on Patrol Handicraft. There you will find the making of many of the things mentioned in the following, described.

When making or purchasing be sure that the boys get the same kind of equipment. Uniformity is very much to be desired, not only for the looks of it but also for its value to the Patrol Spirit. A haversack packed in correct manner ought to advertise loudly enough: "I belong to the Leaping Wolf Patrol" (or whatever the name may be).

## Personal Equipment

On page 241 is given the complete list of the articles necessary on a short term camping trip. Several of the things were discussed while speaking of Patrol Hikes (Chapter VII). The reason for others listed will be found obvious. Left for consideration then is the haversack and the packing of it, as rather special problems.

### The Haversack

Not every haversack will do for camping purposes. There are some definite requirements which it must pass in order to fit the needs of the case.

First of all, it must naturally be *big enough* to contain the necessary amount of equipment. A small haversack will never do for camping purposes. The best way to find the size of haversack which you will require is by getting all of your camping material together and arranging it in the way you would if you

## Personal Equipment

*Complete Scout Uniform*
1 *Haversack*
2 *Blankets or Sleeping Bag*
1 *Poncho or Raincoat*
1 *Clothes Bag containing*:

| | |
|---|---|
| 1 change of Underwear | 1 pair of Pajamas |
| 1 Sweater or Pull-Over | 1 Bathing Suit |
| 1 pair of Stockings | 2 Handkerchiefs |

1 *Mess Bag containing*:

| | |
|---|---|
| 1 Flat Plate | 1 Fork |
| 1 Deep Plate | 1 Spoon |
| 1 Knife | 1 Teaspoon |

1 Dish Towel

1 *Toilet Bag containing*:
1 Piece of Soap in Container
1 Toothbrush in Celluloid Container
1 Tube of Tooth Paste
1 Metal Mirror
1 Towel

1 *Shoe Bag containing*:
1 pair of extra Shoes or Sneakers

1 *Repair Bag containing*:

| | |
|---|---|
| Needles | Safety Pins |
| Thread and Darning Cotton | Buttons |

1 *Cup*

*In outside pocket of haversack or uniform*:

| | |
|---|---|
| 1 Sterilized Bandage | Notebook and Pencil |
| String | Matches in Water- |
| Knife | proof Container |

*If wanted*:

| | |
|---|---|
| Camera | Flashlight |
| Scoutcraft Supplies | Musical Instruments |
| Maps | Canteen |
| Compass | Handbook for Boys |

had the haversack there. Tie a few pieces of string around it and measure its dimensions. If other members in your Patrol are going to purchase haversacks you will help them in the same way.

But the size isn't all. There are other tests of the good haversack.

It must be *light*. The rest of the equipment being heavy enough, naturally you want the haversack light. But the lightness must never be sacrificed for *strength* and *waterproof quality*. The material must be heavy enough and closely woven enough to keep out even the heaviest rainstorm.

One more thing indicates the good haversack. It *rides well*. A pack that rolls from one side to another as you walk along is absolutely no good for your purpose. Neither is one that hangs on the upper part of your back. It makes you round shouldered and tires you out very soon. Part of the weight of the pack falls naturally on the shoulders because of the shoulder straps but the pack ought to come low enough so as to place the biggest part of the weight on the back of the hips. The hips and shoulders constitute the support (no other part of the back). Also be sure that the two shoulder straps are broad enough (so that they will not cut into the shoulders) and that they join each other at the centre of the top of the pack.

In brief these are the requirements: The haversack must be:

(1) *of sufficient size,* (2) *light,* (3) *strong,* (4) *waterproof and* (5) *well balanced and supported by shoulders and hips.*

The Official Camp-O-Sack, which was especially designed for Patrol Camping, lives up to these specifications. Other models are available as for example, the "Comfort" pack, the "Rover" pack, the "Duluth" pack, the "Adirondack Pack Basket" and "Pack Boards." The choosing of a haversack isn't an easy matter. Individual taste enters into it and you may have to experiment a bit before you get your taste satisfied. If you want to make your own haversack you will find directions in Chapter IX for making the Official Camp-O-Sack before mentioned. It is almost sure to meet with your approval.

## Packing the Pack

The art of filling a haversack in such a way that all its advantages are made use of is called packing. This seems to be a rather difficult art to acquire if you look at the many ways in which it may be done. Yet as is the case with all other arts, it becomes easy the minute you discover the secret.

Certain rules govern right packing. We may express them thus:

(1) *Soft padding should be placed at the part of the pack which rests against the wearer's back.*

(2) *There must be a definite position for every piece of equipment.*

(3) *Things that belong to the same class (as, for example, fork, knife, spoon, plate, or soap, nail-brush, towel), should be grouped together.*

(4) *No small articles should lie loose in the pack.*

(5) *You must be able to get at the rain clothing without exposing the rest of the equipment.*

(6) *Pack must not rattle when moved.*

All of these problems are solved by using the "Bags within Bag" system. This means that the pack is to be considered one big bag into which smaller bags containing the different pieces of equipment, as shown in the equipment list on page 241 are fitted.

These smaller bags take up very little space as they are made out of thin linen or canvas. They are easily manufactured by the boys themselves (see Handicraft Chapter) and they are inexpensive—pieces from a discarded sheet or cheap 5 and 10 cent store material can be used.

They are easy to get hold of and they have many advantages.

*First* of all, it is far easier to pack the smaller bags than to fit everything into one big empty space. *Secondly,* in order to get at, for example, your toilet articles, it isn't necessary to dive in one direction for the soap, in another for the towel, in still another for the tooth brush and so on. The only thing necessary is to get hold of the toilet bag which contains all the articles. *Thirdly,* the pack will always be in the most satisfactory and blessed order.

## The Procedure of Packing

In packing your pack you will first put the different articles into the bags in which they belong. Then place

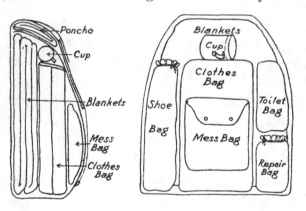

the pack with the back down on the floor or on a table. Fold up blankets properly and place them as flat as possible against the back. Put the clothes bag into the pack on top of blankets. Next place the mess bag on top of the clothes bag. Then the shoe bag along one side of the pack and the repair bag and the toilet bag on the other, the repair bag at the bottom. Put the cup on top in the pack. Roll up the poncho or raincoat into a flat roll and place this directly under the top flap. Close, and the pack is ready so far as the personal equipment is concerned.

If parts of the Patrol Equipment must go into the pack the packing must naturally be varied somewhat to fill the additional needs. In this case it may be necessary to carry the blankets in horse-shoe shape outside the haversack. Roll the two blankets up into a roll and place this inside its waterproof covering. This roll must be of such a length that when fastened to the pack it starts from the bottom edge at one side, goes over the top and reaches to the bottom edge at the other side. Fasten it here with the straps.

Then a tent or a part of tent takes the place of the blankets inside the haversack folded up in the shape

of the back of the pack and placed before the clothes bag is put in. If a cooking pot is in your care you will put that in after the clothes bag has been laid against the back and then proceed by putting in the mess bag (either outside it or on top of it) and filling in the rest of the space with the other bags. Provision bags can be placed in any empty corner of the pack.

## Patrol Equipment

In the same way in which we divided the Patrol organization for camp into two groups one being the "Tenting" group, the other the "Cooking" group, we will divide the equipment necessary for camping into two corresponding groups and use the same terms as before. In the "Tenting" group besides the tents we include material necessary in erecting them and preparing the camp site; also articles that have to do with the general life in camp.  In the "Cooking" group you will find everything that has reference to cooking.

## The Tents

Of this equipment the tents will prove the greatest problem.  A great number of different types are on the market, some for two boys, some for four, some for full Patrols.  The tents for two persons, such as "Camp Tents," "Forester's Tents," "Shelter Tents," "Tramper's Tents," are favored by hikers, but they don't seem to agree very well with the Patrol System, not to mention long term camps in rain and wind. These tents have their justification when a few fellows go out on an overnight hike but they have a queer cooling effect on group spirit, and group spirit or Patrol Spirit is what you are trying to build, not to destroy.  Two boys may have their fun in a pup tent but just imagine how the fun is multiplied when four—or even just three get together.

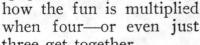

The most suitable tents for a Patrol are those that will give room for half of its members.  That makes two tents necessary, one for a group in charge of the Patrol Leader himself, the other for a group with his Assistant in charge, thus giving to the Assistant an opportunity for making use of his leadership abilities.

The tent must furnish ample space not only for the boys and their packs but also for their moving around in it.  It must naturally be water-proof and provided with a sod-cloth along the bottom.

A good tent is an "A" (or wedge) tent 7 ft. by 7 ft. and 5 ft. high with "side haulers" (see ill. p. 249).  A

## Patrol Equipment

### A. "Tenting" Group

2 "P. L. H." Tents (each with room for 4 boys, divided into halves) or 4 tents, each with room for 2 boys.

4 Peg Bags in which the necessary pegs are distributed.

| | |
|---|---|
| 4 Collapsible Tent Poles | 1 Spade |
| 2 Lanterns with Candles | 1 Axe |
| 2 Ground Sheets | 2 Guard Ropes |

1 Boot Cleaning Bag containing:
Polish, Brush, Rag, Whiskbroom

1 First Aid Kit (Official belt kit)

1 Repair Bag containing:
Canvas Pieces. Carborundum Sharpening Stone. Safety Pins. Yarn and Needles. Thin Wire. String.

### B. "Cooking" Group

2 Cooking Sets (two 6-quart pots, two 4-quart pots, two frying pans. Nesting, in two bags).

| | |
|---|---|
| 1 Axe | 1 Canvas Water Pail |
| 1 Spade | 1 Piece of Oil-Cloth |
| 2 Canvas Water Basins | 1 First Aid Kit |

1 Kitchen Bag containing:
1 Bread Knife. 2 Dish Towels. 1 Ladle or Big Spoon. 1 Can Opener. 1 Dish Mop. 1 Salt Shaker. 1 Pepper Shaker.

2 Bread Bags

6-8 Dustproof Provision Bags for flour, sugar, salt, oatmeal, cereal, dried fruits, beans, rice.

3 Waterproof and Fat-Proof Provision Bags for fresh meat, smoked meat, fish.

2 Aluminum Containers for butter, marmalade, or jam.

still better tent is a 7 ft. by 7 ft. and 5½ ft. high "Wall" tent. And why not aim at the best?

These tents may be made to order. But, instead, why not turn the making of them into a Patrol project which will give many hours of busy work and satisfaction?

In order to help the real active Patrol make its own tents we are giving in Chapter IX a complete description of the manufacture of a practical tent. This may help you considerably in determining the type of tent your Patrol wants.

## Other "Tenting" Equipment

The *ground-sheet* must be waterproof. It may be made out of a closely woven canvas or of rubberized cloth. It must exactly fit the floor of the tent and should be made to fasten to the sod-cloth.

*Illustration above shows: Lightweight Shelter
Tent—"Pup" Tent—Forester's Tent*

*Pegs* and *poles*.  In many localities these aren't necessary but may be cut as needed.  Yet better be prepared
and bring them along when you aren't sure of obtaining
them at the site.  The pegs may consist of 6-inch
spikes.  Aluminum pegs are for sale at the camping
goods stores but are naturally more expensive.  Poles
may be taken full-length and carried to camp as Scout
staves.  Yet one of the rules of the real camper is that
he carries nothing in his hands.  Better stick to this
rule and try to have made jointed poles (preferably
with brass-ferules like fish poles.  Failing this, a piece
of pipe may be used for the jointing) which can be
tucked away in a pack or fastened outside.

*Spades and Axes*.  In the complete outfit are included
two spades (or trenching shovels) and two axes divided
by the two groups with one spade and one axe to each.
You will find that they will come in handy setting up a
good Patrol camp.

*Illustration above shows: Wedge (A) Tent
with Side-Haulers—Wall Tent*

The "Tenting" team will need its spade for digging hip-ditches, latrine, garbage pit, and possibly ditching the tents, while the axe may be used for cutting tent poles and pegs, for pegging the tent down and for the making of special camp constructions.

The "Cooking" team will need a spade for building the fireplace and an axe for constructing the cranes and making the pot-hangers and for cutting wood.

Any of the Official Scout axes are good. The National Supply Department also carries a trenching shovel which fits your purpose.

*Lanterns.* Collapsible camp lanterns are very good. They are worth getting hold of. If you haven't got any of those an empty honey jar hung in a wire and equipped with an illuminating candle is excellent. Just pack it in such a way that you won't break it. Several types of lanterns may be made out of tin cans.

The *Boot-cleaning Bag,* and the *Repair Bag* need no explanation.

Two *First Aid Kits* are distributed with one to each group. These should be adequate. The official kits are specially recommended.

## "Cooking" Group Equipment

For *Cooking Pots* you may choose retinned iron or aluminum. The first is less expensive but aluminum may prove to be the best bargain in the long run. It is clean and it doesn't rust. Be sure that the handle is strong and the lid well fitting. The two pots will rest inside each other and with the pan (with removable handle) fit into a canvas bag. Another plan is to have one 8-quart pot, one 6-quart pot, one 4-quart pot, two pans, and fit these into one bag to be carried by one boy. This makes it more difficult to distribute the equipment.

The *Frying Pans* preferably should be iron ones, though aluminum ones may be used. The trouble with aluminum pans is that if they aren't kept heated and greased correctly, eats like eggs, fish and flapjacks are

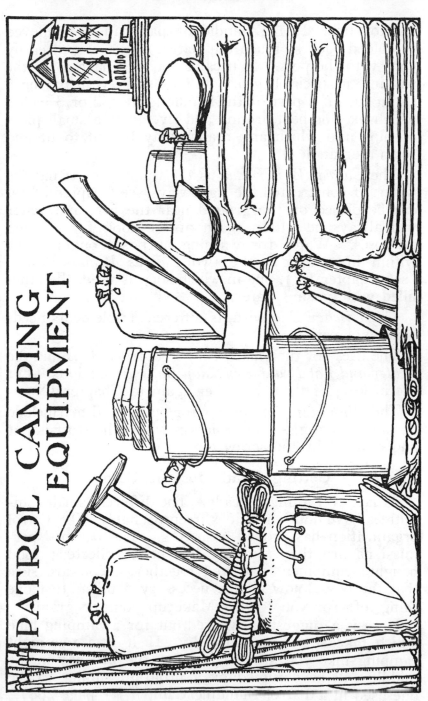

PATROL CAMPING EQUIPMENT

apt to stick. If the handle of pan can be removed or folded back so much the better. Then it will easily pack with the pots. If it can't you will have to fit the pan into a special bag or you may succeed in having a smith cut off a part of the handle leaving 2 or 3 inches which may be bent around and riveted to a small piece of pipe into which any branch may be cut to fit and form the handle.

The *Canvas Water Pail* is *the* thing for getting the water. If constructed the right way (see Chapter IX) it can be placed on the ground near the fire, and water will always be within reach of the cook for cooking purposes. Water for washing purposes ought to be within his reach in the two *Canvas Water Basins,* (see Chapter IX), one in which soap is used, the other filled with rinsing water.

The *Kitchen Bag* with its different implements needs little explanation.

The uses for the *Dust-Proof Provision Bags* and the *Water and Fat-Proof Provision Bags* are obvious. (For the making of them we refer again to Chapter IX).

The *Aluminum Containers* for butter and marmelade or jam have a glass jar inside in which the stuff is put and covered by the screw top.

## Getting Ready for the Camp

At last everything is ready. The different small committees have done their jobs irreproachably. The Patrol organization has proved a success. The parents' permissions are there; money has been collected; food bought; equipment gathered together. You are sure that the boys know all the necessary details. Just one thing left for you to do. Make up your program.

Here is a suggestion worked out for a camping hike which takes in one night only. If it is a two-night camping hike you are seeking for, the full day in the middle will be occupied by a program similar to the one used in a Patrol Standing Camp (See page 288).

# PATROL CAMPING HIKE TO MORRIS HILLS
## May 24th–May 25th

*First Day*

    3:00—Meet at Patrol Den.  Distributing of Patrol Equipment and food stuffs among the boys. Checking up on personal equipment.

    3:45—Starting trip to camp site via trolley, bus, railway or afoot.

    5:00—Arrival at camp site.  Choosing of position for tents, fire, etc.

    5:15—Making the camp and starting cooking.

    6:30—Supper. Clean-up.

    7:30—Resting time or games (tag, etc.)

    8:00—Camp fire. A small one with a happy **group** around, chatting, singing, story-telling.

    9:30—Taps around fire.  Putting out fire.  Making ready for the night.

   10:00—Lights out.  Silence.

*Second Day*

    7:00—Getting out of the blankets. Washing. Starting breakfast.  Airing blankets, cleaning tents.

    8:00—Breakfast.  Clean up.

    8:45—Putting the tents in order.  Camp improvements.

    9:30—Exploration hike from Camp.  Nature study and Scoutcraft.

   11:30—Return to camp.  Preparing dinner.

   12:30—Dinner.  Clean up.

    1:30—Rest.

    2:00—Start striking the camp.  Starting with the kitchen, then getting together personal equipment, the tents being the last thing.

    3:00—Check up to see if site is actually clean.

    3:15—Start home trip.

    4:30—Arrival at Patrol Den.  Collecting of Patrol Equipment and storing it away.

    5:00—Dismissal.

    6:00—The boys will be home in plenty of time.

## Starting the Short-Term Camp

Three o'clock is approaching. The boys are beginning to arrive. The Quartermaster already has been at the Den for some time. He is spreading out the Patrol equipment in small heaps on the floor and table. The Grubmaster has been there with a number of groceries. He has disappeared again with the Assistant Patrol Leader to get the rest of the stuff. He will soon be back. In fact he is just coming in through the door and starts dividing his material up into piles.

Shortly all the boys are there.

The Patrol Leader takes command, looks at the packs, has a few of them corrected, asks if the boys are sure that they have all the necessary personal equipment. They have, O. K.!

### Distributing the Patrol Equipment

The boys put the packs on the floor, open them, receive their share of the Patrol equipment and succeed  in arranging it properly and in such a way as to be able to close the packs again easily. The Quartermaster and the Grubmaster have been working closely together distributing the different articles evenly among all the members of the Patrol taking in consideration, too, how the boys fit into the Patrol camping organization. And when the packs are ready you will find them containing what is indicated on page 255.

In this list we have tried to distribute the different articles in such a way that each boy is carrying about the same weight of material. You may have to adjust this to fit your case. The weight of your tents, your cooking utensils, your rations, may vary from the plan described. Don't do anything half way. Don't strp until you have found the right way of distributing

## A. "TENTING" GROUP

### A 1. Patrol Leader
Personal Equipment
1 Tent Half
1 Peg Bag
1 Pole (jointed)
1 Axe
1 First Aid Kit

### A 2. Scribe
Personal Equipment
1 Tent half
1 Peg Bag
1 Pole (jointed)
1 Spade
1 Guard Rope
1 Boot-cleaning Bag

### A 3. Quartermaster
Personal Equipment
1 Tent Half
1 Peg Bag
1 Pole (jointed)
2 Lanterns with Candles

### A 4. Cheermaster
Personal Equipment
1 Tent Half
1 Peg Bag
1 Pole (jointed)
1 Guard Rope
1 Repair Bag

## B. "COOKING" GROUP

### B 1. Assistant Patrol Leader
Personal Equipment
1 4-quart Pot ⎫
1 6-quart Pot ⎬ In Bag
1 Pan ⎭
1-2 Meat Bags
4 Provision Bags
1 First Aid Kit
1 Piece of Oil-Cloth

### B 2. Grubmaster
Personal Equipment
1 4-quart Pot ⎫
1 6-quart Pot ⎬ In Bag
1 Pan ⎭
1 Kitchen Bag
1 Meat Bag
3 Provision Bags

### B 3. Treasurer
Personal Equipment
1 Ground Sheet
1 Axe
1 Butter Container
1 Marmalade Container
1 Bread Bag

### B 4. Hikemaster
Personal Equipment
1 Ground Sheet
1 Spade
1 Canvas Water Pail
2 Canvas Water Basins
1 Bread Bag
3 Provision Bags

*your* Patrol's equipment even if you have to use eight pennies to put into a slot-weighing machine. Maybe your local grocer will give you permission to use his scales. So much the better. But, find out about the distribution by actual weighing. At a Patrol Camping Contest that took place recently, the heaviest and lightest packs of one single Patrol weighed 35 pounds and 15 pounds respectively. Naturally that Patrol Leader could not have given much thought to the packing of the Patrol equipment. On the other

25 lbs

hand if you have some real huskies and some weak boys in your Patrol you will not think of letting them carry the same amount of pounds. There ought to be a relation between the weight of the boys and of the weight they carry. You will use your judgment and load the packs accordingly. In any case if you find by weighing that the average weight of the packs exceeds 25 pounds you may be sure that there is something wrong about your equipment. Investigate, get rid of unnecessary material and cut down the weight.

At last the packs are ready. The boys sling them on their shoulders and leave the Patrol Den. As you close the door you look around with a last glance. No, nothing has been left. The short-term camp may start.

## Getting to the Camp Site

The camping hike starts like any other hike. You have to get out of the city by using the means of transportation which are at your disposal. You follow the main road for a while, to turn off and start the real hiking through the by-path.

By now the Patrol consists of real hikers who know

how to behave on the way. They get fun out of the hiking but their thoughts reach out toward the camp site. "It can't be far now," "If we were only there already," "What fun we are going to have!" From the boys' remarks you will know that their thoughts roam only in one direction.

Then suddenly a turn in the road or a sudden elevation reveals the camp site. The speed is increased a little. You are there at last.

## Arriving at Camp

Maybe the hike has been strenuous. Maybe the boys feel like throwing themselves in the grass for a real rest. This isn't the time for rest however. There is a lot of work to be done first.

Immediately upon arrival at the camp site the boys put the haversacks down in a neat row, all turned the same way, close together. The "duffel-line" is formed.

This is the token that possession of the camp has been taken.

Then get your boys together and look over the camp site. Stroll up and down with them and discuss how the different parts of the camp may be placed to greatest advantage—so that there will be lee for the wind, so that the smoke from the kitchen fire won't hang around the tents, so that the ground is smooth for bedding, and a lot of other details. This won't take long, but even if it should it is worth it. Never start pitching the camp before you have decided upon the set-up. If you do you may get a lot of extra work to do later and you will regret your heedlessness deeply. You decide with your own "Tenting" group where and how the tents are to be placed and talk over with the "Cooking" group where is the best spot for the kitchen.

As soon as these points are decided the work is started and your camp pitching organization is put to a trial. This organization is made up on the following lines:

## Camp Making Organization

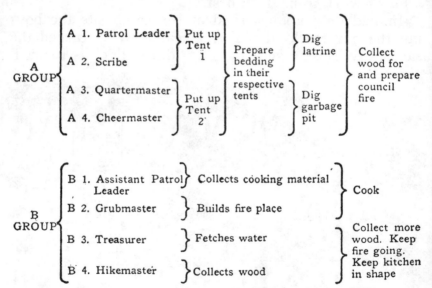

On your signal the work is started.

The "Tenting" group carries its haversacks to the place where the tents are to be pitched and places them in a row, while the "Cooking" group carries its pack to the site of the kitchen and arranges them in a row there.

The boys open up their haversacks, take out the Patrol equipment (leaving the personal equipment).

## Work of "Tenting" Group

The boys of the "Tenting" group each pick up their tent halves, also the tent poles and the pegs and proceed to site where tents are to be pitched. The tent halves are fastened together, back door and front door closed at the bottom. The poles are joined and placed in position and the pegs taken out of their covers.

The tents are spread out and the pitching takes place, two boys working on each tent.

The boys place a peg each in the two back corners of tent, stretching the base line of back at the same time. Then they place two pegs at the front corners, stretching the front base line and side lines simultaneously. One boy raises the front pole to vertical position, while the other pegs down front guy-rope. Then the pole-raiser raises back pole, and his buddy pegs down  back guy rope. The first boy next goes inside tent and straightens up the sod-cloth, while the other pegs down the sides of tent and gets it into correct position.

The other two boys of the "Tenting group" have meanwhile followed the same procedure with their tent as is mentioned above.

As soon as the tents are up, the boys start preparing the bedding.

They clear the ground inside the two tents of stones, humps and branches. If desired they also make a hip ditch in both of them. They lie down all over the floor to be sure that this job is done correctly. A bump sticking into his side may spoil a complete night's rest for one of the fellows. Next they get the ground sheets from the haversacks of the boys who carried them and proceed placing them in the tents. The blankets are gathered together, refolded (if necessary) and placed in the tents on the spot where the owners of them are to sleep.

Then two of the boys bring into the tent which they raised the four haversacks of the "Tenting" group and put them in position at the head of the corresponding blankets, while the other two do the same to the four haversacks of the "Cooking" group, and the tents are ready for the night.

One of the boys picks up the spade from his equipment and with the help of his buddy clears a place for 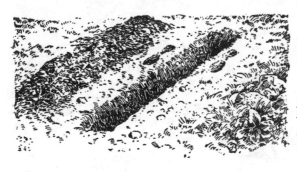 and digs the latrine. No elaborate latrine needs to be built in a Patrol camp. A simple straddle latrine is the best and easiest thing to construct. It should be built away from camp in the direction in which the wind blows, far enough, yet not too far, and it should certainly be kept about two hundred feet away from the water supply and at a lower level. If it isn't naturally protected by a thicket some sort of a screen should be built around it. The dug-out itself ought to be about two feet long, one foot wide, and one to two feet deep. Pile up the earth at one side and provide a whittled shovel or scoop with which to throw down some earth whenever the latrine is used. Toilet paper may be hung nearby protected against rain, for example by a cut up tin can. Be sure to announce to all campers the position of the latrine.

Meanwhile the two other boys prepare with the "Cooking" group spade a garbage pit in convenient proximity to the kitchen to be of real value to the cooks. Make it one foot by one foot and two or three feet deep. Pile up the earth at one side so that it can easily be shoveled down on top of refuse placed in the pit.

The latrine and garbage pit ready, the whole "A" group gets together, decides upon a place for the evening's camp fire, clears the ground, collects a sufficient measure of wood and builds part of it up in such a way that one match will start the fire going while the rest of it is stacked neatly at the side for extra fuel.

## Work of the "Cooking" Group

The four boys of the "Cooking" group get to work at the same time on four different jobs.

Number one goes to his haversack, and brings down to the place where number two is starting to build the fireplace the piece of oil cloth, the utensils and provision

bags which he carried in his own pack. He also fetches the pot and pans, the kitchen bag and provision bags, the butter and marmalade containers and the bread bag and provision bags from the respective "Cooking" group haversacks. He unfolds the oil cloth on the ground and places on it the provision bags in neat rows. He opens up the two packs of pots and pans, takes these out and places them at one side of the oil cloth together with the kitchen bag. This being done, he starts to get the ingredients together for the evening's meal.

In the meantime number two ha~ taken the spade from the equipment with which it was carried and has been clearing the ground preparing the fire₁ 'ace according to the style he thinks most suitable. He may have built a stone or sod fireplace, an open trench fire, or made a fireplace of logs with a crane of forked sticks, cross-piece and pot-hangers big enough to take care of the necessary number of pots and pans for the meal, and, in such a position in regard to the tents that no smoke and no sparks will drift in their direction. As soon as the fireplace is ready, number three will have brought in enough wood to start the fire. Number two proceeds to build the fire and as soon as that is done turns to number one to help in the preparation of the meal.

The third boy of the "Cooking" group has meanwhile collected wood for the cooking fire, first getting tinder together, then larger branches.

The fourth Scout picks up the canvas water pail from his own equipment and goes out to get water for the cooking. He brings it to the fireplace and puts the pail within easy reach of the cooks. Next he takes the two canvas water basins from his pack, opens them up, fills them with water and places them with a piece of soap and a towel where the cooks may easily get at them.

When these four jobs have been accomplished the boys get together in pairs.

The first two boys wash hands and proceed to make the foodstuff ready on the oil cloth for cooking the minute the flames start to leap. Some foresight is necessary. The cooks have to know about how long it takes to prepare the different dishes of the meal so that they can figure out in which order the various things must be started to be ready in time.

The all-important thing is that they *must be served as a meal,* not as any casual mix-up of food stuff. The roast is not to be ready half an hour before the vegetables, nor is the soup to be delayed until after the dessert. This is one of the most important points of Patrol cooking, also one of the points which very few Patrols are able to attain. Another point at least as difficult is to have the meal ready at the exact hour for which it is scheduled. All this can only be learned by training, *training,* TRAINING!

The other two take charge of the cooking fire, or fires. They collect wood, cut or break it into proper lengths and pile it up between three stakes hammered into the ground about 1-2 feet apart, one intermediate space being filled with thin branches, the other with thicker pieces of wood. From these piles they feed the fires and keep them going while the cooking takes place.

## All Hands at Work

The work is getting on splendidly. At last the tents are up, the camp looks like a camp and from the pots ascends a delicious aroma that is a promise of an appetizing approaching meal.

In the above working plan we have figured on the Patrol having eight members. If the Patrol is smaller, some of the jobs will naturally have to be combined. If it is larger, some of the jobs may be divided up for two boys. The whole point is to be sure that every boy has his piece of work to do, that all are occupied.

### Isn't It Wonderful to Be in Camp?

Presently some of the boys of the "Tenting" group finish their work. They remember a rule you have given them: "After having finished your special assignment everything that needs doing is everybody's duty." "Let's set the table" suggests one. They go to the tents, dig down into the haversack and produce the individual eating bags. They place them on the ground in a small circle, open them, take out the plates, put fork and knife and spoon on top of the plates and the plates on top of the corresponding bags. The table is ready—and fortunately so is the meal, as the boys gather around the table.

The two cooks bring the pots and pans with the food and place them in the middle of the circle of plates, and the boys pass them along and around until everybody has filled his plate.

A wonderful meal, well cooked—it is to be hoped. And nothing tastes so good as a meal in the open air.

### Washing Up

While eating, a pot with water has been hanging over the fire, placed there by the fire keeper. When the meal is over the dishes are washed. First everybody goes to the fire or garbage pit and scrapes into it any left-overs from his plates. Next he proceeds to the hot water pot where a boy of the "Cooking" group takes the plates, cleans them with water and the dish mop and gives them back to the boy who himself dries them with the dish towel included in his own mess bag. If hot water is not available the boys will go down to the water (a place sufficiently distant from the spot from which water is fetched for drinking or where bathing takes place), tear up a small piece of sod and scrub the plates first with the bottom side then with the top side of the sod and cold water until they are clean. Rinse in the water, dry and put them into your bag ready for next meal. Forks and spoons are treated in the same way. A table knife may be cleaned by being simply stuck into the ground and wiped.

Also the cooking utensils are to be cleaned. This is done by the two cooks while the other two of their group put out the cooking fire and give the kitchen a general clean-up.

The time is now ripe for the evening's program.

## The Evening's Program

After supper there may still be a few moments of light before darkness sets in. Use them for a not too vigorous game or for a quiet stroll around the camp site. Also make a final check up to see that the beds are actually ready for the night and make sure that some kindling wood from the woodpile is brought into the tent. Maybe rain will come during the night. Better be prepared and have dry wood for making the morning's breakfast fire.

It is getting darker now. The stars are peeping forth. The trees are closing in on you in dark silhouettes. The hour of the council fire has come. The boys get blankets from the tents to wrap around themselves or they put on their sweaters. The night is

getting cool. Then they gather around the council fire circle. You assign one of them to light the fire and to take care of it for the evening. He strikes his match and small flames come leaping out of the wood putting a glow of warmth on the faces of the boys.

Council fires! There is magic in these words! Later on when the memory of the camps has faded the boys may still remember the hours when they were sitting around a glowing fire in a close circle, gazing into the rosy embers in silence or chatting in gay spirits.

Here again everything depends upon the Patrol Leader. The council fires will be just as good as you yourself are. If there is spirit in you, there will be spirit to every council fire you conduct.

At big council fires where many people are present and where the flames leap up from a real bonfire a program of stunts, dramatics, duel contests and big ceremonies are in place. *Not* at the Patrol Council Fire. Here the program must be born of the moment. be spontaneous and free. Yet you may have something in mind that will form a kind of a program. Certain songs to be sung, a story to be told, a discussion to be started. But don't make this a hard and fast program which *must* be followed. Rather drift along with the moods of your boys, and as you sit around the fire you may realize that songs which you thought appropriate before starting are entirely out of place at the fire.

Don't be afraid that too little will happen at the Patrol Council Fire. The fire itself will fill all lapses in a possible "program."

## Around the Fire

Start by talking about the day and about what the tomorrow will bring—actually planning the next day's program. This may get the boys started on general Scouting, or maybe to talking about their life in school, or sports, football, baseball, or maybe talk may start about a movie one of them had seen the other night.

And then some one will say "By the way, that reminds me of . . ." and so forth.  If nobody else says
it, you will.  And you have your story-telling starting
and some of the others will have things to relate.  "Let
us have a song" you will suggest after one of these
typical small camp fire pauses during which the boys
just sit there, gazing into the red coals, dreaming.  Let
them dream a few moments, then bring them back to
earth and have them sing one of the songs they like
best, an old time one or the latest hit, it doesn't matter
what, so long as it is good and they like it.  And after
having hiked with them for several months you ought
to know which songs they do enjoy.  You will then
suddenly remember that Bobby has a song he would

like to sing if you press him.  Give him a chance to
show off.  Also Bill who sits rather quiet in the other
corner.  Everyone ought to contribute to the general
fun.  If one of the boys should produce a "uke" or a
banjo, so much the better for the singing.  If not, the
Patrol's champion harmonica player will no doubt fill
the bill.  Different games may be introduced, a round
robin story to which every one of the boys must sub-
mit a chapter.  Other popular stunts are words mentioned which must be put into a sentence, a line to
which a rhyme must be found, a memory test about
"Mr. Brown" who met "Mr. Smith, who bowed to

him, Mr. Jones, who kicked him, Mr. Sims, who embraced him," and so forth, every boy repeating what has gone before and adding one more thing until the fun has reached its climax.

Another song, an old-fashioned round, another story and the evening has passed,—alas all too quickly and it is already half past nine.

At your signal everybody arises and stands facing the fire. Arms are lifted to horizontal position over the flames and then slowly lowered to the side while you all sing Taps softly, softly:

> "Day is done,
> Gone the sun,
> From the lake,
> From the hills,
> From the sky.
> All is well,
> Safely rest,
> God is nigh."

**"And so to bed."**

Boys of the "Tenting" group start putting out the fire while the rest of the boys go to the tents. The fire men spread out the burning sticks, pour water on them and make sure that every ember is extinguished before they go to their tent. As they turn from what was a few minutes before a blazing fire but is now just a heap of dead black coals, they see the white tents looming through the dark. The lanterns are burning inside and the tents look like the dwellings of mysterious beings.

## Getting to Bed

In the tents everybody is busy getting out of his clothes and into pajamas. All of them know that only foolish tenderfoot campers sleep in the garments they wear during the day and all of them have brought along suitable night clothing. Their uniforms they fold up neatly and put into the space in the clothes bags made vacant by the removing of the pajamas,

whereupon the bags go under the heads of the boys as comfortable pillows. Shoes are placed in a neat row at the entrance of the tent. By and by the boys get into their blankets. Some of them have the blankets
sewed at one end and along the two sides into veritable sleeping bags, others use big blanket pins for the same purpose.

Meanwhile t h e chatter is at its height.

At last everybody is in his blankets and has wiggled himself into a comparatively comfortable position. All except the Patrol Leader. You are ready to turn in. Yet you have still a few responsibilities to attend to. You put on your shoes again and walk out and toward the other tent where the "Cooking" group is to sleep. You look inside. You see if everybody is comfortable and happy. You warn them again not to close the tent flaps, telling them these are only to be closed in case of cloud-bursts or hurricanes. If a tent isn't well ventilated, it is more healthful to sleep in a stuffy room at home than in the midst of the out-of-doors. Everything seems to be all right. You blow out the candle and get back to your own tent. Before entering you glance at the sky. No, there is no sign of approaching rain. Not necessary to slacken the guy ropes. Maybe they might be slackened just a little though to be safe. And you lift up the front pole and place it in a slightly slanting position, or push it down into a small two-inch deep hole which has been made beforehand at the very side of the pole. This does the trick. Then you get into the tent, blow out the candle and creep into your blankets by the light of your flashlight.

The boys are still chatting. You let them continue until your watch shows 10 o'clock sharp. Then you say loudly enough to be heard in the other tent also "Ten o'clock! Silence! Good Night! Sleep Well!" A faint "Good Night" comes back to you. Then silence. And a few minutes later just the deep breathing of eight healthy boys in a sound slumber.

That is the way it is, if you have trained the Patrol that way!!

## Sleeping in Camp

If this is the first night you are sleeping out with your boys you must guard them and yourselves against insomnia. The strange surroundings, the sounds of the night, the hard bed, the excitement of the day, all tend to keep them awake. And if they are permitted to talk they will continue far into the night until exhaustion brings them a few moments of restless sleep. Speak to them about it at the council fire. Tell them that only Tenderfoot Scouts waste the night talking, that real campers go to bed to sleep. Tell them that you must insist that all talking cease at ten sharp when you say "Good Night," not to be resumed before 7 o'clock next morning, when you say "Good Morning." Appeal to the boys' loyalty. Make them understand that even if they can't sleep themselves they must take into consideration the ones that can sleep and instruct your Assistant to carry out your orders in this respect in his tent.

It may be a little difficult at

first. The boys will turn around in their blankets, will want to say something, maybe just whisper. Stop every beginning with a "Sh-h-h." The boys will move around again. Then if he feels that he has to keep quiet he will do so and—suddenly pop off to sleep.

## Next Morning

The boys may start waking up early. Insist that they stay in bed until seven o'clock even if they do not sleep. If they get up they certainly won't get any more sleep. If they stay in the blankets there is still hope. If anybody has to get up and go outside during the night have him understand that he must move as quietly as possible and return to bed immediately again.

You are the guardian of the health of your boys. And enough sleep is the foundation not only of health but also of the fun of the following camping day. If the boys do not get enough sleep they are likely to become cross and quarrelsome later in the day. Therefore insist that they do not rob themselves of their sleep by making them stay put from 10 P. M. to 7 A. M.

At seven you will yell your "Good Morning" so that it may be heard for miles, and immediately the camp will become one big noise.

Get the boys out of their blankets and out of the tents immediately even if you have to have some of them pulled out by force. You may make a run around the camp site in order to get the blood to circulating, then strip to waist, wash, brush teeth, and into the clothes. The day has begun and work is started.

The "Cooking" group builds fire in the kitchen and begins preparing the breakfast while the "Tenting" group pulls out all blankets from the tents for airing. The blankets must be unfolded and the sleeping bags turned inside out in order to get the most benefit out of sun and air. Also pajamas and haversacks are thrown outside, the tents being cleared completely. The tent too is aired. That may be done by opening up the back thereby creating a draft. If it is a wall tent you will roll up the sides also for a while.

Breakfast is served and eaten. Plates and pots are cleaned, kitchen cleared, fire extinguished.

Then after an hour or more of airing, the blankets are rolled according to one plan and put inside the tents again and neatly placed. The pajamas are folded and the haversacks are put at the head of the blankets. The tent is straightened up and the camp looks neat and clean.

## The Forenoon's Program

As soon as everything is cleared up you will start a forenoon program of real Scouting.

Don't stay in the camp during these hours. Get out on a hike in the neighborhood. Go out exploring and use the opportunity for training in the Scout requirements. The activities are very much the same as the ones which were set forth in discussing activities on the one day hikes (page 211). Nature-study, tracking and trailing, signaling, map making, judging and other activities vary as you go along.

If swimming facilities offer themselves you will undoubtedly find that your boys will want to go in swimming. This brings up a serious issue.

You have the responsibility for these boys of yours. Even if they are all supposedly good swimmers, even if their health condition seems to be the best possible, there may be a slip somewhere! And that slip may spell disaster to a boy and be the sinister shadow which will follow you through life because you, who had the responsibility, slipped up. We can't paint this too dark. *You must not permit any swimming whatever without being sure that the necessary safety precautions have been taken. Swimming should never be undertaken on a Patrol hike or in Patrol camp except under leadership of a Senior Life Saver, approved by your Local Council.* He will know about the minimum safety requirements and will make sure that they are lived up to.

After the bathing, run around awhile until you are dry. A sun-bath may be had. But make it short. Half an hour is plenty if the boys aren't already developing a tan. You don't want to have them go home with bad sunburns. Keep everybody moving while sunbathing. Don't permit any boy to lie down and bake. This isn't healthy and besides, by moving, you get far more benefit out of the sunning process.

Dress quickly and proceed on the hike. Or maybe it is time by now to think of returning to the camp to get a bit to eat. Funny how hungry the fresh air makes you!

## The Noon Meal

There can be no doubt about it that the lunch the last day in any camp ought to consist of a meal that is very easily prepared. At this stage of the game there is no reason for going in for elaborate menus. The boys will be getting their dinner at home in the evening, the camp meal is only designed to help them keep up until the return home. Maybe the meal the day before was designed in such a way as to leave something which might be served cold or heated for the last luncheon. If not, provision has been made for something else to be fried or boiled to satisfy the appetite of the boys.

As soon as the meal is over the "Cooking" group will clean up all cooking utensils in order to be prepared for the packing. The pots and pans must be scoured carefully inside and dried thoroughly. If water can be heated you will naturally prefer that; if not, cold water and a few sods will do the trick. Don't make the mistake of scouring the aluminum pots on the outside. Some people do not think that pots are cleaned properly if they do not shine brilliantly. This is a great mistake. First of all it takes a disproportionately long time to do the job. Secondly it serves no purposes whatever (maybe with the exception that it looks nicer seen with not understanding eyes). On the contrary, it delays the cooking on the next trip. Bright metal reflects heat, while blackened metal absorbs it. Therefore it is only after the metal has been blackned that you get the most complete effect out of your fuel. Besides the soot will harm nobody inasmuch as the pots are kept in special bags which do not permit the blackened surface to touch other parts of equipment. On the other hand you should not let the soot layer become too thick. If this happens it must be scoured off with the bottom side of a sod. Yet do not overdo this. This same scouring must be done if the pots happen to become greasy outside.

After this work is done there should be a short rest for all. But the minutes fly quickly by and soon the time comes for breaking the camp.

## Breaking Camp

The first step in breaking the Patrol camp is to provide for all the personal equipment.

When you announce "Let's go" all of the boys will start to get their possessions together. They will put the different pieces into the bags where they belong, and make the haversack ready to be packed.

As soon as the personal equipment is out of the way the four boys of the "Tenting" group will place their haversacks in a row close to the tents and the boys of the "Cooking" group in the neighborhood of the kitchen and start taking care of the Patrol equipment.

The "Tenting" boys will remove the ground-sheets from the tent, fold them up and place them on the haversacks into which they are to go. Then they will, in pairs, return to the tents and start taking them down.

One boy will go to one side of a tent, his buddy to the other. They will take up all tent pegs along the sides of the tent except the corner pegs. Then the first boy will go to the front of the tent, the other to the back. Simultaneously they will take up the front and the back guy rope pegs and let the tent come down flat toward the side from which the wind blows. The next step is to remove the tent poles and take up the front and back corner pegs. The pegs are immediately

put into the peg bags and the poles taken apart (if they are jointed). Next one will grasp the front top of the tent, the other the back top, lift it high, and while stretching the back of the tent, move forward fast, in the direction from which the wind comes, whereupon the tent is quickly placed on the ground. By performing this maneuver the tent is smoothed out and ready to be folded.

It depends upon the size of the tent how many folds have to be made. Usually it is folded in 1/3 of the width from the bottom first, then 1/3 from the top and then rolled from one end.

If the tent is made to be divided into two "halves" the procedure is a little different. After having taken it down you will divide it into the two pieces and then smooth out each piece separately by carrying it against the wind and placing it on the ground, where it is folded up into a shape that will fit the haversacks.

The other two boys of the "Tenting" group will treat the second tent similarly.

As soon as the tents are taken down and packed, the latrine and the garbage pit are filled up and covered with the sod. This done the boys will finish by packing and closing the haversack.

In the meanwhile the "Cooking" group has been busy cleaning up the kitchen. The two cooks have packed the different cooking utensils and have distributed them together with the provision bags between the haversacks where they belong. At the same time the two other Scouts have been picking up wood from the kitchen place. Shavings and c h o p s and twigs and sticks have been burned on the fire which is kept going until the last minute. Surplus wood they have hidden in a place where it may be found the next time they visit the place, or if they do not expect to return they have scattered it among the trees in a way natural for dropped branches.

As soon as these Patrol affairs are attended to the boys will go to their haversacks, finish the packing and make the haversacks ready to be slung on the shoulders.

On a signal from the Patrol Leader the boys will form a line spread over the camp site and while moving slowly forward pick up any trace they find as described on page 220. Not the last scrap of paper or the smallest piece of chip must be left.

Everything picked up is carried to the fire and burned.

Then as the last step the fire is extinguished. Water is poured over it until every spark of life is extinguished. Next earth is put on it. It is stamped down and the sods are replaced on top of what was formerly a fireplace but which is now just a little bit of rising ground which it is hard to distinguish from the surrounding grass field.

If the day is rainy the different things are done in a somewhat different order. Then the tents are left until the very last, all haversacks and equipment being placed and packed inside the tent. When everything else is packed, latrine and garbage pit filled and fire extinguished the tents are taken down, packed, and everything is ready.

The Patrol Leader takes in with a last glance every detail of the camp site. Everything O. K. "Ready to start? Let's go!" And the Patrol is on its way home.

## Storing Away the Equipment

As soon as the Patrol arrives in town it will proceed to its Den. Here the boys will open up their haversacks and take out the pieces of Patrol equipment which they have had in charge.

The Quartermaster will take it over and immediately check up on it to see if anything has been lost. He will then store everything in its proper place.

If the tents are wet from rain he must provide for their being dried before storing them. If not, the result will be that the canvas will be spoiled by mildew, which will shorten the life of the tent. Together with a couple of other boys he will hang up the tents in an airy place and not pack them up before they are thoroughly dry. The same applies to towels, canvas water bag and water basins.

The Grubmaster will look after all of the Provision Bags. If any perishables are left over they must be disposed of—if their quantity is very small by throwing them away, if bigger by having some of the boys take them home and use them there. Meat bags and the like must be carefully washed and dried before they are put away.

## What Did You Learn?

The trip is over but not its effects. Undoubtedly the boys have had experiences and made observations on this camping trip of theirs.

At the next Patrol meeting you will take it up with them before it is dismissed for other experiences.

Three questions you will ask them:

(1) *What did we learn?*
(2) *What was good?*
(3) *What wasn't so good?*

By discussing these three points frankly you may be able to make improvements in planning the coming camps and make them into even bigger successes than the first one.

You may find that the organization ought to be changed somewhat, that the equipment wasn't adequate or maybe was too extensive, that some parts of the menu suited the boys while others did not. And it is only by speaking about these things and by getting the opinion of the boys that you are able to improve the details next time.

Naturally you wouldn't expect everything to turn out just right on the first camping hike you undertake. That would be expecting too much.

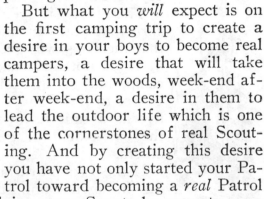

But what you *will* expect is on the first camping trip to create a desire in your boys to become real campers, a desire that will take them into the woods, week-end after week-end, a desire in them to lead the outdoor life which is one of the cornerstones of real Scouting. And by creating this desire you have not only started your Patrol toward becoming a *real* Patrol but you are also helping your Scouts become stronger and healthier and happier boys.

## STANDING CAMPS

The step from one-day hiking to short-term camps isn't so big. The step from short-term camps to standing camps is. In fact it is so big that few Patrols are ever able to undertake it, and certainly no inexperienced Patrol. It can consequently only be recommended for an old Patrol with an older Patrol Leader.

This is not because the equipment is any more expensive or the daily work more difficult to accomplish. The sole difficulty is the building of a program that will keep such a small group as the Patrol is, occupied and interested and happy over a longer period of living together.

Boys want variety, and excitement. And only if they

are used to working together exceedingly well and have something going on the whole time will they be able to enjoy the limitations of the activities of a small isolated gang.

And in this respect the personality of the Patrol Leader counts 100%. Everything depends upon him and his spirit. If he can keep things going, the experiment will be a success; if his grip slips it will become a failure. And the failure of a Patrol standing camp may mean the destruction of the Patrol.

Therefore—if you are *not perfectly sure* that you can undertake the job and that the boys will get real enjoyment out of it, do not undertake a Patrol standing camp, but go instead with the complete Patrol to the Council camp where it may live as a unit its own life and yet have the excite..nent of getting together with others.

If the Troop to which it belongs is having its own camp, the Patrol wouldn't think at all about going Patrol camping. It will stick to the Troop and in the Troop camp do its bit to build Troop spirit together with Patrol unity.

But in case that the Patrol is absolutely to have its own standing camp, go right at it. The obstacles aren't so big that they may not be overcome through grit and perseverance.

## Preparations

Take the matter up with your Scoutmaster. Discuss with him the whole matter, have him help you with the planning. If it is possible for him or for one of the other Troop leaders to go along with the Patrol, so much the better. If not, be perfectly sure that you have the grit yourselves to make the camp a success when alone with your boys.

## Necessary Experience

Before starting an undertaking of this sort, you must, yourself, as well as the boys, have the necessary experience.

Naturally you must, first of all, qualify as a leader of short-term camps for which the requirements are given on page 228. But besides the six requirements there mentioned the following must be added:

For *you* to pass:

(7) *You must have undertaken at least ten short term camps with your Patrol extending over one or two nights to the satisfaction of your Scoutmaster.*

For *your boys* to pass:

(8) *At least 50% of the boys going (yourself excluded), must have taken part in at least ten Patrol short term camps with you as their Patrol Leader.*

You may think that these are rather severe demands to comply with. Yet you are sure to find out by actual experience that they are not too strict. Without the above mentioned experience a Patrol will only in cases of rare exception turn a Patrol Standing Camp into a success.

## When?

The Standing Camp being a matter of one to several weeks it goes without saying that it can only take place during one of the longer school vacations or during the time of the year when the working boys get their days off, in other words possibly at no other time than midsummertime, July - August.

The actual time can naturally not be decided upon without conferences among all of the boys and between the boys and the authorities who have to do with the assigning the vacation periods.

Plenty of time must be given for this, and it would not be too early to start thinking of it in the beginning of May if the camp is to take place in July or August. The sooner the actual date is decided upon the sooner other details can be planned and executed.

## The Site of the Camp

The ideal site for a Patrol Camp was discussed in the preceding pages, yet a few additional remarks may be in place here.

What was said in regard to soil, shelter, water and wood naturally holds good in any case. Only the actual position of the site may be somewhat different. For a camping hike you do not want to get too far away from your home town. Too much money and time is spent this way. But in regard to standing camps one of the most attractive features may just be that it *is* far away, that it is a spot where none of the boys have ever been but which they have longed to see and now get their first chance to visit.

It may be somewhere in a mountainous region, or somewhere at a seashore, at an especially interesting inland lake or some other place famous for its beauty.

In case such a place is decided upon the Patrol must get permission for using it before it starts out on its trip. A certain amount of correspondence is necessary. And in that correspondence it will wish to have the answers clearly settled to several questions besides the ones on shelter, water, wood, etc.

(1) *Is the place exposed to too much publicity?* (This especially if you have the feeling that it might be close to a summer resort of some kind or other.)

(2) *Is there a place within three to four miles where groceries may be bought?*

(3) *Is there a farmhouse within two to three miles from which eggs, milk, potatoes, vegetables, straw may be purchased?*

(4) *Is there a doctor within easy reach?*

(5) *Is the place infested by mosquitoes or other pests?*

The best thing to do would be to have one of your Scouts (if you can't go yourself), go to the camp site, look it over and see if it is fit for use. The next best thing is to get in touch with the local Scout authorities and ask them to help you out.

Without detailed information about the camp site, you may later be sorry because you went there. Therefore, better be too particular than too easy-going.

As you get your information you will put down your notes about the camp site. You will also purchase a topographical map of that section of the country and try to fit the different details into this.

### Equipment

The equipment for a standing camp is mostly the same as the one necessary for camping hikes. Yet some diversities may be considered.

On a camping hike you want to take along as little as necessary yet enough to make you comfortable for a few days. In the standing camp, you may want to arrange everything a little more comfortably. Camp is not, as some people think, a place where you go to rough it. On the contrary, it is a place where you try to make yourself as comfortable as possible with as simple means as possible. Therefore, in order to accomplish this, you may want to take things along which you wouldn't think of bringing on a camping hike. Also a few things may prove to be absolute necessities.

Divided into personal and Patrol equipment you may want to take the following in consideration.

## PERSONAL EQUIPMENT

(In addition to equipment mentioned on page 241)
. Change of uniform—Shirt, Shorts, Neckerchief, Stockings, Extra Underwear, (1-2 sets).

Straw Tick (2' x 6').

Paper, Envelopes and Stamps.

Mosquito Netting (possibly also citronella oil and ointment).

Sport Articles—Football, Baseball, Boxing Gloves, Archery Tackle, Fishing Tackle, etc.

Books—One or two favorites, if possible, suited for reading at camp fire.

## PATROL EQUIPMENT

(In addition to equipment mentioned on page 247)
Store Tent (for food and equipment).

Kitchen Shelter or Tarp.

"Dining Room" Tarp.

First Aid Patrol Pouch.

Felling Axe.

Laundry Soap.

Equipment for Scout Training.

Signal Flag Kit, Tracking Irons, etc.

A few words may be necessary in regard to some articles mentioned.

For the personal equipment in a standing camp, a *straw tick* (browse bag) is very much recommended. It does not take up much space, is inexpensive (made of cheap linen canvas) yet gives a lot of comfort. For a few nights, it is all right to sleep on the ground. But it is tiresome in the long run. A straw tick may be filled with straw rented or bought from the nearest farmer or with dry leaves from the forest and will make up a comfortable bed.

*Mosquito netting* and *mosquito remedies* are only taken along if you think mosquitoes dominate the nights around your camp site. Again—better "Be Prepared" for the worst!

The *Sport articles* mentioned or others you may have may fill some space. But do not let that prevent you from taking them along. They will prove wonderful assets to the program of the camp.

*Books,* if you feel like it, yes. One or two good ones. Cheap books somehow don't harmonize with the spirit of camp.

In looking at the Patrol equipment, *The Flag* of our Country certainly ought to follow the Patrol to camp and wave over it during the long happy days. Impressive hoisting and lowering ceremonies will be a part of the daily program.

A *Store Tent* is a necessity in a standing camp. A pup tent is fine for the purpose. Better still, a small tent of white canvas, pup tents usually being brown, therefore, heat absorbing and rather hot storerooms for perishables.

In case of rain, a *Kitchen Tarp* to place over the fire place, and a *"Dining Room" Tarp* to place over the improvised table and chairs will be a blessing.

The *First Aid Patrol Pouch* ought to contain besides the material mentioned on page 204 one small bottle of Aromatic Spirits of Ammonia, one bottle of castor oil, tablets of Permanganate of Potassium, tablets of Boric Acid, one tube of Ungentine or cold cream, preferably the first.

*Felling Axe* may come in handy (i.e., if you are permitted to use it), for pioneer work.

And most certainly *Soap* for laundry purposes is necessary in a camp extending over a week or more.

PUT UP WITH SPEED          PUT UP WITH CARE

## Eats

The menus must be very carefully prepared before-hand, every detail taken into consideration. It would be a good idea to get in connection before the camp with the grocer and the farmer who are going to provide you with the necessary provisions to send them a copy of your provision list and get their ideas on it. There isn't any fun in making up a list with strawberries and watermelon and fish when none of these things are to be had.

Don't make the menus too complicated. Wholesome food well prepared is better than any fancy dishes.

It is very much to be recommended that you bring along food-stuff for the first day in camp and only start to depend upon the local supplies when the camp is well established.

## Your Part of the Planning

The equipment and eats being taken care of by the proper experts of the Patrol, again we come to your planning of the program for the adventure.

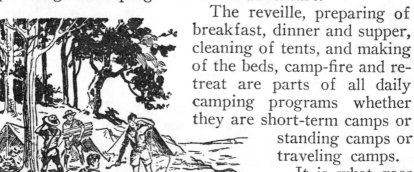

The reveille, preparing of breakfast, dinner and supper, cleaning of tents, and making of the beds, camp-fire and retreat are parts of all daily camping programs whether they are short-term camps or standing camps or traveling camps.

It is what goes in between breakfast and dinner and supper, the activities of the forenoon and the afternoon periods that make all the difference in the world.

And that is exactly the point that must be planned extremely carefully before you go to camp with your boys. All hours of the day must be filled to over-flowing.

The first day and the last day give no trouble. You will probably not arrive so early that you get more accomplished than just establishing a camp in its simplest form and the last day is filled with the excitement of packing.

The second day in camp is usually occupied by making all of those camp improvements which add to your comfort, while the remaining days must be filled with a variety of activities depending upon the ingenuity of the Patrol Leader.

As a general rule it may be said that the forenoon period is best spent away from camp on some sort of a hike while the afternoon periods are spent in camp in sports, games and special training.

In regard to the first part you will find a number of suggestions on page 221. In regard to the latter the activities will depend to some degree upon the equipment which you have brought along, even if it is possible to plan quite a few things right in camp.

No definite suggestions can be made in regard to the afternoon activities. They depend upon the taste of the Patrol and its members. And you are the only one that will know about that, having had a chance to study them for months. Therefore, talk it over with your boys or find ideas yourself.

Whatever you do, be sure to have a program for every hour of every day, if you want the camp to become a success. The following outline for a general daily program may help you in your planning.

# PROGRAM FOR DAY IN STANDING CAMP

7:00—Reveille.  Get up, wash, start breakfast, etc., air blankets, clean tents and camp site.

8:00—Breakfast. Clean-up.

8:45—Putting tents in order, camp improvements.

9:30—Hike from camp.  Scoutcraft.

11:30—Return to camp.  Starting dinner.

12:30—Dinner. Clean-up.

1:30—Compulsory rest.  Writing of letters and diary, reading.

2:00—Different sports and games, archery, axe throwing, rope spinning, lariat throwing, ball games, etc.

3:30—Scoutcraft training or short hike in neighborhood of camp. Possibly bathing.

4:45—Return to camp.  Rest.

5:00—Preparing Supper.

6:00—Supper.  Clean-up.

7:00—Rest.

7:30—Evening games.

8:00—Council Fire.

9:30—Taps, extinguishing of fire.  To bed.

10:00—Lights out.  Silence.

## Starting the Camp

So you are off at last.  Every bit of equipment is there.  Nothing has been forgotten.  And it is with high spirits that the Patrol gets into the train, with high spirits it rolls toward the adventure of the summer, and with high spirits it arrives at its camp site after a hike that possibly tested the perseverance of every one of its members.

Following the same system which they have been following on all their camping hikes the boys put up the camp in a few minutes, and the cooks start preparing the first meal while all the boys who have nothing to do have left for the farm with their ticks, returning a short while later with a comfortable straw mattress for every one of the members of the gang.

The supper is eaten, the utensils cleaned. A bit of rest and then—the first council in the camp.

So far away from everyday life surrounded by a group of good friends! And just think of the days ahead!

The camp fire is short. The boys are sleepy from the excitement and the travel. "Day is done" is sung softly. To bed. "Good night! Pleasant dreams!"

Maybe you don't go to sleep immediately. Maybe you suddenly get a feeling of your great responsibility, the responsibility, the happiness of these sleeping boys around you for days to come. Maybe a silent prayer moves your lips while you bend your head. "Give me power and give me ability to justify all of their expectations!" Then you too are carried off to slumber.

## Camp Improvements

The first day was used for setting up camp, the second day is used for improving it and to introduce all of those things which may add to the comfort or glory of the days to come.

As soon as breakfast is over with and the tents are straightened up you will, everyone, get to work. The first thing you will think of is to do what the discoverers used to do in the days of old when they found their way into an unknown land, to hoist the symbol of their own country. You have taken the camp site in possession as real American boys and you show it by

hoisting the symbol of the United States over the grounds—Old Glory. Get a *flag-pole,* and get it quick. It ought to be found without difficulty. Fasten an eye to its top, bring the halyard through it, dig a hole in the ground, raise the pole in it, fill up and stamp the earth hard around it, finishing up with a small mound of rocks. Have your boys come to attention and sing one verse of "The Star Spangled Banner", while one of their number hoists the Flag to the top of the pole and fastens it there. This ceremony is used every day as long as the Patrol occupies the camp. In the morning The Flag is hoisted. It is lowered again at night and every time the boys pay it their tribute.

The raising of the flag pole is the start of making camp improvements. Many others may be suggested. We shall describe some in a few words and hope that the accompanying illustrations will make the details clear.

First let us consider the kitchen.

A *permanent fireplace* may be built with side logs and crane. It may be constructed of rocks, dug into

the ground, or raised over it on some kind of an altar. A bottomless water pail provided with holes for draught makes a wonderful Patrol stove.

*Camp ovens* of different designs may be constructed from an old biscuit tin. Don't forget that top heat is just as important as the bottom fire.

*Fire thongs* and a *fire broom* will be a real help in handling the fire and keeping the fireplace clean.

A *wood pile* is made to contain the ready-cut wood for the fire assorted in different thicknesses. A shelter

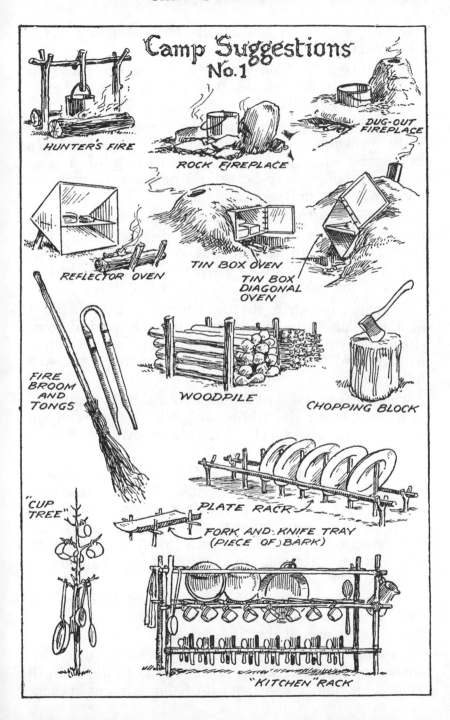

Camp Suggestions No. 1

HUNTER'S FIRE

ROCK FIREPLACE

DUG-OUT FIREPLACE

REFLECTOR OVEN

TIN BOX OVEN

TIN BOX DIAGONAL OVEN

FIRE BROOM AND TONGS

WOODPILE

CHOPPING BLOCK

"CUP TREE"

PLATE RACK

FORK AND KNIFE TRAY (PIECE OF) BARK

"KITCHEN" RACK

may be built over it to keep it from becoming wet on a rainy day.

A *chopping block* on which to cut the wood and into which the axe is sunk when not in use is a necessary part of every fireplace.

A *rack* may be built for the cooking pots as shown in the drawing. Another will come in very handy for the plates, while a *"cup-tree"* consisting of a much branching bough may be set up and a bark container made for fork, knives and spoons.

A *cooling cellar* is an excellent thing to have in the kitchen. It may be a 2 x 2 x 2 foot hole dug in the ground lined with stones and covered by a wooden cover. In this the butter may be kept hard, and the milk and the meat fresh even on a hot day.

If a river is flowing by the camp it is even better to dig the cellar in the river bank and line it with stones. The water will fill the cellar and surround the butter, the milk and the waterproof meat container and keep them cool.

Another way of keeping the meat is by putting it on a plate, cover the whole with cheese cloth and suspend it from the branch of a tree in shade of the sun as a *fly cabinet*.

So much for the kitchen. But the other rooms of the apartment must also be considered. Just outside the tent you may want to place a *shoe scraper* for the use of the boys before they enter the tent. Another good arrangement for shoes is a *shoe rack* just inside the tent door. On this all shoes which are not in use are kept neat and out of the way.

A *towel rack* for drying towels and bathing suits may be set up behind the tents. A few poles and a piece of rope are all that is necessary.

A *dining table* with *benches* may be constructed in a number of different ways. One way is to dig it in the ground, another to construct it of thin straight branches

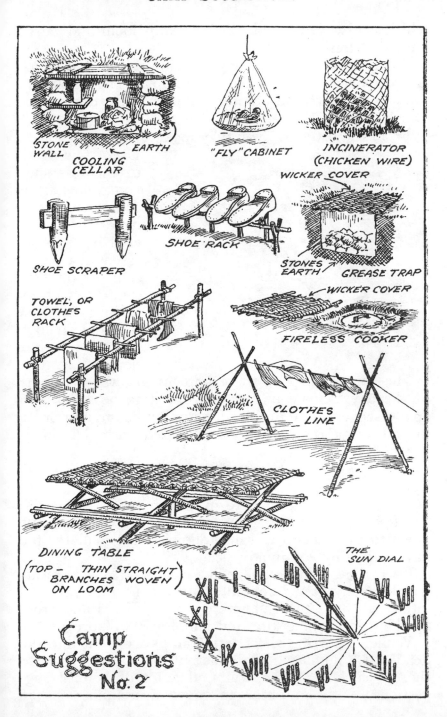

STONE WALL — EARTH
COOLING CELLAR

"FLY" CABINET

INCINERATOR (CHICKEN WIRE)

SHOE SCRAPER

SHOE RACK

WICKER COVER
STONES EARTH — GREASE TRAP

TOWEL, OR CLOTHES RACK

WICKER COVER
FIRELESS COOKER

CLOTHES LINE

DINING TABLE
(TOP — THIN STRAIGHT BRANCHES WOVEN ON LOOM)

THE SUN DIAL

Camp Suggestions No. 2

which are woven together on a camp loom and raised on a skeleton of poles.

As the last thing we may mention a *sun dial* which is a favorite in a number of camps. The important thing is to have the pointer point directly toward the North Star.

From the list above you may make your own choices.

Use a few or all of them as suits you. Some of the equipment c a n - n o t  b e  consid-ered in any way essential t o t h e comfort o f t h e camp y e t t h e y b r i n g  i n  just enough civiliza-tion to make it a camp.

The constructing of these implements will take part of the day. Some of the day ought to be spent also on a discovery hike in the surrounding country in order to get yourself thoroughly acquainted with the neighborhood.

Then supper, rest, camp fire! And the second day has gone.

### The Life in Camp

After the first two days are over with, you settle down to the general routine following the plan for the days as laid by you in advance.

Everything will be going like clockwork. The meals will be ready at the appointed hour, the different activities will have the full interest of the boys and from morning to evening fun and happiness will prevail.

While discussing short term camps we went into the details of a number of daily activities. By referring to those (page 265) you will find a lot of helpful suggestions. Still in order to cover a camping day in

chronological order it may be considered wise to sum up
the suggestions and add other worth while hints.

## Morning

The camping day starts at seven sharp. Either with
your "Good Morning" or with reveille sounded on the
bugle by the Cheermaster. While bugle signals aren't
exactly necessary in the Patrol camp yet they help to
put special emphasis on certain occurrences, and it is
well to start the day in a festive way. So let him go
ahead exercising his lungs even if some of the tones
seem to stick inside the bugle.

Get the boys out of the tents immediately and into
the morning wash. Be sure that they actually wash,
that they even go "as far" as clean-
ing necks and ears. Also tooth
brushing must be attended to, no
one being permitted to sheer away
from this.

After the wash the day's work
is started. The "Cooking" group
lights the fire and gets the break-

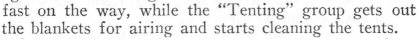

fast on the way, while the "Tenting" group gets out
the blankets for airing and starts cleaning the tents.

In the meantime the two boys who have been given
that special assignment are on their way to the farms
to fetch the milk and other things which have already
been ordered here. They will return to camp in time
for breakfast and take part in this meal with the rest.
If the grocer is on the way they will see him too, get
hold of the foodstuff for the day and leave the order
for next day's meals. If the grocery is so far away as
to prevent the boys from getting back for breakfast if
they market at this time the collecting must be attended to at some other time of the day, preferably the
early morning hours before the special activities are
started.

Breakfast is eaten, pots and plates have been cleaned,
the tents are fixed. The Patrol gathers at the flag pole

for the Flag Raising ceremony. They salute The Flag as it slowly ascends.

## Forenoon

The program of the forenoon is laid away from camp, on a hike in the surrounding country, with nature study or training in the Scout requirements. (See page 221). If some of the boys have special hobbies as for example photography, collecting of minerals, butterflies and other nature articles, this is the place for satisfying them.

If a bathing place can be reached during this period,

so much the better. A plunge into the coolness of the water will be welcomed by all of the boys. Be sure to live up to the rules as given on page 272.

Naturally all of the boys ought to take part in these activities. Yet sometimes it may be necessary, if the camp is close to any roads and exposed to publicity, to leave one or two of the boys in camp as guards. We should not like to have happen to your Patrol what happened to another Patrol which we have read about. On returning from a hike they found that their kitchen tent had been razed, and all their foodstuff had disappeared. To the tent flap was fastened a piece of paper with the following words: "Wy dontcha keep sum beer?" That is one of the reasons why we insist upon the fact that the *ideal* camp site must be withdrawn from public view.

## Noon

As soon as the Patrol returns from the forenoon's hike the noon meal is started. There has always been some difference of opinion as to what kind of a meal this ought to be. Many insist upon making it the most important meal of the day and reducing the evening meal to a light supper while others want the noontime meal light and the evening meal more elaborate.

This is mostly a matter of taste, with both pros and cons. The meal should be such as can be made to apply with the program of the day. In many cases when the Patrol has special training to do it will prefer to keep the day as free as possible and therefore will decide upon an easily prepared luncheon and save the bigger meal for the evening. At other times the Patrol may think that the preparing of a big meal in the evening after a strenuous day is too much and will decide upon making the noon meal the chief feast of the day. It is up to you and to your Patrol to decide upon which procedure to follow.

It is very much recommended that you do not stick to the procedure of having one group of boys prepare all the meals in camp. The "Cooking" group will do

its share, but the "Tenting" group must also be given an opportunity to try its culinary skill. If this is not done, too much specialization will be going on and half of the Patrol will be deprived of the possibility of training in Patrol cooking. By rotating the responsibilities all the boys will get an insight into all of the things which make a camp run smoothly. If the "Tenting" group isn't sufficiently versed in the art of cooking to prepare the meal it will call in a little help from the other group until it has acquired the necessary skill.

The noon meal and cleaning up after it ought to be

folldwed by a compulsory rest period. The boys will
need it.

Have them lie down in the shade of some tree (the
tent is not to be used during the day), preferably on
a blanket taken from the tent. Even if the ground
doesn't feel damp it may still be able to give the boys a
chill.

A quiet talk may fill the rest hour. Maybe even the
reading of a chapter from a good book or a story from
the current issue of "BOYS' LIFE". Some of the
boys may have special activities to attend to. Writing
up their diaries for example, or getting that letter finished for father and mother. Also repair work may be
going on, as patching a hole in the shorts, getting that
button fastened, that stocking hole darned and shoes
cleaned. Still others may take a nap. Don't disturb
them. They will be so much better off later in the day.

An hour ought to be sufficient for rest. Extended too
long, the rest period may result in a tendency to loafing
that will continue the rest of the day.

## Afternoon

After the rest hour get some real activity started. An
active game from the Handbook for Boys or a sport of
some kind. You may rig up an athletic field with broad
jump, high jump, race track and try out the boys. If
they are interested in archery and have brought their
tackle along, bow and arrow work may fill the afternoon. Ropes will suggest lariat throwing and rope
spinning (why not make this a Patrol specialty?), also
a baseball or a football will create a lot of fun.

Later in the afternoon a short walk may be undertaken. And then the time has come for another meal.

## Evening

After the evening meal is over with, have a short rest
followed by a couple of comparatively quiet games as
the dusk comes creeping on, until the hour arrives for
the council fire.

Be sure that the boys are warmly clothed as they come to the fire, either by a sweater or by a blanket wrapped around them. If the dew fall is heavy go easy with the blankets. You do not want the boys to creep into cold or damp blankets for the night. This may be remedied by holding the blankets close to the fire for warming just before the boys turn in.

Before starting the more entertaining part of the council fire it is necessary to have a short business meeting during which the program for the coming day is discussed and the different duties distributed. Here you decide who will be getting tomorrow's milk and food stuff, who will cook, who will take care of the camp site, and so on. When this is over with the fun begins

and the council fire continues on the lines described on page 266.

Half past nine already! Taps sung around the fire, taps sounded on the muted bugle. Fire extinguished. To the tents!

Then 10 o'clock. The day is over. "Good-night. Sleep well!"

## If it Rains?

The activities as described above are for the good-weather day in camp. But you are right! It might rain.

We all know that rain muffles even the highest spirits and may even go as far as putting disconsolateness into camp. There is only one thing to do: Get as much out of it as possible. If you are prepared to receive rain when it comes you will be able to offset some of its disadvantages.

But before thinking of the activities the camp itself must be prepared for the rain.

First of all get all equipment which can't stand rain into the tents. Pots and pans may be left outside, but clothing, spades and axes must be brought inside. And teach the boys that it is not enough for them just to take care of their own equipment. If rain starts it is their simple duty to help bring in the other fellow's possessions too.

Next think of the tents. You certainly do not want the inside of them transformed into bathtubs. And they

 will be if some provision is not made to lead off not only the water which streams down the tent sides but also the water which runs toward the tent in brooklets. All spades must be put into activity digging a trench, (or as it is sometimes called because of its form, a "diamond ditch"), around the tent.

This is done by first cutting down into the ground close to the tent with the spade about 3 inches deep, the whole way around, next by cutting around the tent about 4-6 inches further out and then by turning over and away from the tent the long sods loosened in this manner. Don't ever permit your boys to merely cut up a spadeful at a time and turn it against the tent side. The sods thus placed will absorb the water as a sponge and tend to ruin the tent. If trenching has to be done, it must be done correctly, also in such a way that the sod can be easily replaced when the camp site is abandoned, thus leaving no trace of the camp.

Also do not forget to slacken the guy ropes, or the tent pegs may pop out of the ground. If your tent isn't perfectly waterproof, if it is rather old or of comparatively loose woven material you may find that the rain breaks through and falls inside as a fine spray. Don't be alarmed. If the tent isn't all to the bad this will stop as soon as the canvas becomes thoroughly wet. Worse it is if drops start to drip from the tent side. This may usually be remedied by putting a finger on the spot and running it along the canvas to the ground. Instead of coming through, the drops will then follow this course. Warn your boys against ever touching the inside of the canvas when it is raining. Unpleasant consequences may follow. Also move every piece of equipment which touches the canvas.

When the necessary work is over with, then is the time to think of the rainy day activities.

Always have a number of stunts or competitions ready which might be pulled inside the tent. Also different instruction may be in order. Try some advanced knotting or splicing, some simple first aid, some signaling by sound or by flashlight, whittling or different projects. Competitions may include spell downs in any of

the Scout requirements or it may be remembering of messages for a certain number of minutes while a general conversation is going on, a Kim's game or one of the games mentioned under camp fire (page 266). You will also find that a musical instrument (a banjo, a "uke" or a harmonica) is worth its weight in gold on a rainy day. If you can get your boys started singing you are not so badly off.

Or why not try a vigorous tag in the midst of the rain? Take off shoes and stockings. Keep on as little clothing as possible. If bathing suits have been brought along get into them and get out in the downpour. As long as the boys keep moving they won't feel cold. When the game has lasted long enough, if the players strip, creep inside the tent door, take a real rub down until they glow, then get into their clothes again, they will all feel so much better after the fun.

Also a hike through the rain has its attractive aspects, provided you have suitable rain clothing. You can smell the fragrance of the earth streaming toward you. The trees look different. The plants seem to be more alive.

If the rain is a warm summer one, the cooks may prepare the meals in their bathing suits. If it is rather cool, they will put on their rain clothing. As long as they keep their feet warm they will feel no discomfort.

The meals are served in the tents, the boys sitting as close to the door as possible and looking out not to spill

any foodstuff on ground-cloth o r on blankets, or under the "dining room" tarp, i f y o u brought one along. After t h e m e a l the plates are put into the pots and set aside to be cleaned a l m o s t

automatically by the drizzling rain outside.

An indoor camp fire program with singing, story telling (what about ghost stories?) may follow. Or discussions may be improvised in the evening around one of the lanterns. This doesn't need to be of long duration. Rain makes one sleepy and the boys will want to turn in rather early. Let them. The monotony of the falling rain-drops on the canvas will soon lull them to sleep.

But do not have the tent closed hermetically even if it is pouring outside. Ventilation is necessary. If the wind comes from the back of the tent it may be possible to keep the front entirely open. If not, you may close it at the bottom, leave the top open and put in a square peg to form a kind of window.

## Breaking Camp

Whether it is a short-term camp or a standing camp, the procedure of breaking camp is the same with the exception that the clearing of the standing camp may have to be started earlier.

Start by pulling down all of these things with the sole exception of the flag pole from which The Flag has been waving since the morning's ceremony. Next proceed in packing the personal equipment, cooking gear and tents.

When the camp site has been cleared of all traces and the packs are ready to be slung on the boys' backs, gather around the flag pole and take down The Flag with appropriate ceremony. Then remove the flag pole and clear the place where it stood.

If the camp site is private property the Patrol will now proceed to the house of the owner who has been kind enough to put it at their disposal. The Patrol Leader will express to him the thanks of the Patrol and the boys will show him their approval by a heartily rendered Patrol cheer.

The camp is over. The Patrol returns home knowing that it has lived up to the counsel of Baden-Powell when he says there are two things which a Scout camper leaves behind him, namely—

1. *Nothing.*
2. *His Thanks.*

"Nothing" on the camp site to show his having been there. "Thanks" to the people who have helped him by their kindness to enjoy his camping experience.

## TRAVELLING CAMPS

Without a doubt the most complicated form of camping and the one that requires the biggest amount of capability of its leader is the hiking camp.

The standing camp is difficult enough for a Patrol to manage, but the traveling camp with its questions of leadership responsibilities, knowledge of the country to be traversed, choice of equipment, provision for suitable meals, its heavy expenses is very much harder.

Also the travelling camp is a decidedly older boy proposition for which reason it can never be advised that any but old and well cemented together Patrols should so much as think of such a camp.

If the Patrol has been existing for at least three years, if it has had all the training a Council camp, a Troop camp, and an individual Patrol camp can render, it may be considered capable of undertaking a hiking camp, but not before. And even so it must be insisted upon that adult leadership is present and has the actual responsibility of the hike.

If your Patrol has the above qualifications, go ahead and try to arrange such a hike. If it hasn't, keep away from the attempt.

Should a travelling camp be undertaken, it will be necessary to start planning early, decide upon where to go, what to see, means of transportation and expenses involved.

Maybe a certain part of the State in which the Patrol lives attracts the boys because of its natural beauty or because of its historic interest or the Patrol may want to go even farther away, exploring other states or visit-

ing cities at considerable distance. Much of this planning for such a journey depends upon the way in which the Patrol expects to travel. If it wants to go afoot, the territory to be covered must necessarily be a small one. If it can get a car at its disposal the "sky may be the limit," provided there are enough days in which to get there. Other means of transportation may be used.

If walking, don't expect to cover much more than 10-12 miles a day at an average. More will prove a great discomfort. For canoe or boat trips 15 miles may be considered the maximum, while bicyclists may cover 30-35 miles without getting exhausted. For automobile hiking, journeys of not more than 150 miles a day are to be recommended if you want the hike to be a pleasure trip.

These distances may seem rather small to you but you will find when you get on the road that a shorter daily journey brings more satisfaction. After all it isn't the distance covered but the experiences encountered that are the main issue.

As soon as your dreams of place and conveyance have taken shape you will confer with your Scoutmaster, who in turn will confer with the Local Council. They together will decide if the travelling camp should be permitted to take place. If it is agreed that the plan is practicable, these leaders will help you to secure the necessary adult leadership and to work out the definite plans for the trip.

As it will be easily seen from the above only in cases of rare exception will a Patrol have an opportunity to undertake a travelling camp. It will also be seen that as the planning of the travelling camp depends upon the local conditions and upon the means of transportation no hard and fast rules can be laid down and no advice given which will suitably cover all possible combinations. Therefore we shall not in this book further elaborate on the subject beyond advising Patrols which have enough ambition to think of undertaking such a trip to seek the co-operation and consent of the local authorities and help in regard to the planning and the actually carrying out of the project.

A well-planned, worth-while journey of this sort makes an unforgettable and valuable experience for a Patrol that is ready for it, but no Patrol should rush into this sort of thing inadvisedly.

# CHAPTER IX

## PATROL HANDICRAFT

A BUSY Patrol is a good Patrol. And a good Patrol Leader keeps his eyes open all the time for worth-while, interesting Handicraft Projects to offer to his boys. He and his Patrol should find in this chapter enough ideas and suggestions from which to start making a selection for Patrol activities, which can be turned to good account for the Patrol's own use and satisfaction, for money earning possibilities and for gifts. Many other projects not here given will undoubtedly occur to you and your boys. A wide awake Patrol is a Patrol with ideas of its own, and enough persistence and imagination and Patrol Spirit to put them through. Insist always that whatever is attempted should be done well and finished. Don't let the boys skip from project to project, but also be always ready with a new idea as soon as the old one has become fact.

Probably its own needs will make your Patrol decide first to work on its camp equipment or the outfitting of its Den. And such a shared dream and effort is the best possible foundation for real Patrol Spirit and co-operation, for getting to be real friends with each other.

As has been said elsewhere, the Patrol Leader will

try to utilize and develop the individual gifts and special abilities of his boys. Let the boy who is handy with tools make the Den bookcase, the boy who is artistically inclined design the Patrol emblems or totem pole, the boy who is interested in special craftwork like woodcarving or metal work or photography make his particular gift to the Patrol Den furnishings. Let the knot-tying enthusiast supply the knot board, the nature study lover provide the leaf or track casts. Let each boy offer some definite contribution to the Patrol life accessories. And this, in addition, of course, to the group projects such as making camping equipment, tents, and so forth, in which all work together on a common task, for a common end. Thus everybody has a share in everything.

## Patrol Specialties

In selecting Patrol projects for money earning remember that specialties pay best and are most satisfactory to develop. The Patrol which is known to be expert makers of neckerchief slides, or celluloid ornaments and utilities, or pine needle trays will have a better opportunity to market its wares profitably than one which tries to do a little of everything and doesn't bother to do any of it with the highest degree of excellency and beauty.

In this connection, too, it should be noted that "mass production" is best conducted on a specialist-within-your-group plan. For instance, if your Patrol is producing and selling linoleum prints for Christmas greeting purposes, let one boy—your best artist—make the designs, another transfer the designs to the linoleum, while two others cut the blocks, still another inks them, and two others work together in making the actual prints. In this way the work is done more rapidly and more satisfactorily and with a generally higher standard of results than can be otherwise achieved.

## Other Helps

Though naturally, in so brief a space, it has not been possible to treat these subjects in great detail, we have endeavored, nevertheless, to make the descriptions of procedure involved in the Handicraft activities so complete that by the aid of the illustrations it can be easily followed by you and your boys. For your convenience also, in case you wish to dig deeper into any of these specialties, we have listed with each subject discussed a few good practical books, which will be of interest and help. Most of these books and probably others on the same lines you may be able to secure from your local libraries.

And so to work!

Be a busy leader of a busy Patrol. Make Expert Handicraft a tradition in your Patrol. Use it for fun, for training, for self expression, for thrift, and above all—for Service.

## PATROL DENS

The value of a Patrol having its own room, which it can furnish and decorate as it sees fit, can not be over - estimated. The possession of a Patrol Den is a tremendous help in developing Patrol Spirit, and at an early stage of its life the Patrol should certainly try to get one.

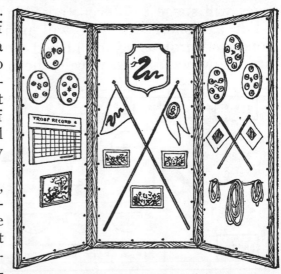

To start with, however, the Patrol may have its meetings at the Troop meeting room. Consequently it wants this, its own corner, to represent the

BSA PATROL ROOM

personality of the Patrol. This may be done by building up a Patrol screen, as shown on page 309, decorated with Scoutcraft articles, record charts, photographs, shields, etc.

When you are lucky enough to procure a room for the Patrol, get together with your boys and decide upon how it is to be decorated. You may want to make the room into a Scouting den, a woodcraft den, a pioneer log cabin, an Indian tipi, or into something else specific for your Patrol. The pictures on these pages will suggest different possible lay-outs.

For a pioneer den you will naturally stick to the pioneer style of using unfinished wood for your furniture, snowshoes, skins, powder horns, old firearms and

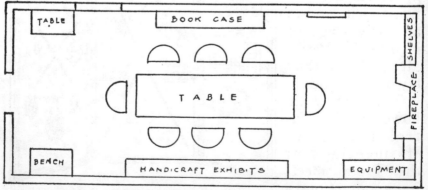

PLAN OF PATROL ROOM

A PATROL DEN IN THE PIONEER SPIRIT

the like for wall decorations. An appropriate chandelier may be made out of an old wagon wheel.

For an Indian room you may build a tipi within your den, furnished with stump seats and fireplace on which incense may be burned. Or you may decorate the room with Indian blankets, bead work, head dresses, skins, totem poles, and build an artificial camp fire for the center.

There are many other ways of furnishing and decorating a Patrol Den.

You may build rustic furniture consisting of chairs or benches, tables, desks, library shelves. Or you may use old wooden boxes for the making of your furniture.

On the walls may be hung The Flag of our country, flags of other Scouting countries, signal flags, stream-

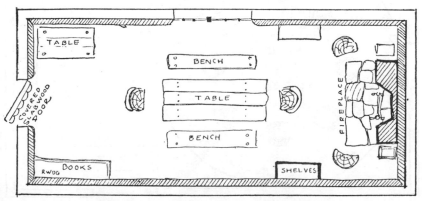

PLAN OF PIONEER PATROL DEN

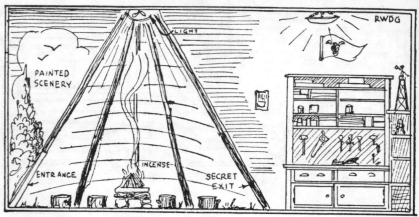

INDIAN TIPI BUILT WITHIN A ROOM—FOR PATROL DEN

ers or bunting. Also a poster with the Scout Oath and Law, pictures of James E. West, Dan Beard and other well known men inside or outside the Scout world.

On one wall you may want to arrange a Patrol Hall of Fame with a shield for each boy with his photograph, his Merit Badges, his record in the Patrol. Or what about a Patrol historical exhibition of photographs and souvenirs brought home from the Patrol's

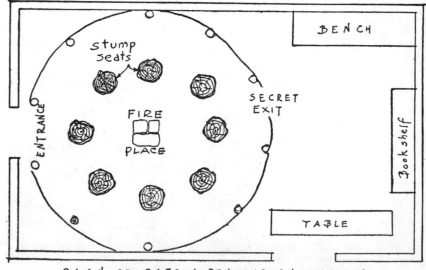

PLAN OF PATROL DEN—INDIAN FASHION

many trips? Another good idea is to have a big topographical map of the country around your town on which may be painted the routes of trips undertaken by the Patrol.

On another wall you may have knot boards, instruction charts, or a blackboard which may help you in the training of your boys. Also shelves for your Patrol library and chests for your Patrol equipment.

In the corners of the room may be arranged different nature exhibits, models of camp fires and tents and bridges or the Patrol flag or totem in majestic solitude in a stand made especially for it.

There is no limit to the number of ways in which a Patrol Den may be decorated. Use your imagination, but be sure that the Den expresses the personality and spirit of the Patrol.

## EQUIPMENT HANDICRAFT

### Making the "P. L. H. Tent"

As mentioned in Chapter VIII, tents which can accommodate half of the members of the Patrol are by many considered the best for Patrol camping. But at the same time transportation must be considered. Naturally a tent for four weighs more than a tent for two and is consequently more difficult to handle. On page 315 are given the patterns and working drawings for a tent which has the advantages but not the drawbacks of a 4-person tent. It consists of two halves. If only two boys want to use it, they put up one half as a complete baker tent. If four boys want it for shelter they will make two halves into one wall tent.

For your tents it is up to you to choose your own material. You may want to use 7 or 8 ounce duck, white, khaki or green, or a lighter, tightly woven material.

Before cutting it make up a miniature model of tent in paper, two inches representing one foot. Figure out how material may most economically be used, how many widths go into making the roof and side, how many the flaps.

*Remember that on the pattern, page 315, no extra measure is allowed for seams. Leave enough for a strong seam when cutting material.*

The procedure of assembling the tent is evident from the drawing. Detail drawings explain a few points. One sketch shows the sewing of the eave, one, the fastening of ribbons to flaps for closing, one, the loops through which side pegs go, one, the correct way of putting together and attaching guide ropes.

Ordinary clothes line may be used for guy ropes.

Two poles, 6½ feet long, are necessary for wall tent. For baker tent, poles are halved, two 3¼ feet poles being used.

The dimensions of wall tent are 6½' x 7', 6½' high with 2½' side walls. Dimensions of baker tent are 4' x 7', 3½' high, with 3½' x 7' veranda.

For necessary tent accessories, see chapter on Patrol Camping.

## Patrol Equipment Bags

On plate, page 317 appear the patterns with dimensions and drawings of a few pieces of the Patrol camping equipment which a Patrol can make for itself, namely, canvas water pail, canvas water basin and provision bags for dry rations and meat.

The *canvas water bag* is made of heavy waterproof material. The largest piece is turned over with a wide hem at top and bottom. Next the sides are sewn on, the pail turned inside out and sown again along the seam. Two grommets are fastened at front and back of top and a couple of rope ends inserted for a handle. If bag leaks at seam rub with a piece of beeswax.

The sides of the *canvas water basin* are sewed to the bottom separately, starting at center and working to either side. Next, the sides are sewed together.

# MAKING *the* P.L.H. TENT

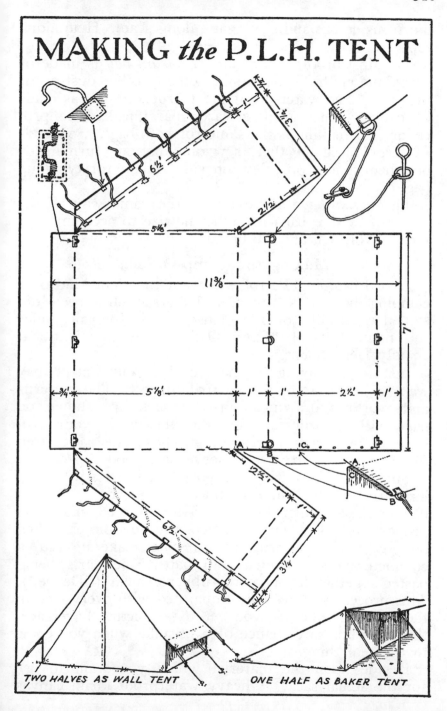

TWO HALVES AS WALL TENT          ONE HALF AS BAKER TENT

Turn inside out and sew again along seam. Hem along top.

The dust-proof, *dry ration provision bag* is made of aeroplane cloth, "balloon silk" or any other dust-proof material. The water-proof *meat provision bag* is made of canvas which is afterwards paraffined. The procedure for making is the same for both bags. Sew ends of large piece together, sew onto bottom, turn inside out, hem along top. Sew on side ribbon for tying up bag.

The *bread bags* are made in the same way as the above provision bags in sufficient size to accommodate your favorite brand of bread.

## Making the Camp-O-Sack

A real camping Patrol will want the right kind of a camping haversack. Such a haversack has been designed especially for Patrol use and is for sale under the name Official "Camp-O-Sack" at the National Supply Department.

Instead of buying the haversacks, your Patrol may want to make its own as a real project. The patterns and working drawings for the sack are shown on page 319. It will facilitate the making of your own haversacks, however, if you purchase one sack from the Supply Department to serve as a model.

Supply yourself with two large sheets of stiff paper. Transfer in duplicate on these sheets the design of haversack as shown on page 319, enlarged in correct proportions. Cut out the two sets of pieces, using one set for a pattern, the other to make up into a complete model haversack in paper, the parts being pasted together firmly with rubber cement ("Devoe"). This process will get you acquainted with every step in the procedure before you get to the actual haversack, thus avoiding any chance of a mistake when you come to the real thing.

Decide upon the material which you want to use for the actual sack. A heavy waterproof khaki canvas

# PATROL EQUIPMENT BAGS

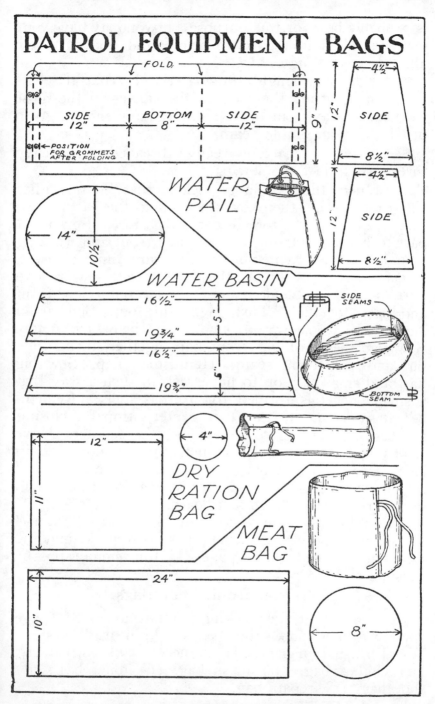

FOLD

SIDE 12"    BOTTOM 8"    SIDE 12"

9"

POSITION FOR GROMMETS AFTER FOLDING

4½"
SIDE
8½"
12"

4½"
SIDE
8½"
12"

*WATER PAIL*

14"
10½"

*WATER BASIN*

16½"
19¾"
5"

16½"
19¾"
5"

SIDE SEAMS

BOTTOM SEAM

12"
11"

4"

*DRY RATION BAG*

*MEAT BAG*

24"
10"

8"

is probably best for this purpose, but you may have your own pet ideas in regard to colors and weave. After all, this is *your haversack*.

After having bought the material lay out the patterns on it, fitting them on to the canvas in the most economical way. Cut out. The measurements as given provide for an ample seam.

Get a sewing machine ready, threaded with heavy thread, and start the sewing.

First hem the two long pockets that go on either side of the back, then sew them on to the back. Also sew straps on to bottom in correct position. Sew front part to bottom, starting from center front and working to either side. (Remember at the same time to insert, in center, strap for tying the flap). Next sew back to bottom in same fashion. Turn inside out. Sew front and back together. Turn right side out. Sew again along seam whole way around. Next hem sack at top. Sew two pieces of big front flap together, turn inside out and sew along seam. Hem small flap. Sew big flap and small flap on to haversack in such a way that a small pocket is formed for a cross stick. (Remember at same time to insert, in center, strap for closing the bag.) Take bag to a sailmaker or saddler. Have straps riveted on, six grommets put in top (two in back strap, two in front, one in each side center) and one in flap. Also have leather straps for closing flap pocket riveted on. Two ash boards, 13" x 1½" x ¼", are fitted into the side pockets, another board, 9" x ¾" x ¼", into the cross pockets at top of pack, and the haversack is ready. See page 245 for photographs of finished sack.

## Personal Equipment Bags

In speaking of the packing of the haversack (page 243) we mentioned the "bags within bag" system. We also listed on page 241 the necessary bags, namely, (a) clothes bag, (b) mess bag, (c) toilet bag, (d) shoe bag, (e) repair bag.

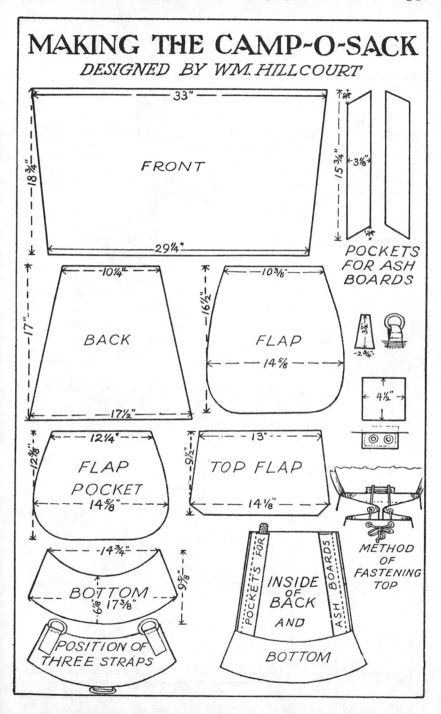

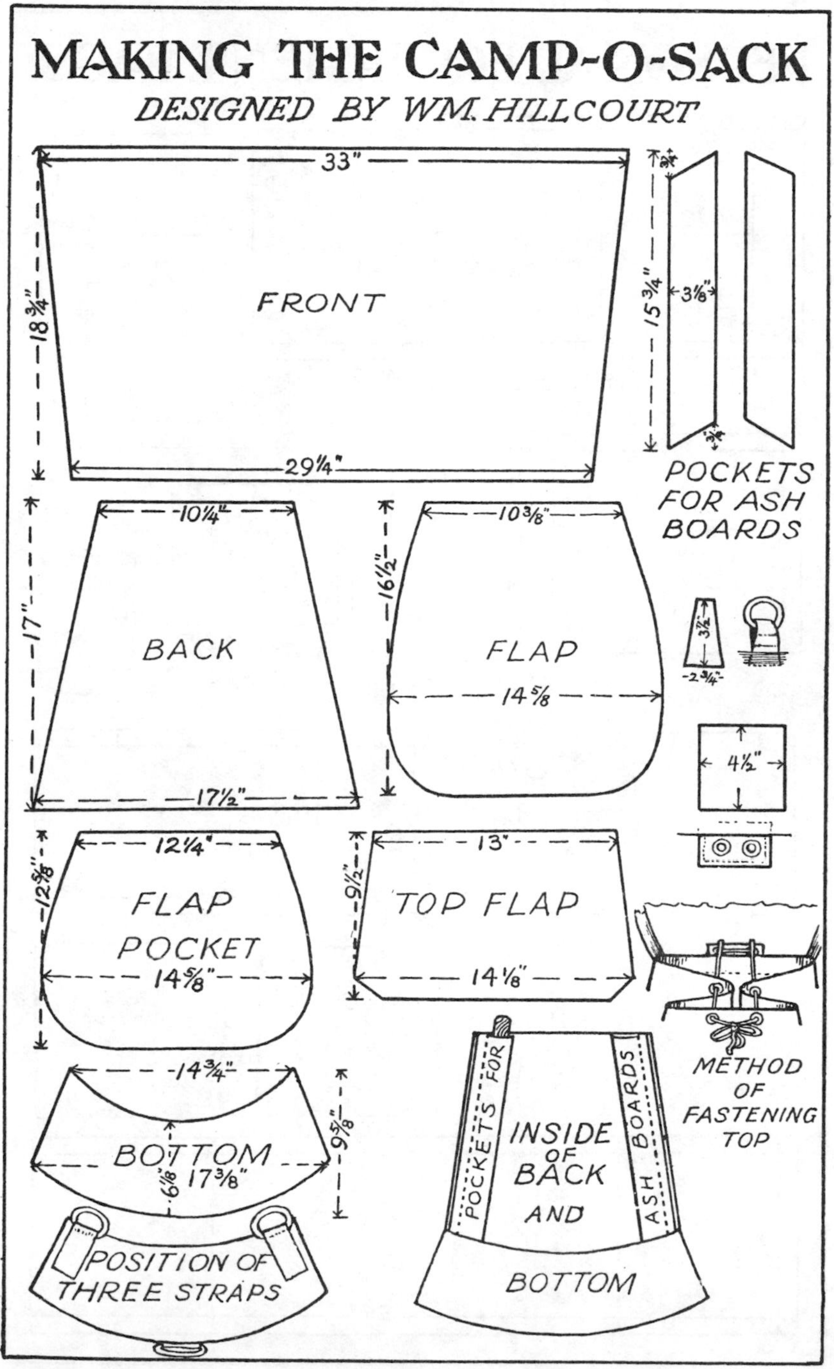
MAKING THE CAMP-O-SACK
DESIGNED BY WM. HILLCOURT
33"
18¾"
FRONT
29¼"
15¾"
3⅛"
POCKETS FOR ASH BOARDS
17"
10¼"
BACK
17½"
16½"
10⅜"
FLAP
14⅝
3½
2¾
4½"
12⅝"
12¼"
FLAP POCKET
14⅝"
9½"
13"
TOP FLAP
14⅛"
METHOD OF FASTENING TOP
14¾"
9⅝"
BOTTOM
17⅜"
6⅛"
POSITION OF THREE STRAPS
POCKETS FOR
ASH BOARDS
INSIDE OF BACK AND BOTTOM

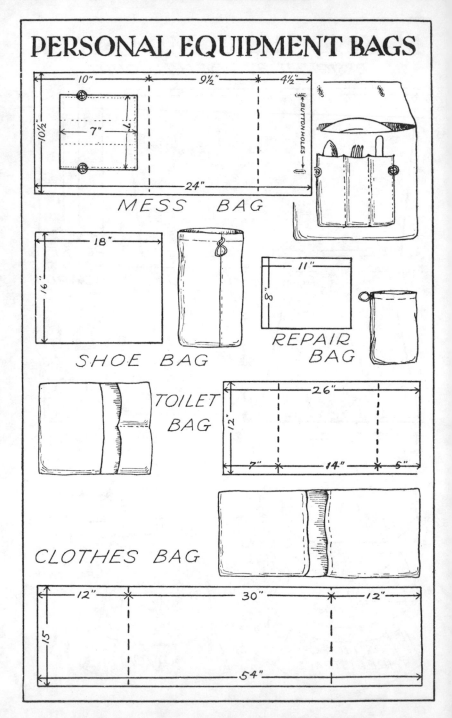

# PERSONAL EQUIPMENT BAGS

MESS BAG

SHOE BAG

REPAIR BAG

TOILET BAG

CLOTHES BAG

The patterns and dimensions for these bags, with pictures of finished bags, are given on page 320.

Inexpensive 5 and 10 cent store material may be used for these bags. The cutting and sewing is very simple.

For the *clothes bag* the cloth is hemmed the whole way around. Next a piece is folded up at both ends and seamed along the side. Bag is turned inside out and is ready for use. One compartment is for night clothes, the other for extra day clothing.

For the *mess bag,* also, the cloth is hemmed the whole way around. Next a smaller piece is sewed on front piece of bag as indicated on illustration, making three small compartments for knife, fork and spoon. Seam along sides. Make button holes and sew on buttons in front, or use snap fasteners.

The *toilet bag* is made in the same way as clothes bag. Larger space is left for towel, smaller spaces for soap, tooth brush, paste, comb. One or two tapes may be sewed on outside for tying around bag.

*Shoe bag* and *repair bag* are made as square bags with a wide hem at top through which draw strings are passed.

## NATURE HANDICRAFT
### Leaf Printing
(Plate Page 322)

**Projects:** Leaf collections.

**Material and Tools:** Dependent upon procedure to be followed.

**Procedure:** *Smoke print.* Rub a little vaseline evenly on a piece of paper. Soot over candle flame. Place leaf under side down on sooted surface. Place paper on top and rub with finger ends. Move leaf to clean paper, place paper on top of it and rub again from center of leaf outwards. Remove paper and leaf. *Spatter print.* Fasten leaf on paper with pins. Dip tooth brush in ink, pull bristles toward you with finger or nail, and let them snap back. This throws a fine spatter of ink on to the paper around

# LEAF PRINTING

SMOKE PRINT

SPATTER PRINT

PRINTER'S INK PRINT

PHOTOGRAPHIC PRINT

BLUE PRINT WITH SPECIAL BACKGROUND

BLUE PRINT OF SKELETON LEAF

BLUE PRINT     COMBINED INK AND BLUE PRINT

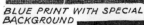

the leaf. Continue until even spatter is made. Dry. *Printer's Ink print.* Spread out printer's ink on glass plate with rubber roller. Continue as under Smoke Print. *Blue print.* Place leaf on sensitive blue print paper, cover with glass. Expose to bright sunlight till blue around the edges. Wash in running water 2 to 3 minutes. Dry between dry paper under pressure. Special background effect with wire netting, cheese cloth, etc. *Photographic print.* Same process as making blue prints. Expose to light for twenty minutes.

**Bibliography:** *Nature Collections,* by Cornelius Denslow, Boy Scouts Service Library, *SCOUTING,* March, 1929, page 114.

## Nature Casts
### (Plate Page 325)

**Projects:** Leaf casts, twig casts, casts of tracks.
**Material:** Plaster of paris, "Plasteline" or "Plasticum."

**Procedure:** For *Leaf or twig casts,* take some "Plasteline" and flatten it out on a board. Then carefully lay leaf underside down in the position desired, lay sheet of paper over and rub thoroughly with tips of fingers to make deep impression. Remove paper and leaf. Print name of leaf or any other information in the clay backwards as though you were seeing it in a mirror.

Next build a wall of "Plasteline" around the negative (see plate) to form the mold. Mix plaster, slowly sifting the plaster into water. It will sink to the bottom of the dish. When it rises above the water level just slightly you have sufficient plaster. Now stir thoroughly. It should be about the consistency of thick cream. If too much plaster has been put in, it can be thinned with water.

Pour plaster into the leaf impression. In about twenty minutes the cast will be hard enough to remove. When you can tap it fairly hard with your finger nail without making a dent in it, it is ready. Remove "Plasteline" walls and lift off the cast. If it sticks carefully insert a blade under the edge. After trimming it neatly with a knife leave it until dry, then paint with water colors, or show card colors (opaque water colors).

*Track casts* are made from animal or bird tracks found in the ground. Choose the best track you can find. Place a ring made of a strip of cardboard and a clip around it. Pour plaster of paris into the ring to sufficient thickness of cast. Leave for twenty minutes. Wash in running water. By making an impression with cast in plasteline a mold may be made that can be used for producing other casts in the form of letter weights, book ends, etc.

**Bibliography**: *Tracks and Trails* ($1.25) by Leonard Rossell, Boy Scouts of America. *Nature Collections* by Cornelius Denslow, Boy Scouts of America.

## Nature Collections
(Plate Page 326)

**Projects**: Collections of wood specimens, rock samples, butterflies, pressed flowers, bird feathers.

**Material**: Dependent on subject chosen.

**Procedure**: On plate are given several suggestions. The wood specimens are cut with grain, cross grain, slantwise of grain in order to show clearly how grains run. Half of each cut may be polished. Specimens are mounted on board. For the rock samples two boards are used. In one, circular holes are cut, and then the boards are nailed together. Plaster of paris is poured into the holes, the specimens placed in correct position and the whole thing put aside to harden. The other pictures on the plate are self explanatory.

**Bibliography**: *Nature Collections* by Cornelius Denslow, Boy Scouts of America. *Insect Life Merit Badge Pamphlet* ($1.50) Boy Scouts of America. *SCOUTING* (Collecting and Preserving Plants), May, 1928.

# NATURE CASTS

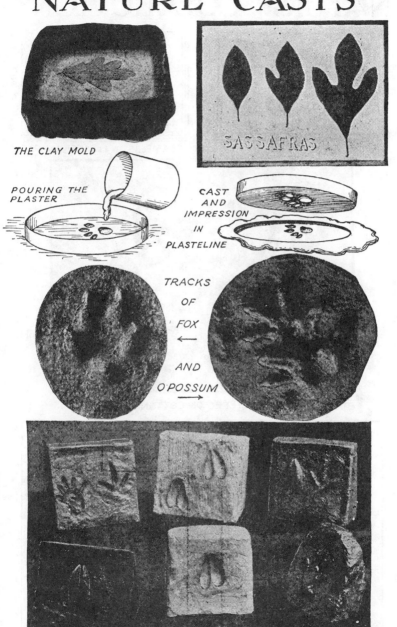

THE CLAY MOLD

SASSAFRAS

POURING THE PLASTER

CAST AND IMPRESSION IN PLASTELINE

TRACKS OF FOX ← AND O'POSSUM →

PLASTER BOOK ENDS WITH TRACKS COMPLETE AND INCOMPLETE

# NATURE COLLECTIONS

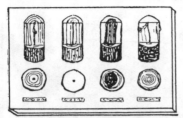

WOOD SPECIMENS

ROCK SAMPLES IN PLASTER-OF-PARIS

BUTTERFLIES MOUNTED ON COTTON UNDER GLASS

PRESSED FLOWERS

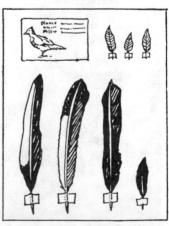

MOUNTED FEATHERS

# MISCELLANEOUS HANDICRAFT

## Art-Stone Craft
### (Plate Page 328)

**Projects:** Vases, frames, candle sticks, bird houses, flower pots, etc.

**Material and Tools:** Art-Stone powder, working plate, spreading knife, marking point.

**Procedure:** To about a quarter of a cup or less of cold water add enough Art-Stone to make a smooth thick paste. Art-Stone should be put on only one-sixteenth inch thick. More is waste. Wet the sponge on working plate No. 1 (see page 328), then clamp projecting rod on corner edge of table No. 4 as shown above No. 2, placing vase No. 3 on end of the projecting rod No. 4, so that it will roll freely while working. Clean spreading knife No. 5, and marking point No. 6 now and again on the wet sponge while working. Art-Stone may be applied to glass, china, metal, cardboard, wood and worked into artistic finishing, imitating bark or smooth stone. Vines, stalks, cones, acorn cups may be used for added effect.

**Bibliography:** *"Art-Stone Craft".* Dumouchel's Art-Stone Co., 919 South Westnedge Avenue, Kalamazoo, Michigan.

## Basketry

**Projects:** Baskets, trays, lamp shades and stands, etc.

**Material:** Reed, raffia, pine needles, paper rope.

**Procedure:** Depending upon subject.

**Bibliography:** *Basketry Merit Badge Pamphlet* ($.20), Boy Scouts of America, *The Basketry Book* ($3.00), by Mary Miles Blanchard, Scribner's Sons, New York, N. Y. *Practical Basket Making* ($1.25), by G. W. James, J. L. Hammett, Cambridge, Mass. *Inexpensive Basketry* ($.45), by Marten, Manual Arts Press, Peoria, Ill. *How to Make Baskets* ($1.50), by Mary White, Doubleday, Page Co., Garden City, Long

# ART-STONE CRAFT

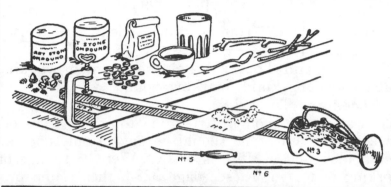

MATCH HOLDER

TRINKET BOX

WREN HOUSE

CANDLE HOLDER

BLOTTER PAD WITH CALENDAR

| VASE BARK FINISH. | VASE ANTIQUE FINISH | CALENDAR SALT SHAKE | VASE WITH ACORNS | VASE & CEDAR BUDS |

Island, N. Y. *Pine Needle Basketry* ($.75), by L. L. Milikin, J. L. Hammett Co., Cambridge, Mass. *Long Pine Needle Weaving,* Prang Co., 1922 Calumet Ave., Chicago, Ill. *Weaving with Paper Rope,* Dennison Mfg. Co., New York, N. Y.

## Beadwork
### (Plate Page 330)

**Projects:** Watch fobs, medallions, necklaces, bands for Indian headgear, belts, garters.

**Material and Tools:** Beads, loom, strong linen finish thread or silk, fine needle, pattern.

**Procedure:** Cut one more thread than the bead pattern is beads wide, threads being twelve inches longer than article to be made. Draw threads tight and fasten them on either end of the loom. Thread fine needle, tie end of thread to left hand warp thread, pass needle under warp threads, string beads enough for once across pattern (one less than warp threads), press beads up through, and between each warp thread, pass needle back *again* through each bead (see double weft bead weaving, page 330), being sure it is above every warp thread, then back under warp. String enough for another row and repeat process. Continue until pattern or required length has been made, and finish by weaving warp threads back into the article.

**Bibliography:** *Bead Work* ($.10) Boy Scouts of America Supply Department Pamphlet, *Indian Beadwork* ($.50) American Museum of Natural History, New York, N. Y., *Beads and Beadwork of the American Indians* ($2.50) by William C. Orchard, Museum of the American Indian, New York, N. Y., *The Book of Indian Crafts and Indian Lore* ($2.50), by Julian H. Salomon, Harper's, New York, N. Y., *Handbook of Craftwork* ($.50) Lester Griswold, 623 Park Terrace, Colorado Springs, Colo.

## Celluloid Craft

**Projects:** Paper knives, pendants, napkin rings,

# INDIAN BEADWORK

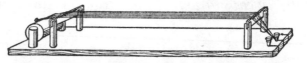

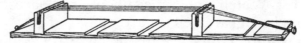

THE SUPPLY DEPARTMENT LOOM

A HOME MADE LOOM

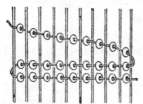

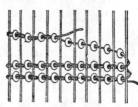

SINGLE WEFT
BEAD WEAVING

DOUBLE WEFT
BEAD WEAVING

SIMPLE DESIGNS ~

ACTUAL INDIAN BEADWORK

calendar pads, combs, book marks, place card holders, etc.

**Material:** Celluloid or Ivorene sheets in various colors, 8" jeweler's saw, No. 0 or No. 1 saw blades, a few jeweler's needle files, small hand-drill, sharp knife blade. "Enamelac" or lacquer for decorating.

**Procedure:** First plan your design. Transfer to celluloid through carbon paper if painted design is desired. Draw on onion skin paper and paste on celluloid if cut-out design is desired. In sawing, use long strokes with light pressure. Edges are finished by filing. Celluloid or Ivorene may be softened in hot water and bent into interesting shapes for napkin rings and the like. Finished celluloid articles may be bought inexpensively and with "Enamelac" turned into articles of art.

**Bibliography:** *1929 Supplement to Handbook of Craftwork*, Lester Griswold, 623 Park Terrace, Colorado Springs, Colo., *Ivorene Craft,* write Prang Co., 1922 Calumet Ave., Chicago, Ill.

## Half Hitching
### (Plate Page 333)

**Projects:** Belts (imitation wampum).

**Material:** Two lengths of cords (any two colors) about 75 feet each, one buckle ⅝" wide.

**Procedure:** Cut two lengths of white and then two lengths of black, each 8 feet long. This will give convenient lengths of cord to start with. (As the original cords are reduced to about 6 inch lengths new cords should be added later). Arrange them as indicated on plate. Make the buckle firm either by catching it on a hook, closing a drawer on it or in any convenient way.

The knot used in making the belt is a simple half hitch as illustrated in the center drawing. The filler (the straight cord in the illustration) must be held taut and the knot made *over* it with the other cord as the illustration shows. After the knot is made draw it up tightly, being careful not to let the filler buckle up. It is important to notice that these knots are always made two at a time with the same cord over the filler (double half hitch)—the second knot binds and locks the first. Pull the knots up tightly and keep them close together.

There are two methods of working the belt called Method "A" and Method "B".

In Method "A" you work from sides toward center, in Method "B" from center toward sides.

By arranging cords in different ways on buckle and by using varying numbers of Method "A" and Method "B" rows you are able to make different belt designs, as shown on plate. "A" is made by alternating three rows of Method "A" with three of Method "B", "B" is five rows, "D" nine rows and "F" seven rows of each. "C" and "E" show whole belt worked with Method "A", the cords being arranged in two different ways.

**Bibliography:** *SCOUTING,* March, 1929, page 89, *Square Knot Book* ($1.00), P. C. Herwig, 97 Sands Street, Brooklyn, N. Y., *Making Wampum Belts* ($.15) D. P. Winne Co., Inc., 76 Reade Street, New York, N. Y.

## Horsehair Craft
### (Plate Page 335)

**Projects:** Belts, hatbands, watch fobs, quirts, lanyards, etc.

**Material:** Horsehair in various colors.

**Procedure:** Horsehair strands to be plaited should be prepared from hair of uniform length. Five to ten horsehairs are placed side by side and an overhand knot is tied at one end. A slight twist, about three turns, will make the hair into a strand. Then tie an overhand knot at the other end. The plaiting may be done with eight or twelve strands. For convenience in starting the plait, the strands are separated in two equal groups and supported as indicated in sketch A (plate page 335).

# HALF HITCHING

METHOD A
CONTINUED
IN METHOD
B

METHOD B
CONTINUED
IN METHOD
A

MAKING THE
HALF
HITCHES

ARRANGING
CORDS

STARTING
THE HITCHES

A    B    C    D    E    F

Eight plaits are made as indicated in sketches A-H. The principle is: Bring highest strand around behind the plait, under two and over two. Change hands and repeat, using the highest strand on the opposite side of the plait. K, M, O, Q show three patterns made by following color arrangement J, L, N, P. The procedure in plaiting twelve strands is similar to that above, only the working strand is brought under three and over three. Sufficient plaits to make the desired width are sewed together as indicated on plate.

**Bibliography:** *Handbook of Craftwork* ($.50), Lester Griswold, 623 Park Terrace, Colorado Springs, Colo.

## Leather Thong Plaiting
### (Plate Page 337)

**Projects:** Neckerchief slides, lanyards, watch fobs, hat bands, etc.

**Material and Tools:** Leather discs, sharp knife, cutting stand.

**Procedure:** Cutting the thongs from discs is accomplished by following one of the methods indicated on plate.

For plaiting, arrange two thongs as shown in first drawing. Grasp the two crossed center thongs with left hand. Reach through between the white thongs and grasp the black thong.

Bring the black thong around behind the crossed pair up between the white thongs, and carry it over the lower white thong, over in left hand.

The procedure from here on is identical, but the manipulation changes from the left to the right hand, as indicated in the sketches. This completes the cycle for both hands.

**Bibliography:** *Handbook of Craftwork* ($.50) Lester Griswold, 623 Park Terrace, Colorado Springs, Colorado. *Leathercraft* ($.10), *Graton & Knight Co.,* Worcester, Mass.

# HORSEHAIR CRAFT

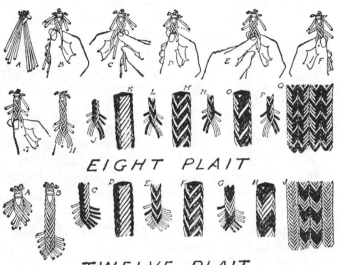

## EIGHT PLAIT

## TWELVE PLAIT

## STRAP ASSEMBLY

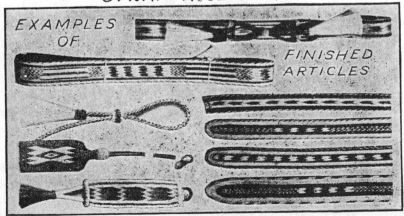

EXAMPLES OF

FINISHED ARTICLES

## Leather Work
(Plate Page 338)

**Projects:** Bags, purses, watch fobs, belts, camera cases, axe and knife sheaths, first aid kits, quivers, brief cases, desk sets, photo frames, billfolds, book covers, buckskin clothes, moccasins, etc.

**Material and Tools:** Leather depending on article to be manufactured, leather thongs (see plate on leather thongs), punch, knife, stamps made by filing 16 or 20 penny nails.

**Procedure:** Make your own design or choose one from any of the books mentioned below. Cut leather in correct shapes, punch holes and sew together pieces following methods indicated on plate, page 343. Different designs may be made on the leather before assembling.

**Bibliography:** *Handbook of Craftwork* ($.50) and *1929 Supplement to Handbook of Craftwork* ($.25), Lester Griswold, 623 Park Terrace, Colorado Springs, Colo. *Leathercraft* ($.10) Graton & Knight Co., Worcester, Mass. *Leathercraft* and *Leather Work Merit Badge pamphlets* ($.20 each) Boy Scouts of America. *Leather Work* ($.85) by Mickel, Manual Arts Press, Peoria, Illinois.

## Linoleum Blocks
(Plate Page 339)

**Projects:** Greeting cards, book plates, book covers, etc.

**Material and Tools:** One-fourth inch "battleship" linoleum, penknife or stencil knife, two woodcarver's gouges (one "V" shaped, the other "U" shaped), printer's ink or linoleum-cut water colors, rubber roller, glass plate, clothes-wringer.

**Procedure:** Use a design that consists of strong shadows and bright high-lights. Popular magazines may suggest such designs. Put a piece of transparent paper on the design and trace the outline with a pencil. Put a piece of carbon paper on the linoleum; place

# LEATHER THONG PLAITING

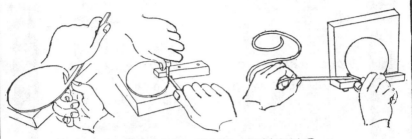

*CUTTING THE THONG*

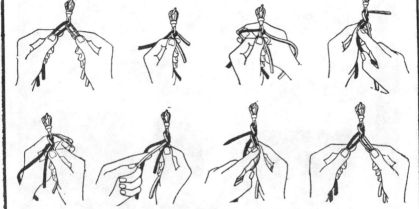

*FOUR PLAIT ROUND*

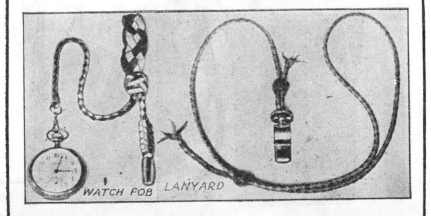

*WATCH FOB   LANYARD*

# LEATHER WORK

FRONT    BACK      FRONT   BACK

**EDGE TO EDGE LACING**     **CORNER LACING**

**SIDE BY SIDE LACING**     **ROUND CORNER LACING**

STAMPING TOOLS
AND
IMPRESSIONS

# LINOLEUM BLOCKS

THE CUT BLOCK

PRINT PULLED FROM SAME

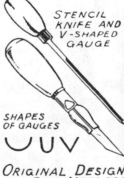

STENCIL KNIFE AND V-SHAPED GAUGE

SHAPES OF GAUGES

ORIGINAL DESIGN AND FOUR METHODS OF CUTTING IT

your drawing on top of it, face down, and trace the lines from the back, remembering that the design must appear reversed on the block. Next cut the outline with your stencil knife or specially sharpened jack-knife. Hold the knife slanting so that it cuts away from the outline of the design. The next cut is made in the opposite direction, i.e., following the outline but a little further out and with the point of the knife pointing toward the outline. Thereby you cut out a fine "V" shaped sliver which must be removed carefully. This may also be done with one cut of your "V" shaped gouge. After outline has been cut, the rest is cut away with the "U" gouge. When block is finished you make your prints. Press a little ink out on a piece of glass. Take rubber roller and roll it up and down, back and forth, criss-cross over the glass, until the ink is evenly distributed over the surface. Place block on a piece of newspaper and ink with roller. Put a piece of paper on top of the block and rub the back of a spoon over the paper until you are sure that it has been pressed firmly against every relief part of the cut. Then re-move paper by lifting it slowly and carefully, begin-ning in the corner. If you have a clothes-wringer in the house, this may be used to great advantage. Pad cut with newspaper.

**Bibliography:** *SCOUTING,* November, 1928. *Es-sentials of Linoleum Block Printing* ($2.00) Manual Arts Press, Peoria, Ill.

## Metal Work

**Projects:** Trays, pendants, bowls, lamps, candle-sticks, lanterns, desk sets, jewelry.

**Material:** Copper, brass, silver.

**Procedure:** Depending upon subject.

**Bibliography:** *Metal Work Merit Badge Pamphlet* ($.20), Boy Scouts of America. *Art Metal Work* ($3.85), by Arthur F. Payne, Manual Arts Press,

# MODEL MAKING

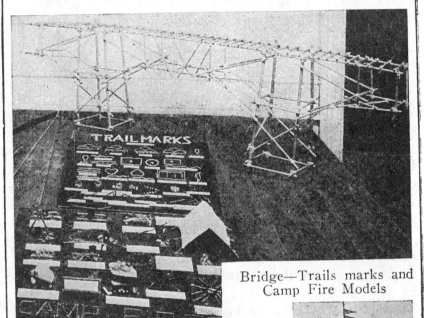

Bridge—Trails marks and
Camp Fire Models

Bridge Models

Signal Tower

Peoria, Ill. *Metalcraft and Jewelry* ($2.00), by Kronquist, Manual Arts Press, Peoria, Ill. *Handbook of Craftwork* ($.50), Lester Griswold, 623 Park Terrace, Colorado Springs, Colo.

## Model Making
(Plate Page 341)

**Projects:** Models of bridges, signal towers, camp fires, trail marks, camp furniture, log cabins, camp site, tents, ships, etc. Knot boards.

**Material:** Sticks, stones, red paper for fires, string for rope, colored sponges or dry goldenrod for trees, dried and crushed moss or colored sawdust for grass. Mirror for lake, boards for mounting models, etc.

**Procedure:** Depending upon subject.

**Bibliography:** *Pioneering Merit Badge Pamphlet* ($.20) Boy Scouts of America, *Junior Engineering* ($.50) Boy Scout Foundation of Greater New York, N. Y. *Camp Fires and Camp Cookery* ($.25) Boy Scouts of America, *Games and Recreational Methods* ($2.00) Charles F. Smith, Doubleday, Page, Garden City, N. Y., *Handbook for Boys* ($.50) Boy Scouts of America, *Camp Buildings and Scout Shelters* ($.15) Boy Scouts of America, *Rope and Its Uses* ($.05) Boy Scouts of America, *Camping Merit Badge Pamphlet* ($.20) Boy Scouts of America.

## Neckerchief Sliding
(Plate Page 343)

**Project:** Neckerchief Slides.

**Material:** Wood, cow horn, leather, leather thong, vertebrae, birch bark, insulated wire, bamboo joint, turtle shell.

**Procedure:** Depending on material used. Use your imagination.

**Bibliography:** *Knife Craft* ($.20) Boy Scouts Service Library, *SCOUTING*, March, 1929, page 120.

CARVED BONE

TORTOISE SHELL

# NECKERCHIEF SLIDES

CARVED LEATHER

FUNGUS

(WITH TWO
COCKSPURS)

CARVED     WOOD

SHEEP AND LAMB VERTEBRAE

BIRCH BARK

## Pottery
(Plate Page 345)

**Projects:** Bowls, jars, vases, ash trays, flower pots, candlesticks, etc.

**Material:** Artists' clay or "Permodello".

**Procedure:** Roll your clay into a ball. With your fist make impression into the ball and form it with your fingers into a bowl. Place on board or plate. Roll out coils of clay. Fasten them in spiral form to inside of bowl and build up your bowl by adding coils. Smooth surface and inside as you go along. When necessary size has been reached form the pot into its final shape with your fingers. The pot is left to dry in the air and afterwards fired. This may be done in a kiln as shown on page 345. After the first firing the pot may be decorated and glazed. For this process, see Pottery Merit Badge Pamphlet. If you use "Permodello" (Prang Co., see below) no firing is necessary.

**Bibliography:** *Pottery Merit Badge Pamphlet* ($.20), Boy Scouts of America, *The Potter's Craft* ($2.50), by Charles F. Binns, D. Van Nostrand Co., New York, N. Y. *How to Make Pottery* ($1.50), by Mary White, Doubleday, Page Co., Garden City, Long Island, N. Y. *Pueblo Pottery Making* ($4.00), by Carl E. Guthe, Yale University Press. *"Permodello" Modeling* ($1.50), by Snow and Froehlich, Prang Co., 1922 Calumet Ave., Chicago, Ill.

## Soap Carving
(Plate Page 347)

**Projects:** Small sculptures, bas relief, models, bric-a-brac.

**Material:** Cakes of soap, a penknife, one orange wood stick, such as is used for finger nails, another orange wood stick to which is fastened a bent hairpin by the help of a string or a piece of wire, (the projecting end of hair pin is filed to a sharp edge), sealing wax paint for decorating.

# POTTERY

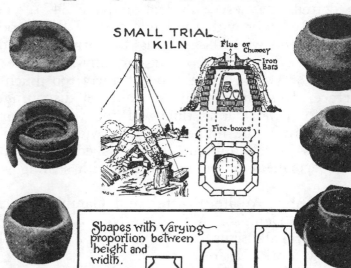

SMALL TRIAL KILN

Flue or Chimney

Iron Bars

Fire-boxes

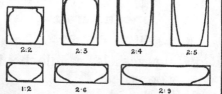

Shapes with varying proportion between height and width.

2:2   2:3   2:4   2:5

1:2   2:6   2:9

BUILDING
UP THE
POT FROM
A FLAT BASE
AND CLAY
COILS

FORMING THE
POT AND
ATTACHING
THE EARS.
THE FINISHED
PRODUCT

INDIAN POTTERY DESIGNS ~

**Procedure:** Draw design on soap with pencil or point of tool. Next cut away the soap with the knife, leaving the rough outline of your model as indicated by the dotted lines (see illustration page 347). This time proceed slowly with the blade end of the wooden tool or with the wire tool, trying to form a rounded surface. Do not work too long on any one side of your model or you are likely to cut away too much of the surface. Keep turning it. Do not get discouraged. It is well to spend a long time working for the form, noticing carefully the highest, lowest, widest and narrowest parts of the animal. The finished article may be made permanent by being covered with sealing wax paint.

**Bibliography:** Write Procter and Gamble, Cincinnati, Ohio, or Dennison Mfg. Co., New York, N. Y., or National Small Sculpture Committee, 80 East 11th Street, New York, N. Y.

## Tincandicraft
### (Plate Page 348)

**Projects:** Cooking vessels, candle holders, lanterns, trays, cups, pens, scoops, etc.

**Material and Tools:** Empty tin cans, wire, nail, cutter.

**Procedure:** The drawings on the plate are self-explanatory.

**Bibliography:** *SCOUTING,* July, 1928. *Making Tin Can Toys* ($1.50) by Edward Thatcher, J. P. Lippincott, Philadelphia, Pa. *Tin Can Toys and How to Make Them* ($1.50 paper cover) by Carrie Williams, C. Williams, 5454 Page Avenue, St. Louis, Mo.

## Wood Work
### (Whittling Page 349)

**Projects:** The number is unlimited. It may rank from small carved items to complicated cabinet maker's articles.

ANIMAL SCULPTURES IN SOAP

# SOAP CARVING

NECESSARY TOOLS

LIFE CYCLE OF FROG—4 MONTHS

BEETLE

FRONT          BACK

MONARCH   BUTTERFLY

CICADA

MAPLE LEAF

CARTHAGINIAN
COIN 280-190-BC

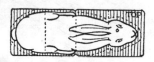

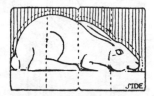

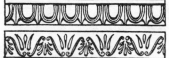

GREEK BORDERS

AN EASY DESIGN
FOR BEGINNERS

BAS-RELIEF from NATURE
AND HISTORY

# TINCANDICRAFT

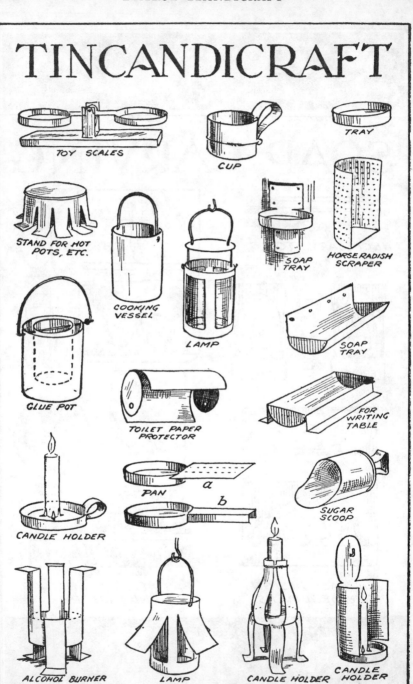

TOY SCALES

CUP

TRAY

STAND FOR HOT POTS, ETC.

COOKING VESSEL

LAMP

SOAP TRAY

HORSE RADISH SCRAPER

GLUE POT

TOILET PAPER PROTECTOR

SOAP TRAY

FOR WRITING TABLE

CANDLE HOLDER

PAN

a

b

SUGAR SCOOP

ALCOHOL BURNER

LAMP

CANDLE HOLDER

CANDLE HOLDER

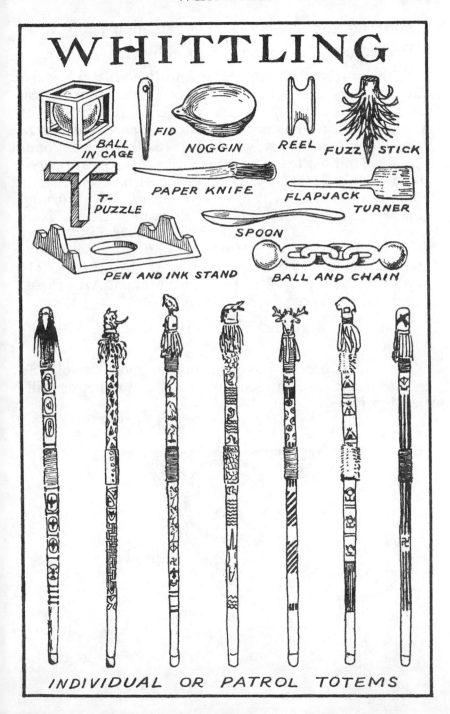

# WHITTLING

BALL IN CAGE   FID   NOGGIN   REEL   FUZZ STICK

T-PUZZLE   PAPER KNIFE   FLAPJACK TURNER

PEN AND INK STAND   SPOON   BALL AND CHAIN

INDIVIDUAL OR PATROL TOTEMS

**Material and Tools:** Dependent upon subject.

**Procedure:** Dependent upon subject.

**Bibliography:** *Woodcarving* and *Wood Work Merit Badge Pamphlets* ($.20 each) Boy Scouts of America. Current issues of *BOYS' LIFE* ($.20) Boy Scouts of America. Also *Popular Mechanics, Science and Invention. Boy Mechanics,* Vol. I-III ($2.00 each) Popular Mechanics Press, Chicago, Ill. *American Boy's Handibook* ($3.00) by Dan Beard, Chas. Scribner's Son, New York, N. Y. *A. B. C. of Woodcarving* ($2.00), by Wheeler, G. P. Putnam's Sons, New York, N. Y. *How to Build Bird Houses* ($.20) Boy Scouts of America. *Home Handicraft for Boys* ($2.00) by A. Neely Hall, George H. Doran Co., 244 Madison Avenue, N. Y. Books by Manual Arts Press, Peoria, Ill. (Write for catalog).

Visit your local library for great selection of books on wood work.

As said before: A busy Patrol is a good Patrol. So go ahead and use this chapter freely. Or better still: Develop ideas of your own.

# CHAPTER X

## PATROL STUNTS

THE Troop camp fire is well under way. It has been a glorious day. The hike was a success, and so far the camp fire which closes the day's program has done credit to everything else that has happened. Then suddenly somehow or other it starts to slacken. There isn't the same attention, not the same spirit. Then perhaps from a corner comes a voice "Wet Moccasins, pull us one of your stunts!" And in a moment all the others join in: "Moccasins! Moccasins! Up! Up! Up!" And you simply have to get your Patrol up, because yours is it, even if the name we have hit on doesn't happen to be the one that is on your Patrol flag. And the reason why all the others depend upon your Patrol for entertainment is that you have proved before at Troop meetings and hikes that you and your boys were always ready to do their bit to amuse the rest.

### "Be Prepared" for Fun

This is a thing that must not be overlooked when we speak about being "Prepared." Our motto applies not only to serious business but also to fun. So "Be Prepared" to pull a stunt whenever it may be asked for or needed. This will not only help entertain others, but it will also be a good thing for your own group. There will be many a time when a stunt will help your boys along and pep up their spirits. Whether these stunts consist of a song on the twenty mile hike, a yell before entering a competition, an inspirational story around a camp fire or a more elaborate piece of dramatics that needs plenty of training which will add to the fun of the Patrol meeting, or something else, it will be well worth this effort if it livens things up for yourselves and others.

## PATROL YELLS

Let us start with Patrol yells, maybe the simplest form of a stunt, yet, maybe, also the one for which you will find use most often.

Yells are great fun. You can't get away from that. Yet there is far more to them than just their entertaining qualities.

They may be considered a safety valve for over-abundance of enthusiasm and suppressed energy, or just a means of giving the boys an opportunity to indulge in their favorite sport of making a noise. But also—and this is equally important—at the same time that they are offering the boys a chance to express their bubbling spirits, they are also helping to build up unity in the group and helping to make the boys feel more closely knit to each other. In short, Patrol yells make for Patrol Spirit and close comradeship.

So by all means encourage the yelling. Naturally not at any time, whether suitable or not, but every time there is something to yell for or a reason for yelling. But before starting to yell you must necessarily know what you are going to yell. Also you ought to have somebody lead the yell in order to get it loud enough and keep it in rhythm.

## Develop Your Cheer-Leader

Generally in every Patrol there is a boy who knows something about how a yell is rendered. Let him step in front of the boys and try out his abilities along that line. If you haven't a natural cheer-leader you must try to develop one. Our Patrol organization calls for a "cheermaster," and having one, is well worth while. Try to make a few of the boys interested in leading, have them try to learn the trick by watching real cheer-leaders in action, or by simply going to one of them and asking him for a few pointers. In most cases the high school cheer-leaders won't mind teaching their secrets to a boy whom they find actually interested in the subject.

To start with you may find your boys rather shy when they are to lead, but if the Patrol responds to their efforts they will speedily warm up to their job and sooner or later develop into the real stuff.

## Making up a Yell

In regard to the yells themselves, the best thing would naturally be if the Patrol tried to make up its own and put its personality into them. A simple two-line rhyme with a few "Rah's" in front and a few "Rahs" behind can easily be made up, as for example:
"Rah, Rah, Rah, Rah, Rah, Rah, Rah!
Yellow Foxes are in line,
Whether it be rain or shine!
Rah, Rah, Rah, Rah, Rah, Rah, Rah!"
In the above, the first line of Rahs may even be omitted. The last line, too, for that matter, maybe leaving one Rah only for a closing effect. It is as simple as that to make up a yell for any special occasion!
To help you in making up a yell for your Patrol we are offering a number from which you may choose

# YELLS FROM MANY COUNTRIES

## AMERICAN SCOUT YELL

A-M-E-R-I-C-A
Boy Scouts! Boy Scouts!
U-S-A!

## AMERICAN SKY ROCKET

Sssss-s-ssss! (long sizzing sound)
BOOM! Ah! (very loud)
Boy Scouts! (followed by clapping of hands)

## BRITISH RANK YELL

Be Prepared! Be Prepared!
Shout it! Shout it! Shout!
Tenderfoot! Second Class!
First Class Scout!

## BRITISH

Leader: Who are we?
Chorus:
We are the boys who make no noise!
Hoo-ha! Hoo-ha! Hoo-ha-ha!
Rambling Buf-fal-oes! (or other Patrol name)

## BRITISH LOCOMOTIVE

Rah! Rah! Rah! Rah!
Boy Scouts! Boy Scouts!
(Repeat three times, imitating a locomotive with increasing speed. Arm movements like the piston)
Ray! Ray! Ray! Ray! Ray! Ray!
(Rays without arm movements and gradually diminishing to finish)

## CANADIAN
### (In Norwegian Disguise)

I, gee, itta, keeh!
I, ee, jip!
Speidere, Speidere! Rip, Rip, Rip!
Kanta Teta Vah Vah!
Kanta Teta Tar!
Fremad Speidere! Fremad Speidere!
Rah! Rah! Rah!
("Fremad" means Forward, "Speidere," Boy Scouts, pronounced "Spider")

## DANISH

Teh Rikkeh, Teh Gikkeh, Teh Geffen!
Viola, Vo-ola, Effen!
Leve Spejderchefen!
(Last line pronounced "Leh-vay Spider—chefain" meaning ''Long live the Chief Scout")

## DANISH APPLAUSE

B-R-A-V-O!
Bravo! Bravo! Bravo!
(Pronounced short and sharp, like: Brow! Brow! Brow!

## FRENCH

Adidgi, Adidgi, Ah, ou, ah!
Adidgi, Adidgi, Zim, bom, bah!
Ah, ou Ah, Zim bom bah!
Ah! Ah!! A-a-ah!!!
(The last Ah representing the air escaping from a balloon, the force of it decreasing)

## DUTCH

Ric! Tic! Ric-a-tic-a-tic!
Hopsa! Hopsa! Hie!
(Repeated three times)

## MISCELLANEOUS AMERICAN YELLS

Buffaloes! Bis! Boom! Bah!
Buffaloes! Rah! Rah! Rah!

Rocky-eye! Rocky-eye! Zip,
  zum, zie!
Shingerata! Shingerata! Bim,
  bum, bie!
Zipzum! Zipzum! Rah, Rah,
  Rah!
Karabora! Karabora! Ah,
  ah, a-a-ah!

Urah, rah! Urah, rah! Urah,
  rah!
Tiger! ! !

H-O! R-S-E! Rah, rah, rah!
Boom-a-laka, Boom-a-laka!
Boom! Horse! Boom!

B-B! B-O-Y! S-S! S-C-O!
  U-U! U-T-S! Of Amer-
  ica! ! !

Who are we? Who can
  guess?
Boy S-C-O-U-T-S!
Boy Scouts! Boy Scouts!
Yes! Yes! Yes!

Boom-a-racket!
    Cheese-a-racket!
Sis, boom, bah!
Foxes, Foxes!
Rah, rah, rah!

Chee-hee! Chee-hie!
    Chee-ha-ha-ha!
Silent Panther!
Rah, rah, rah!

Rah, Ry! B-O-Y!
Rah, Ry! B-O-Y!
Rah, Ry, Ree!
Scouts are we!

Razzle, dazzle! Razzle, daz-
  zle!
Sis-Boom-Ah!
We're the "Flying Eagles"!
Rah! Rah! Rah!

Wang, bang! Sis-Boom-Bah!
Kangaroos! Kangaroos!
Rah! Rah! Rah!

Hac-a-lac-a, boom-a-lac!
Hac-a-lac, zim-a-sac!
Hallo, hoo! Hallo, hive!
Number five!

Clickety, clackety!
Sis, boom, bah!
Mohawk Indians!
Rah! Rah! Rah!

Breketex! Koax! Koax!
Breketex! Koax!
Alala! Alala!
Siss-s-s!
Boo-oo-m!
Beavers!

Rah, rah, ree! Rah, rah, ree!
Scouts of Red Patrol are we!

Hobble-gobble!
    Razzle-dazzle!
Sis, boom, bah!
Mohicans! Mohicans!
Rah, rah, rah!

Rackety! Hackety!
    Wah, who, wah!
Rackety! Hackety!
    Wah, who, wah!
Zip, boom, bah!
    Zip, boom, bah!
Eagles! Eagles!
Rah, rah, rah!

Razzle, Dazzle, Never Frazzle,
Not a Thread But Wool,
All Together, All Together,
That's the Way We Pull—
Beavers!

Boom-a-lacka,
Boom-a-lacka,
bow, bow, wow!
Ching-a-lacka,
Ching-a-lacka!
chow, chow, chow!
Boom-a-lacka!
Ching-a-lacka,
Who are we?
We're the Otters!
Can't you see? ! !

One, Two, Three, Four,
Who Are We For?
Three, Two, One, Four,
Who Do We Yell For?
Foxes!

Nails and Tacks,
Rails and Cracks,
Beaver Patrol Are Crackerjacks
Yeh, Beavers!

Razzle, dazzle, sis, boom, boo!
Wallica, sooka, sooka, soo!
We are Boy Scouts, who are you?
Razzle, dazzle, sis, boom, boo!

Boom-a-lacka,
Boom-a-lacka!
Boom-a-la-buss!
We are the clever guys!
Take it from us!

Karo, Keero, Kiro, Kee!
(Kore, Kive, Kate, etc.)
Rah, rah, rah for Forty-three! (four, five, eight, etc.)

Tutti-Frutti, Punch and Judy,
Beaver Patrol Will Do Their Duty.
Don't You Worry, Don't You Fret!
Beaver Patrol Will Get There Yet!

The above ought to give you ideas a-plenty. And when you have chosen the yell (or the yells) you like the best, go ahead practicing it till you can deliver it with the best possible effect.

If you want to honor any special person or places with a yell you can usually make your favorite yell more effective, or anyway more up to the minute, by adding the name of person or place three times to the yell.

But remember that a yell that is only a yell is not a yell at all. It isn't the noise that counts. It is the spirit and the meaning that is behind it that make it of value in a Patrol's life.

# PATROL SINGING

A singing Patrol is a live Patrol. No Patrol can count itself perfect if it does not feel joy in singing. The habit of singing may help it through many discouraging experiences. It lightens the spirits and shortens the road. It fits into the Patrol meetings as well as on the tramp or around the camp fire.

You certainly are fortunate if you yourself as Patrol Leader are able to lead in the singing, if you have even a just middling-to-good singing voice. But even if you haven't, there is almost sure to be some one in the Patrol who can and will start the singing going when the right moment arrives.

## When and What

If the Patrol has a hard job of some kind or other to do it will find that a song helps it along. It puts up the speed and makes the boys forget it's hard. It works the same way on a hike. In the beginning of the trip a real marching tune helps to set the pace, and when the boys, tired out, are swallowing the last few miles a crazy song with a crazy refrain helps to keep the feet a-moving.

But after all, it is around the camp fire that the most important part of the singing in a Patrol is done. And the biggest point for the Patrol Leader is to be able to choose the right songs to fit into the spirit of the thing.

Many second-rate songs are published every year, featured and distorted on the vaudeville stage. Let us show that Scouts have a better taste. Let us choose songs that are worthy of our brotherhood. This does not mean that all the songs must be serious or high flown. "A Scout is cheerful." He wants his funny songs and "crazy" songs, too, but he knows how to choose them with a little tact and appropriate to the occasion.

## Everybody in It

One thing is necessary if the Patrol wants to enjoy its singing, and that is that everybody should be in it. The boys may none of them be Carusos. This isn't necessary if they only do their best when joining in the choruses. And then try to make your boys *sing*. All too often boys intone with a yelp and make singing into yelling. It isn't necessary to make the singing loud.

In fact boys' voices usually need to be toned down. So help them to use the "soft pedal."

Be sure before you start a song that everybody knows the words. Alas, generally we don't seem to care much for learning the texts even of our national songs, and the result is that before we get through the first verse, half of the people are just humming, not to mention what happens when the second verse is started. Have your boys learn the words to the songs which the Patrol like to sing. First of all learn the old familiar ones, then later go to new ones which you or your song leader may teach your boys around the camp fire.

## Choosing Your Songs

When choosing your songs, take into consideration the mood of the moment. Only when their own mood and the sentiment of the songs are related do the boys get the full benefit out of singing. On the other hand you may sometimes want to change their mood. If you know how to choose the right song you will have no difficulty in making your boys follow you from gay to serious, if you so desire.

Fortunately we have a wonderful treasury of American songs, and fortunately boys still like to sing good songs. The songs of Stephen Foster, "Swanee River," "Old Black Joe," "Old Kentucky Home," are great favorites with them.. So are others like "Love's Old Sweet Song," "Till We Meet Again," "The End of a Perfect Day," "Long, Long Trail," "Far Northland."

Many of these songs the boys will even enjoy harmonizing. The same applies to several Negro spirituals and a few sea chanteys.

Rounds are also generally well liked. "Row, Row, Row Your Boat," "Sweetly Sings the Donkey," "Scotland's Burning," "Three Blind Mice" are just a few of the many that might be mentioned.

Of semi-sentimental character we have songs like our good old "Clementine" and our "Bonnie Who, Lies Over the Ocean." They are sung time and again and the boys seem never to grow tired of them.

Then again we have the more or less funny songs, the songs with the many verses or with the queer refrains, like "Old McDonald Had a Farm," "Alouette," "There Was a Bee-i-ee-i-ee!" "John Brown's Baby," "Johnny Was a Parlor Scout," "Three Good Turns." This list also can be continued indefinitely.

## Song-Collecting

Make up a list or even a scrap-book of the songs which your Patrol sings and occasionally add to this new ones for your boys to learn. Also, of course, have them know all the songs their Troop knows and likes. Many Councils get out excellent song sheets. There is also, of course, the Boy Scout Song Book, ready for use.

Maybe you will some day find a tune which you would like to make the special song of the Patrol, with

words that fit it and which is appropriate to your
Scouts. In many Patrols a boy may be found who has
a bit of a poetical vein and who can put together words
and rhymes to make a suitable Patrol song. If your
Patrol isn't as fortunate as that, maybe a versifier may
be found in another Patrol or in the family of one of
the boys. One of your teachers,—a newspaperman, an
author who lives in the town may also be willing to
help you. Don't be afraid of asking this favor of them.
They won't bite off your head. And it is very likely

that they will agree to help you if
you put it up to them in the *right*
way. And if you succeed in getting a Patrol song, train your boys
to sing it well and render it whenever the occasion offers itself. It
will be an effective contribution to
your Patrol tradition treasure.

If any of your boys has a musical instrument, whether it be a
"uke," a banjo, a clarinet, or a
saxophone, encourage him to take
it along every once in a while. It
will help you immensely in your efforts of making a
singing Patrol out of your group.

## STORY-TELLING

You will often find that it is a tremendous help to
you in your task as a Patrol Leader to be able to tell a
story which will hold the interest of your boys. This
is especially valuable in camp, around the council fire or
in the rest hour, but also it fits in well at Patrol meetings in order to put variety into the program.

Boys enjoy hearing a story, provided it is a good
one well told. And also it is a satisfaction for the
teller of the story to feel the breathless attention with
which the boys follow his tale.

You may think you have not the ability to be a good

I search for the Right Story. Many I enjoy reading are discarded because I should not enjoy telling em.

Hurray! I've found one!

I read it again— and again.

story-teller. You may feel that you lack the imagination necessary or the power of adding words to words, to build up a picture. Don't let these things discourage you. Few people have a natural gift of story-telling, but almost any one is able to develop it if he goes at it the right way.

## How to Get at It

Some day you may discover a book or a short story which attracts your interest and you start thinking: "This would be the very one to tell the Patrol at our next meeting!" Don't lay down the book and say, "But I can't." Go at it and you will see how easy it actually is.

There are people who can hold their audience by simply reading the story. Generally, however, it may be said that it is better among boys to retell it in your own words in order to put it across. If you want to do this you must first of all try to memorize the story. Read it once more. Then read it again for the third time. By this time the plot sticks in your brain, and you have learned to know the different characters by heart.

Then sit down for a minute and think over the relation between the characters and their relation to the plot, so that you are sure you have it right. If there are points that do not seem clear to you, go back to the story and straighten things out.

When the story is fixed in your mind go ahead telling it, for example, to the alarm clock or the table lamp in

I make clear in my own mind the appearance and traits of the different characters.

I think of each scene in relation to the climax

I try telling it to a group of imaginary kids

your room. You may find that your first telling of it will be rather dry, a sort of a synopsis without the picture-power of the words which the author had at his disposal. Don't let this worry you. Go ahead and tell it a second time and a third time, every time adding to it a little more life, making the telling more descriptive and at the same time more vivid. Try to have your characters speak with different voices, find ways of making the tone of your voice indicate the various moods which run through the story.

And at the next meeting or camp fire go ahead and tell it when the right time comes. Don't be afraid of not being able to do it well enough. If the story is interesting the boys will forgive any crudeness in its telling. And as you go along with the tale you will gain confidence in yourself, or rather forget yourself entirely and get into the sweep of the thing, and when it is over the applause around you will tell you that you have succeeded.

## The Right Kind of Story

But as said above, so much depends upon the story that you ought to be very discriminating in your choice. Do not select anything but a first-class story. You may find it in a library book, or in one of the leading magazines, or maybe a news item in a paper will be your basis for building up a story to tell. Just be sure that your boys do not know the story already. There isn't any fun in hearing a boy whisper to his neighbor, "Aw, I fell out of my cradle laughing at that one!"

I refresh my memory where it is weak.

I discard the book.

NOW — I'M READY

(adapted from Warren H Wardle, Auburn,Me)

Whatever story you chose, be sure that there is action in it and a meaning to it. Things must be moving, there must be a climax and a good finish. Without those essentials the telling may fail. And then when the story is over, stop. Do not go back again and try to drag out a moral from it to put up to your boys. They will find that for themselves, if it's there.

Story-telling is largely a matter of courage. If you have been brave enough to plunge into it once you will find it easier afterwards. Indeed each story you tell will come easier.

## All the Boys Story-Tellers

Also try to make your boys into real story-tellers. If you show them the example and encourage them you may start an interest going that will not only benefit the Patrol but every one of the boys. Have a definite story-telling period at every Patrol meeting and every camp fire, expect your Scouts to do their bit and you will be surprised to find how much enjoyment they get out of it when they once are started.

## PATROL DRAMATICS

And so by and by we get to what we might term Patrol dramatics, in which the use of words combined with the actions which the words indicate, make up an entertainment which can be used to amuse the rest of the Troop whenever amusement is called for.

Patrol dramatics is a field inside Scouting into which few so far have penetrated. This is too bad because it has the power to develop some points of boy nature which other things may leave undeveloped. It helps to cure boys who are naturally shy, and it gives others a means of expression, and in still other cases it helps boys with the too bubbling spirits to control themselves. And besides this, the rehearsals for the dramatics and the actual performances create a lot of fun which cannot be overestimated.

## What to Choose

As a general rule it may be said: Don't go in for anything serious. A funny skit even if it doesn't contain much that will live in the memories of the boys is ten times easier to put over than one that tries to put

across some great truth. A slip in the latter, and it may become unintentionally f u n n y, which might kill it entirely. A slip in the first mentioned, and the fun is increased. Only in cases of rare exception is a Patrol able to put across Patrol dramatics with serious trend. Better stick to the more or less funny bagatelles and keep seriousness inside the stories told around the camp fire.

Also it is recommended that the skit be as simple as possible. Any complicated dramatics that need a lot of training in order to be performed in the right way should be avoided. Choose instead plays with a plot easy to grasp, with as little talk and as much action as possible.

Very often a story you read may suggest a dramatic action to you. Even a joke may be transformed into a playlet, and the same is the case with several old and new songs. Only a little imagination on your part is necessary to do the trick.

In the public library in your town you may find books that will contain stunts suitable for a Patrol.

And several of the Boy Scout Service Library Pamphlets will help you. For example, "Camp Fire Helps" contains a number of ideas, so also does "The Father and Son Idea." Below you will find a number of Patrol dramatics, chosen from many different sources, which will illustrate the points and which may be easily performed by one to eight boys.

## STUNTS FOR ONE BOY

### The Magician

Boy enters (if possible made up like a magician such as you see on the stage, in old dinner jacket borrowed from home, and with the indispensable magic wand in his hand. He speaks incessantly, elaborating on the following):

"Ladies and Gentlemen: I am going to perform for your approval the marvelous trick called "the flying coin." I should be very happy if some of the audience would trust me with two hats! Thank you! Also I shall need a half dollar. A quarter will do. Thank you! As you see this hat is empty (turns it around) and so is this (turns the other around). Now I place this hat here. And the other over here. They are still empty (lifts hats and shows them). Now I take this coin which is, as you will see, an or-

dinary United States Treasury Quarter, and place it under this hat over here. Just to assure you I will let you see again that the other hat is empty (lifts hat). Now I take my magic wand and make the coin fly from this hat over under the other. (Makes mysterious gestures as if bringing up the coin from under hat and throwing it in direction of the other at the same time making queer noises. Then he moves toward the empty hat.) The magic has been performed. The coin has flown through the air from the hat under which I placed it and is now by magic transferred to this. (Magician doesn't lift the hat, just continues his stream of words.) But that isn't much of a trick. Thousands of other magicians have performed it successfully. My art goes farther. I am actually going to make it fly back again. That is my great feat. (Makes mysterious gestures again as if making coin fly from hat under which it supposedly is back to the hat under which it has been the whole time.) And as you will see, Ladies and Gentlemen, the trick is performed to perfection. (Lifts hat, picks up coin and shows it around, bows and disappears.)

## The Cough Drops

Boy enters (made up as street vender with tray in front of him supposed to contain boxes of cough drops and speaks in a voice made as hoarse as possible, elaborating on the following):

"Ladies and Gentlemen, please come nearer. I have something to tell you that may benefit you. I have in this box the most wonderful cough drops ever manu-

factured in all the world. Simply marvelous, I tell you! If you take just one of them your cough will disappear almost immediately and you will feel 100 per cent better. And not only coughs are cured with this marvelous medicine. Every other ailment too. Headaches, stomach-ache, earache, toothache, and hoarseness. It is simply wonderful for hoarseness. Why do I not take it myself and get rid of my own? Why I never thought about that. Thanks for the suggestion. I will do it immediately. Just follow me. I open the box, take out one of the cough drops, open my mouth, place it on the tongue (falls back

into normal voice) and the results show immediately."
(Everything in this little stunt depends upon the boy's
ability to render an imitation of genuine hoarseness and
to throw himself instantly back into his normal voice
when getting to the last sentence.)

### In the Jeweler's Shop

Boy enters (ordinary boy's clothes. It is necessary
to announce beforehand that the action takes place in
a jewelry shop. He starts immediately to put his hand
quietly into one pocket after another as if he were
seeking something).

"My father told me to ask you if you would be kind
enough . . . (searches other pockets; starts again).
My father told me to ask you if you would be . . .
(More search. He gets more and more alarmed as he
does not find what he is searching for.) My father
told me to ask . . . (he is weeping now searching fran-
tically in one pocket after another). My father told
me . . . Boo-huh! My father . . . Boo-huh . . . (Suddenly he stops wailing. A smile comes over his face.
He drags forth a coin) . . . wants to know if you
would be kind enough to change this quarter?"

## STUNTS FOR TWO BOYS

### The Sign

First boy on stage, second boy enters with sign on
which is written "Fresh fish
for sale here."

2nd boy: *"Are you the
proprietor of this fish shop?"*

1st boy: *"Sure, that's me!"*

2nd boy: *"I am an artist.
Maybe I could interest you in
buying this nice sign for your
shop?"*

1st boy: *"Maybe. Let us see it!* (reads) *'Fresh fish*

*for sale here.' Not so bad. But why the dickens do you have that word 'fresh' there. Did you believe we could ever think of selling rotten fish, huh? Cross that out."* (Second boy does so). *"And what about that 'here.' Naturally it is here. Did you think it was on the other side of the street? Out!"* (Crosses out). *"And 'for sale.' Are you crazy?"* (Works up a rage). *"Did you imagine that we gave them away?"* (Second boy crosses words out). *"And 'fish'! You dumb-bell! Absolutely out of place. Anybody can smell that! Get out of here, fool, and quick."* (Kicks boy off stage).

## In the Insane Asylum

It is announced that the action takes place in an insane asylum. 1st boy enters, starts walking up and down. 2nd boy comes in, looks at him for a while in silence, then starts questioning.

2nd boy: *"Don't they treat you well?"*

1st boy (continues walking up and down): *"Yes."*

2nd boy: *"Don't you get enough to eat?"*

1st boy: *"Yes."*

2nd boy: *"Don't you ever get any liberty?"*

1st boy: *"Yes."*

2nd boy: *"Have you been here for a long time?"*
1st boy: *"Yes."*
2nd boy: *"Haven't you any father or mother?"*
1st boy: *"Yes."*
2nd boy: *"Have you a brother?"*
1st boy: *"Yes."*
2nd boy: *"Did he send you up here?"*
1st boy: *"No."*
2nd boy: *"Have you a sister?"*
1st boy: .*"Yes."*
2nd boy: *"Did she send you up here?"*
1st boy: *"No."*

2nd boy: *"Did you commit murder?"*
1st boy: *"No."*
2nd boy: *"Did the police send you up here?"*
1st boy: *"No."*
2nd boy: *"Then how the dickens did you get up here?"*
1st boy: *"By train. I am the director of this asylum!"*

## Two Black Crows

Two boys may be able to make up a dialogue in the style of the two popular entertainers Mack and Moran. The original dialogue of the two may give some ideas, but it is best to build up others and especially to put into the dialogue references to the people present. Needless to say that the faces of the boys must be blackened and the drawl of the negroes imitated as carefully as possible.

## STUNTS FOR THREE BOYS

### The Beefsteak

It is announced that the action takes place in an eating place in the Far West.

Waiter comes in, dusts off imaginary table with napkin. Two cowboys come in, place themselves at imaginary table.

1st Cowboy: *"Waiter!"*

Waiter: *"Yes, sir!"*

1st Cowboy: *"Something to eat! What have you?"*

Waiter: *"I am awfully sorry,*

*sir, but all we have left is one beefsteak, sir!"*
1st Cowboy: *"All right! Bring me the beefsteak!"*
2nd Cowboy: *"No, bring me the beefsteak!"*

Waiter: *"Awfully sorry, sir, but only one left, sir."*
1st Cowboy: *"Bring me the beefsteak!"*
2nd Cowboy: *"Bring me the beefsteak!"*
1st Cowboy: *"We can't both get it. We must settle who is going to have it."*
2nd Cowboy: *"Easily settled."* (Pulls toy gun. Shoots. 1st cowboy falls. 2nd cowboy calmly to waiter): *"Bring me the beefsteak!"*

## At the Railroad Crossing

Sarah, her husband, and the guard. The husband may be represented to be deaf and a stutterer. Railroad tracks may be indicated by a short ladder or two sticks.

Sarah and her husband walk up to the tracks but do not cross.

Sarah: *"Go up and ask him when the train comes through from the North."*

Husband: *"Huh?"*

Sarah: *"Ask him when the train comes through from the North."*

Husband: *"Oh."* (Walks up to guard). *"Please tell me when the train from the North comes through?"*

Guard: *"At two o'clock this afternoon!"*

Husband: *"Huh?"*

Guard: *"At two o'clock this afternoon!"*

Husband: *"Oh."* (Walks back to Sarah). *"At two o'clock this afternoon."*

Sarah: *"Ask him when the train comes through from the South."*

Husband: *"Huh?"*

Continuing in the same manner as above, Sarah gets the answers to when the trains come through from the South, the East and the West, namely, six o'clock this evening, two o'clock at night and six o'clock tomorrow morning, respectively.

Sarah (after some reflection looks at watch): *"Then I believe that we may cross the tracks in perfect safety."* (Proceeds to do so carefully, followed by husband.)

**Dumb Dave.**

1st boy (made up as woman calls): *"Dave."*

Dave (enters): *"Yes, ma!"*

1st boy: *"Here is a quarter. Go and fetch me a quart of milk."*

Dave: *"Yes, ma!"* (Both out).

2nd boys enters (with white apron, as grocer).

Dave: *"May I have a quart of milk?"*

2nd boy: *"Do you have a pitcher to carry it in?"*

Dave: *"No, sir!"*

2nd boy: *"How do you expect to carry it then?"*

Dave: *"Oh, I can use my hat!"* (Takes hat off. Water is poured into it from pitcher).

2nd boy: *"But there isn't room for it all!"*

Dave: *"Here is room for the rest."* (Turns hat upside down. Water streams out. Makes room for rest by pressing down the crown. 2nd boy pours it in. Both out).

1st boy and Dave (in).

1st boy: *"Did you get the milk?"*

Dave: *"Certainly. Here it is."*

1st boy: *"Is that all?"*

Dave (turns hat, water flows out; shows inside): *"No. Here is the rest."*

## STUNTS FOR FIVE BOYS

### The Jubilee Quartet

Conductor: *"Ladies and Gentlemen, it gives me great pleasure to introduce to you the famous Jubilee Quartet,*

*who will render for your approval the well-known song,*
*"Old Black Joe."*

Quartet enters, bows to the audience, starts singing led by the conductor. When the singers have sung a few lines a false note is heard. Conductor stops song immediately and has the last line sung over. False note again. Turns to the audience saying: *"Excuse me a minute. I shall be right back."* Goes to the side, waves at the Quartet to follow. All out. A shot is heard outside. Presently the conductor appears again and begins all over:

*"Ladies and Gentlemen, it gives me pleasure to introduce to you the famous Jubilee Trio, who will render for your approval the well known song, "Old Black Joe."*

Trio enters. Starts singing. False note. The same procedure is followed as above. Shot. And the conductor enters announcing *"The Famous Jubilee Duo."*

Same thing as before. False note. Shot. Conductor announces *"The Famous Jubilee Soloist."*

Again a false note. Repeating of last line. False note. But before conductor can wave soloist off stage the latter brings from his back a rubber club and chases out the much confused conductor.

## The Dagger

As one of the very best stunts of this sort we may recommend to you "The Dagger" which is contained in the Service Library Pamphlet "Camp Fire Helps." It has become a Boy Scout classic because of its simplicity and its very amusing qualities.

## STUNTS FOR THE FULL PATROL

### Indian Dancing

If the Patrol is interested in Indian lore, it may take up Indian dancing and the Indian handicraft which goes into the making up of the necessary equipment as war bonnets, shirts, loin cloths, leggins, moccasins, rattles, tom-toms, etc.

Indian dancing isn't a stunt that can be performed after just a few hours of instruction. It requires a thorough study, and if the Patrol isn't prepared to take it up with perseverance and seriousness it might better not attempt to imitate the dances of the American aborigines.

On the other hand if the Patrol is actually interested in Indian lore it can do nothing better than to take it up as a special Patrol proposition, always pro-

viding *everybody* wants to join in it. If only a few have the necessary interest, the introduction of Indian lore may mean the break up of the Patrol.

If the inclination is there, by all means get started. And the Patrol will have a real project and a mutual interest which will help link the members together.

The subject of Indian lore is so big that naturally it can not be treated in this volume. For Patrols interested we refer to Scout Executive Julian Harris Salomon's "The Book of Indian Crafts and Indian Lore" which was written especially from the viewpoint of adapting the theme to Scouting.

## Pyramus and Thisby

An excellent Patrol stunt is the little playlet on "Pyramus and Thisby," contained in Shakespeare's "A Midsummer Night's Dream" which you can get in an inexpensive edition at any book store. The number of actors necessary is six, filling the parts of Prologue, Pyramus, Thisby, Wall, Moonshine and Lion. A seventh actor may be used to represent Moonshine's dog.

The skit must be played as a farce, as exaggerated as possible, Pyramus trying to use a man's deep voice, Thisby a falsetto, Moonshine popping off to sleep in the middle of the acting and Wall forgetting what he has to say.

The costumes ought to represent Greek dresses. They may be made in the following way: Wear bathing suit. Put a towel in front of you and one in back and fasten them together with a safety pin on either shoulder. Tie a string around the waist and drape the dress neatly. On the feet: moccasins or gym shoes. Put a wreath of green leaves around the brow of Pyramus. Use for Thisby's dress a sheet instead of the two towels.

If played in the right spirit this will always be found amusing.

## Casey at the Bat

This old favorite (found in a number of books; ask your librarian to help you get hold of it) may be played as a pantomime, one boy reading, or better reciting the poem while the rest of the Patrol play the baseball game as the persons mentioned with an imaginary ball and imaginary bats.

## The Parade of the Wooden Soldiers

This tune performed as a stunt was introduced by Russian actors in "Chauve Souris" and may easily be performed by a group of Scouts. The music may be purchased from any music store and is easily learned by the boys.

The equipment necessary consists of a paper soldier's cap and a wooden sword for each of the performers. Rouge applied on the cheeks in a round hectic spot adds to the effect of the makeup.

The boys start humming the tune outside the stage. Then they enter with small stiff tripping movements of the legs, the arms being kept perfectly quiet, and go through a drill consisting of turning one way, then another, moving forward, backward, and so forth, the whole time humming the tune. Toward the end of the tune they get into one line, and as they arrive at the last note the right file leader falls toward the left, causing the whole row to fall like a row

of real wooden soldiers being overturned.

## Circus

As a last stunt for a Patrol we shall mention Circus which is really a combination of several stunts, namely, Sharp Shooter, Wrestling Match, Strong Men, Tight Rope Dancer, and Performing Horses. And besides these actors required naturally we must have the Director of the show who introduces the different acts.

The parts must be divided between the boys in such a way that no boy takes part in two or more stunts successively.

## Sharp Shooter

Equipment: Toy gun, an enamel plate, a spoon. One boy holds the target, i.e., the plate between his hands overhead with the spoon in such a position behind it that a slight movement of the fleshy root of the thumb causes it to strike the plate making a noise as if real bullets were hitting the target. Naturally he must stand facing the audience. The shooter starts shooting in different positions, with front, side, back toward target, bending down, standing on head, etc. Every time he shoots the gun the sound of hitting is heard from the plate. The fun comes in the end when suddenly no longer the taps on the plate correspond with the shots and therefore the fake is exposed.

## Wrestling Match

Director announces a match between Mr. Slaposnutski (the boy introduced bows) and the famous Mr. Nobody (who isn't there at all). The match starts, the boy fighting the imaginary person. He seems to be flung up into the air, falls down; makes bridges, succeeds in getting up, is caught in a half Nelson, down again in bridge, etc. In the end his shoulders touch the ground and the imaginary Mr. Nobody is declared the winner.

## Strong Men

Two boys enter in gym shirts and pants. A third acts as helper. He carries a handkerchief in his hand. The two strong men get into position. They lift arms to horizontal position, then bend right arm at elbow, hand held up. They look at the hand and start moving it at the wrist. Suddenly they yell "Hep" and turn their attention toward the left wrist which is moved likewise. A "Hep" again, a bow to the audience, the first stunt is performed. The helper throws handkerchief to first performer, who rubs hands and forehead also the armpit and throws it to second strong man who does the same and throws it to the helper who repeats action. Next stunt consists of the strong men each standing on one leg with the other leg lifted and moving the ankle in small circles. A "hep" and they do the same with the other leg. "Hep" again, a bow to the audience, and the handkerchief goes around as before. Other similarly crazy stunts are performed. Then the act is ended by the "Death Spring". One of the boys takes position with hands interlocked as if going to help the other perform a double somersault. The other boy walks back some steps. He starts running toward the first one. He stops in front of him and corrects the position—not of the hands but of the head. Walks back again, makes a start, stops up again, corrects head position and walks back. The third time he runs forward he is caught in the arms of his friend and carried off the stage. The "Death Spring" has been performed.

### Tight Rope Walker

Two boys bring in a rope. Stretch it out in front of them in height with their shoulders. The rope walker enters. Bows to the audience. Walks toward rope. Says "Far too high". The boys put rope down a few inches. The rope walker tests it with his hands. "Still too high". This procedure is continued until the rope lies on the ground. The two strong men carry in the balancing pole. They seem hardly able to carry it, because of its weight. The rope walker snaps it up in one hand, throws it into the air and catches it again. Starts walking the rope and performing the stunts of a rope walker. Walking forward, backward, running, standing on one foot, bending down, turning around, etc. As a last stunt he walks the rope blindfolded, takes off the bandage, discovers that he is off the rope and disappears apparently much embarrassed.

### Performing Horses

Ringmaster enters with long whip. He snaps it, and three helpers lead in three hobby horses made out of sticks with heads of cardboard in the form of horses' heads. They walk around the ring once. Another snap, and in come three jockeys. They follow the ringmaster around the ring once, then run up to the horses and mount them while the helpers disappear. The three horses now perform the stunts of trained horses, they gallop, waltz, turn in one direction and another, etc. As last stunt they are gathered in front of the director and made to stand on the hind legs, i.e., the jockeys lift up the hobby horses in front of them while imitating the tripping of horses in such a position. When the horses get into ordinary position again, the director takes from his pocket three lumps of sugar and gives them—not to the horses—instead he puts one piece into the mouth of each of the jockeys. One more round in the ring, then out, and the whole circus performance is over.

## Merely Suggestions

The above mentioned stunts are merely suggestions. Some of them are old favorites, others are new, all of them have in common that they, performed in the right spirit, are sure to entertain, and amuse the audience.

Which is, after all, all that Patrol stunts are for.

## CHAPTER XI

## PATROL RELATIONSHIPS

HOWEVER strong a Patrol may get to feeling itself as a unit, a group existing "all for one, one for all," it must never lose sight of the fact that it doesn't and cannot stand by and for itself alone. It has definite obligations and loyalties to other people and to other groups. If Patrol Spirit developed into a selfish self-absorbed attitude of conduct and way of thinking it would be very far from an ideal thing. But then it couldn't so develop. If it did it wouldn't be the real thing. True Patrol Spirit is the true Scouting spirit, doing one's best to be helpful and friendly and loyal, all along the line, in all one's contacts with other people.

We have already spoken in an earlier chapter of the Patrol's relationship to the Troop and discussed the particular importance of the contacts of the Patrol Leader with the Scoutmaster and other members of the Troop Officers' Council. In this chapter we shall speak briefly of other important relationships and contacts.

### The Home

If the Patrol Leader has followed the suggestions already given as to starting his Patrol meetings in the various different homes of his boys, he has laid the right foundation. From the beginning the fathers and mothers of his boys have had a chance to see what it was all about. They have had a chance to understand why their Bill or Bob or Pete wanted to be a Scout and if the thing has been started right, long before the Patrol Den has become a full fledged meeting room, most

of the parents will be almost as much interested in the Patrol hopes and plans and activities as the boys themselves.

You will want to encourage the boys to be careful to live up to their Scout Law in the homes, to be trustworthy, loyal, cheerful and all the rest of it. There's nothing that will serve better to convince parents that Scouting is really worth while for their sons than to have them see that the boys really are trying not only to pass interesting Scout tests and get ahead in Scoutcraft, but also to be more responsible, helpful members of the home circle, because they are Scouts and their Scout promise really means something to them.

You will need also to be on your guard lest in their enthusiasm for Scouting your boys neglect home or school tasks. Try to get the parents to help in seeing that the boys show up 100 percent in attendance at Troop and Patrol meetings, but on the other hand, don't let Scouting swallow up too much of the boys' time. Parents want to have a chance to see a good deal of their sons too. Scouting should help develop comradeship between a boy and his parents, not take him away from such a comradeship.

If fathers and mothers see from the very beginning that you and your boys want and need their help and are ready, in turn, to give service cheerfully, you will have sympathy and support in the various homes represented and a sure understanding that Scouting is helping their boys to be happier and healthier and better in every way.

## Some Suggestions

*Meeting in Homes.* This has already been mentioned. It's the best opportunity possible to start on a right footing so far as the homes are concerned. Even after you have your own Den, arrange to meet at the homes of the various Patrol members, now and then, so as to keep in close touch. Don't forget that Scouting will be judged not by what the books say about it, but by the way your boys conduct themselves as Scouts. Here is a test and a challenge to you as a leader.

*Interest Parents in Scout Progress.* Naturally you will encourage your boys to talk over with their parents what they are doing and learning. Bill's mother will be tremendously interested to know he has been successful in passing his Second Class Cooking test, especially if he has already demonstrated to her that he's a "handy man" about the kitchen and can even cook a supper for the family if need be. Dan's father will, if he has been kept in touch with the march of affairs, be exceedingly proud when his son gets his first Merit Badge or shows the family how many knots he can tie and how many first aid uses his Scout neckerchief has.

But it needn't stop even here. It isn't difficult to get parents to be interested, not only in Bob's or Dan's prowess and achievement but to carry the interest over to the whole Patrol—in its honors won, its handicraft

projects, its worth while exhibits, the day the Den is fully fitted, the hour when the Patrol has at last earned its camping equipment. Let fathers and mothers in on the fun.

## Keep in Touch

As Patrol Leader keep in close touch with your boys' families. Call on each boy early in the game and keep

your eyes open. Learn as much as you can of his home conditions so as to be able to understand any special kinks of his character or any difficulties there may be in the situation. Talk freely whenever you get a chance with your boys' parents. Talk especially about Scouting and the Patrol, its aims and activities, what it is doing and what it hopes to do.

## Insist on Loyalty to Promises

One of the things that can easily throw parents out of sympathy with Scouting and with a Patrol is any failure to keep strictly to the letter of an agreement. If you tell your boys to inform their parents that they will be home from a meeting at 9:30 see that they are home. Don't let the meeting drag on after the hour set for closing and don't let the boys stop to chat on street corners or drift into a drug store for a soda. "A Scout is trustworthy" and his word is given upon honor. If you keep to your side of the bargain and insist upon reliability, precision and obedience, in your turn, you may expect the parents' help in seeing that the boys get to meetings on time and are not prevented by errands or other distractions from being at the appointed spot, at the hour the hike is scheduled to start. It is co-operation all along the way that establishes the right attitudes on both sides.

## Other Contacts with Homes

A Parents' Night Program has its place in Patrols as well as in Troops. Arrange for such an occasion quite early in the life of the Patrol. Make it an all round friendly occasion and show parents as a group how the Patrol is progressing and what it can do.

A Father and Son Hike is especially appropriate for a Patrol. It can be made a camp supper or overnight hike. Get fathers to try to do Scout work and play Scout games. Get them to "reminiscing" round the camp fire. You'll be surprised what grand yarns you'll get, adventures you never suspected these hard worked busy "dads" ever had. Just get somebody to start with, "When I was young we didn't have any Scout Program but——" and you're off.

No need to leave out the mothers. Maybe they would like a camp meal too, or perhaps you can all— fathers, mothers, Patrol as a whole, have a picnic or jolly excursion of some sort. Anyway, whatever you do keep the home contacts close, friendly and sympathetic. This is all important and unless you are making a genuine effort along these lines, you are not living up to your responsibility and privilege as a leader.

## Church and School

Closely allied with what has been said in regard to the home comes the Patrol's responsibility to the church and school.

You will try to live up to the resolution of the Executive Board of the Boy Scouts of America in regard to camping and hikes (see page 191). But if by chance, you are in

camp on a Sunday as a Patrol Leader you will arrange a brief but reverent service of your own, if you are too far away, or it is not convenient for some reason for you to attend a local church. You will also encourage your boys to attend Church and Sunday School regularly and to enter into any church Good Turn that may be decided on, particularly if you are members of a Troop sponsored by a church. It goes without saying that you will see that your boys are careful to respect the religious convictions of others and neither to do nor say anything at any time which could possibly hurt the feelings of anyone else in this connection.

Similarly, you will quietly but firmly influence your boys to make the most of their school opportunities and

fulfill their school obligations faithfully. Scouting must not be allowed to conflict at any time with the latter. A word here and there to your boys either individually or in a group will easily make clear that you expect them to be a credit to the Patrol in the schoolroom or school yard as well as in the Den or in camp. Scouting goes through all the ways of everyday life and isn't kept in a neat compartment by itself. School Good Turns are also in order. Keep your eyes open for opportunities to be of service as a Patrol to teachers or the school as a whole.

## Sponsoring Institution

Naturally, the Patrol as well as the Troop owes special loyalty and service to the sponsoring institution or group, that is, the particular church, or school or Legion post, or Rotary Club or whatever it is, which has been good enough to make itself responsible for the success and continuous operation of the Troop.

If the church wants ushers, or somebody to distribute

notices or clean up its garden see that your Patrol
stands by to offer its services. Better still don't wait
to be asked. Be "mentally awake" enough to think
up something for yourselves—something that needs doing, but which nobody else thought to do. A Scout is
resourceful.

Apply this to your sponsoring institution whatever
group it is. If it is a school offer to take charge of a
crossing nearby, run up and lower the flag, manage the
fire drill. If it's a group of Legionnaires or Rotarians
or Kiwanians find out what they would like done and do
it as an expression of your appreciation for all they are
doing for you and the Troop.

Ask one of these Legionnaires or Kiwanians, your
pastor or teacher to come and talk to your Patrol some-
time. Perhaps one of them is a specialist in some subject in which your fellows are particularly interested.
Get him to help you if he will. Contacts like this are
very helpful.

A word of warning here, though. In all this, don't
go ahead, on your own initiative, without first con-
sulting your Scoutmaster. Anything your Patrol undertakes as a service to your sponsoring institution, any
special contacts you desire to establish with any one
representing these institutions are to be arranged for
only with the full approval of your Scoutmaster. It is
fine to be full of ideas and action, but be careful always

not to exceed your own authority and power to act. With the best of intentions you may make trouble this way, get the wires crossed so to speak.

## The Patrol Good Turn

We have already touched on the subject of the Good Turn. Of course, as a Patrol Leader you will from the beginning, try to make your boys accept seriously and faithfully the obligation to the individual Good Turn on which so much stress is laid in the Scout Law. The Patrol Good Turn also has an important place in Scouting.

Eight boys can accomplish a Good Turn which one boy alone might not be able to undertake. For example one boy keeping a wood box full all winter for an aged couple might have a rather heavy task on his hands, but the same responsibility shared by seven other boys, would be easily carried through. Snow shovelling, guarding dangerous crossings, hoisting a school flag daily, distributing church bulletins, maintaining bird shelters, gathering books or toys for

Christmas distribution, visiting an invalid or taking him out in a wheel chair are all worth doing by a Patrol and divided among eight boys is no burden at all, whereas for one boy alone it might be too much to pledge himself to do.

Special Scouting Good Turns are always in order as when a Patrol on a camping trip volunteers to help a farmer mend his fences or get in hay or apples, or when the Patrol as a whole earns money to give a boy who otherwise could not afford it, his chance for a week in camp.

All these things are not only worth doing in themselves but bring a fine flooding back of good to the

Patrol itself for a service and sacrifice undertaken by the group and loyalty shared by each and all is one of the best possible means of developing Patrol Spirit and Patrol unity.

## Who Thinks up Good Turns?

That is as it may be. If the Patrol Leader challenges his boys to bring in suggestions he is likely to get some ideas worth following up. He may, on the other hand, have a pet idea in his own head, which he suggests to the boys. If they like it they will soon enough make it their own, if they don't, they will say so; which will open the way for you to challenge. "Very well. Suggest something better." If they can, good. If they can't, then there is still your idea. It doesn't matter so much who thinks up the idea in the first place. The main thing is to have every fellow in the Patrol "sold." to it when you do decide on it.

## Carrying It Out

Whatever you decide on, decide only after full discussion. Then plan how the thing is to be done. Assign everybody his share and see that each feels his responsibility to carry through whatever he has pledged himself to. Let them feel that here, too, the honor of the Patrol is at stake. They can't afford to fail in this, any more than they can afford to fail in knot tying or signaling. Indeed, better fail at these than to go back on a pledged responsibility, undertaken in the spirit of the Scout Law. It is by the Patrol Leader's success in making these things really mean something deep and serious to each boy in the Patrol, that he may really dare to measure himself.

## Making an Adventure of it

The Good Turn Hike mentioned elsewhere is an excellent way of stimulating interest in the Good Turn idea and practice. The clever Patrol Leader and his Assistant may plan this kind of a hike and get every boy so eager and alert that he will feel like a knight of old going out to find some service to perform. Given a breath of romance and adventure, the Good Turn becomes doubly worth while and adds to the Patrol's traditions as well as its spirit. Get your boys to feeling that tracking and trailing the opportunity for the Good Turn either for the individual or the Patrol to do is as much a part of Scouting as other kinds of tracking and trailing are, and takes fully as much observation and training, too.

## The Spirit of It

Incidentally, of course, you will want to help your boys to realize that a real Good Turn, big or little, must be done simply, unpretentiously, not looking for any reward except the satisfaction of having done it. If it is done in any other way, it loses its charm and spirit, becomes perfunctory or worse. Tell your boys the story of the "Unknown Scout," where a small Good Turn was instrumental in bringing the Scout Movement to the United States. The story shows the real meaning and value of the Good Turn idea in compact and unforgettable form.

## Chapter XII

## THE PATROL LIVES ON

AND so the Patrol lives on.

Weeks pass by, months, years. And while they go the Patrol becomes a still stronger unit, unbreakable ties binding its Scouts together. Traditions are fostered and Patrol Spirit grows. The Patrol is all the time becoming more and more a living thing.

We wish in our hearts that it could go on forever, that the thrill and happiness of meetings and hikes and camp fires could be continued throughout the years with the reflection of the flames flickering always over the same familiar faces.

But alas, this cannot be. Some day the boys will have grown into manhood. They drift away from the old town out into a new life, a fact that must be faced by every Patrol at some point of its existence.

And yet, even if the boys are scattered all over the world, still there is one thing that keeps them together, their common memories. And the same thing makes them stand loyally by the young Patrol that has grown from the old roots.

For even if life takes the boys away as they grow up, the Patrol does not die. For every one that steps out another and a younger one takes his place ready to carry out the traditions of the old Patrol.

That is an ideal to which the boys will aspire. *The Patrol must never die.* The torch must be carried on, its old name must be kept intact. But this can be done only if the old boys are animated by the right spirit, if they realize what the years in the Patrol have meant to them.

Again the Patrol Leader plays a very important part. It rests on his shoulders to get the thing started going that will keep the boys in close touch with each other and with the Patrol for whose honor they have been working.

As the boys disappear from the Patrol be sure that a link of correspondence is kept up with them. Make

the new boys that join realize what such a connection may mean for the future of the Patrol, and interest them in writing to these older fellows even if maybe they have never met them.

One wonderful idea which a Patrol carried out for many years was a thing which they called "The Book of Traditions." It had another name too, "Verbit," this name being made up of the initials of the six original members of the Patrol. This book was kept moving between the old members and the living Patrol. And every time it came back to them from its travels they would write down on its pages their experiences since the last time they had been visited by the book. What stories that book could tell! And how it helped to keep alive the spirit of the Patrol!

But there are other ways.

One Patrol met with all the old members that could possibly get home once a year. Everybody went out on an overnight hike, and around the camp fire memories were refreshed and the old life lived once more, while the young members of the old Patrol listened in with veneration. In the beginning these annual meetings took place in September, on the birthday anniversary of the Patrol, but as the years passed by some of the members moved farther away from the old home town, and the camping hike was moved to the last Saturday of the year, when the largest number of the members returned home for Christmas and New Year's. And what did it matter that snow covered the ground? They had all been hardy Scouts, they knew how to live the life in the open, and the hike was spent in comfort.

Still another Patrol succeeded for many years in getting its old members together for a few days in camp in the summer months. One year they undertook a real Patrol camp with the younger group of boys and another year they met with their old Patrol and Troop at the camp of the Local Council.

And always the Patrol received its old members with open arms. They always brought with them a glimpse of earlier greatness, and helped the Patrol to carry on their work in the old spirit.

And the old boys themselves?

There was something touching in their attitude. There were feelings in them that had never before risen to the surface. There was gratitude in them because of the fact that they had once been an active part of a real Patrol and lived through its days of glory and despair.

And then their thoughts would turn toward their old Patrol Leader.

He had never heard them tell him what the life in the Patrol meant to them. Boys do not do such things. He had been plugging along because he felt that after all they were *his* boys and it was up to him to try to make them happy.

But did not the very knowledge of the old boys coming together now to celebrate with the Patrol tell him everything? That his work was still going on, that his dream, as well as the Patrol's, still lived?

It did. And wherever he was his heart filled with gratitude for the power that had been given him to be a *real Patrol Leader* for a *real Patrol*.

# A Cooking Outfit

## FOR THE
# Whole Patrol
### HERE ARE THE 61 PIECES

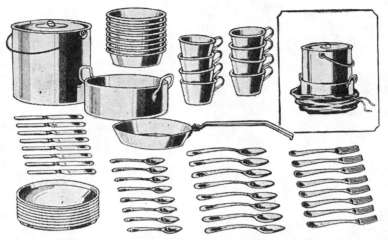

THE task of arranging this outfit included a number of problems. Suitable appliances were necessary for the various cooking operations; also enough articles to serve food; a second requirement, fitness, for close packing. This Outfit covers them all.

It is of aluminum, each piece stamped out of a single sheet so that there are no seams to leak.

The pans and other equipment are made in sizes to nest between the pots. A really complete outfit of cooking, serving and eating utensils. Scouts and Scout Patrols will appreciate the lightness of the load and the Patrol cook will appreciate the articles for his use and the Scouts will not find lacking any necessity for the table.

Outfit is as follows:

1 Stock Pot 3⅜ Qt.          8 Bowls 14 Oz.
1 Stock Pot 4¾ Qt.          8 Plates
1 Stock Pot 6¾ Qt.          8 Teaspoons Nickel Silver.
1 Stock Pot 11⅜ Qt.         8 Tablespoons Nickel silver.
1 Polished Steel Fry Pan.   8 Table Forks, Nickel silver.
8 Drinking Cups, with handle 8 Table Knives, Stainless
   11 Oz.                        Steel with solid handle.

This Outfit nests compactly and is provided with canvas carrying bag.

No. 1326 .......................................$18.75

# INDEX

To avoid duplication, all subjects of which the word Patrol is an essential part are given in their regular alphabetical position only, not under Patrol. Chapter Headings, however, appear also under Patrol.

# How Does Your Patrol Rank
# *In First Aid?*

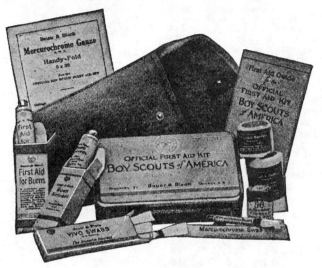

O F course you want your Patrol to be the best in every-
thing—whether you happen to be the Eagles—the
Bears—or the Wolves—you want your Scouts to be good
Scouts—and your Patrol to be the best Patrol.

An Official Scout First Aid Kit is a necessary part of
every Scout's equipment. You don't want accidents of
course, but when they happen, as they will now and then,
you want to "Be Prepared."

Why not do a little active work to put your Patrol up
on top in first aid—teach your Scouts first aid work—give
them practice—and above all, be sure that every member
has correct official equipment?

# Bauer & Black

**DIVISION OF THE KENDALL COMPANY**

**CHICAGO**          **NEW YORK**          **TORONTO**

*The Official Boy Scout Kit—Made to the specifications of Boy
Scout Headquarters.*

395

# Eyes Right! Steady Front!

### EVERY TROOP SHOULD HAVE THE U. S. FLAG

**No. 1102. United States Flag.** "wool" bunting, sewed Best quality throughout and finished in first-class manner. Stars sewed on both sides. Canvas heading, teeth grommets. Size 3x5 ft..............**$3.15**

**No. 1103.** Same, "parade" size 4⅓x5½ ft. Regulation flag ...................................**$5.50**

**No. 1104.** Same size 5x8 ft., suitable for decorative purposes. Special lot, each.................................**$7.00**

**No. 1111. Silk United States Flag.** Best sewed flag silk. Sewed silk stars. Size, 3x5 ft...................**$20.50**

**No. 1120. Silk United States Flag.** Superior banner silk. Sewed silk stars. Size, 3x5 feet..................**$21.50**

**No. 1123.** Same, U. S. National Regulation flag, 4⅓x5½ feet. Sewed silk stars....................**$36.50**

**No. 1293. United States Flag Set.** Includes absolutely fast dye cotton bunting flag, size 3x5 feet, canvas heading, metal eyelets; jointed pole with halyards, and bracket for fastening to window ledge or other support...............................**$1.65**

**No. 1010. Parade Size Troop Flag.** Design same as No. 1009, but 4⅓x5½ feet. **$6.00**

**No. 1005.** Troop Flag, 3x5, Same design as No. 1009 but size 3x5 feet.............**$4.50**

**No. 1399. Cotton Bunting Official Troop Flag.** These flags of best quality, durable cotton bunting will be found an excellent substitute for wool bunting. Size 22x36 inches ...................................**$1.20**

**No. 1400. Cotton Bunting Parade Size Troop Flag.** Best quality cotton bunting. 4⅓x5½ feet...................**$3.50**

**Note**—When ordering your Troop Flag have it lettered. 10c per letter, showing on both sides. 20c per letter on Pacific coast. Remittance should cover the word Troop.

## SUPPLY DEPT. — BOY SCOUTS OF AMERICA
**2 PARK AVENUE**      **NEW YORK**
New York Retail Store, 20 E. 33rd St.
37 So. Wabash Ave., Chicago    583 Market St., San Francisco
**Chicago and San Francisco have retail stores too.**

# Recognize
# Outstanding Ability

## CREATE AN INCENTIVE TO WIN !

BRONZE ....... $ .85
SILVER ........ 1.00
GOLD ......... 1.25

A new set of medals designed to stimulate the interests of Scouts in their many activities. They are of the best workmanship and are all fitted with red, white and blue ribbons.

Available in the following subjects:

No. 5060. Track.
No. 5063. Field.
No. 5075. First Aid.
No. 5111. Swimming.
No. 5121. Signaling.
No. 5125. Cooking.
No. 5129. Bugling.
No. 5133. Knife and Axe.
No. 5137. Knot Tying.
No. 5141. Camping.

No. 5145. Wall Scaling.
No. 5149. Firemaking.
No. 5153. Handicraft.
No. 5157. Tent Pitching.
No. 5161. Tower Building.
No. 5165. Archery.
No. 5169. Canoeing.
No. 5173. Bridge Building.

# Has Your Patrol a Name?
## If Not, Take Your Choice

Shoulder Medallion
No. 851

| | | |
|---|---|---|
| Alligator | Flying Eagle | Pelican |
| Antelope | Fox | Pine Tree |
| Bear | Hawk | Raven |
| Beaver | Hound | Ram |
| Black Bear | Horse | Rattlesnake |
| Bat | Hyena | Raccoon |
| Bob-White | Hippo | Rhinoceros |
| Buffalo | Jackal | Seal |
| Bull | Kangaroo | Stag |
| Blazing Arrow | Lion | Stork |
| Cat | Mongoose | Swallow |
| Curlew | Moose | Tiger |
| Cobra | Owl | Wolf |
| Cuckoo | Otter | Wood Pigeon |
| Crow | Panther | Wild Boar |
| Eagle | Peacock | Woodpecker |
| Elephant | Peewit | Whippoorwill |
| | | Wolverine |

# Patrol Leaders—

As a Leader, it is up to you to see that the new boys of your Patrol are told where to buy Official Boy Scout Equipment.

Tell them the quality is the best and the price most economical—

Trade thru your own Boy Scout Supply Department. It has everything a Scout needs for every Scout activity.

## Boy Scouts
### It's Yours!
#### Patronize It.

---

### SUPPLY DEPARTMENT

# Boy Scouts of America
### 2 PARK AVENUE       NEW YORK

---

**New York Retail Store:   20 East 33rd Street**

---

| 37 South Wabash Avenue, | 583 Market Street, |
|:---:|:---:|
| **CHICAGO** | **SAN FRANCISCO** |

---

*Chicago and San Francisco have retail stores, too.*

# The Service of the Supply Department

From start to finish the operations of the Supply Department are conducted from the standpoint of satisfactory service to Scouts and to the Movement.

SERVICE, effective helpfulness—the final test of the Department's worth—is its aim, watchword, and sole reason for being.

To you this means assurance of high standards in quality, suitability of equipment selected according to your needs, moderate price for what you order, and promptness in supplying your requirements. Indeed it is a fact that most orders are shipped within 24 to 48 hours from their receipt.

With everything goes a double guarantee—ours and the manufacturers. Unless you are satisfied, the transaction is not completed, or our service finished, until you have allowed the Department opportunity to make good with you.

Supply Department

## Boy Scouts of America

### 2 Park Avenue, New York City

New York Retail Store: 20 East 33rd Street

583 Market Street
San Francisco

37 South Wabash Avenue
Chicago, Ill.

*Chicago and San Francisco have retail stores, too.*

# A Twelve Year Old Recruit!

Patrol Leader, make sure that your new Scouts will get the most fun out of Scouting by insisting that they have an Official Boy Scout Uniform.

Outside of the Scoutmaster, you are the first Scout Leader the new recruit speaks to and, as a Leader, the responsibility is yours to see that he gets the Official Boy Scout Uniform.

# Sigmund Eisner Company

### Red Bank, N. J.

**Sole Manufacturers of Official Boy Scout Uniforms.**